Asking for Eyes

The Visual Voice of Southeast Africa

Asking for Eyes

The Visual Voice of Southeast Africa

The Southeast African Collection of the
Edward M. Smith Family Art Foundation

Edited by
Teri L. Sowell

Essays by
Mary Axworthy
Beth Baniadam
Ruth Broudy
Nancy El-Haddad
Marilyn Jolley
Sara Mandel

University Art Gallery
School of Art, Design and Art History
San Diego State University

This book was published on the occasion of an exhibition of works from the Edward M. Smith Family Art Foundation at the University Art Gallery, San Diego State University. The exhibition was curated and designed by students from the Spring 2004 Curatorial Practices Seminar in SDSU's School of Art, Design and History, under the direction of Dr. Teri L. Sowell and with the assistance of Professor Tina Yapelli, director of the University Art Gallery.

Asking for Eyes: The Visual Voice of Southeast Africa
Selections from the Edward M. Smith Family Art Foundation

8 November through 4 December 2004
University Art Gallery
San Diego State University

Students of the Spring 2004 Curatorial Practices Seminar

Mary Axworthy Budget/Finance Chair
Beth Baniadam
Suki Baz Education Chair
Michael Boyd
Ruth Broudy Research Chair
Kaitlin Cron
Nancy El-Haddad
Caroline Emmerson
Adrian French Exhibition Design Chair
Fadi Haddad
David Harris Photography Chair
Marilyn Jolley Development Chair
Jayna Lee
Lindsay Magnuson
Sara Mandel
Rian Medlin
Nicole Newman Design/Advertising/Public Relations Chair
Nicole Rossi
Lisha Ryan

Catalogue design by Nancy El-Haddad, Jayna Lee and Nicole Newman
Design advisor: Lori Palmer, Instructional Technology Services, SDSU
Printed by Spectrum Printing, Inc., San Diego
Cover images: ***Northern Nguni puppets***
Edition of 1200

Photography by Kevin Walsh, with the following exceptions:
Mary Axworthy (figures 10, 18, 40, 55, 68, 71, 72 and 87), William Dewey (figures 6, 7 and 9),
Fee Halsted-Berning, Ardmore Ceramic Studio (figures 115 and 116), Dan Kramer (figure 52) and
Matt McInvale (figures 19, 31, 56 and 102)

Copyright © 2004
University Art Gallery
School of Art, Design and Art History
San Diego State University
San Diego, California 92182–4805
619.594.5171
www.sdsu.edu/artgallery

ISBN 0-937097-01-2

Table of Contents

v

Wilhelmina and Edward Smith

Foreword

Wilhelmina Wilkie-Smith

*"Eyes which have met have
established relationship."*
    –Shona of Zimbabwe proverb

It is with great pleasure and excitement that we present our collection in the exhibition and catalogue *Asking for Eyes: The Visual Voice of Southeast Africa*. It has been the Edward M. Smith Family Art Foundation's goal to increase public awareness and appreciation of the value and importance of diversity in our world. The Foundation has worked to provide the local community with educational programs related to the indigenous cultures of Africa, the Pacific Islands and the Americas, and *Asking for Eyes* takes that goal even further by expanding our outreach to national and international venues. Through a mutually beneficial partnership with San Diego State University, the Foundation is realizing its goal and has hopes for future collaborations with SDSU, its dedicated faculty and talented students.

The Edward M. Smith Family Art Foundation was established in 1996, after having assembled a large and diverse collection of non-Western art. It was, and continues to be, Ned's and my wish to preserve and promote the visual arts from these historically overlooked regions. Ned has always been drawn to the non-Western arts and yearns to connect with and understand the messages these unrecognized artists were communicating within their societies. I was exposed to the arts of the world at a young age. Born and raised in South Africa, I was surrounded by the sights, sounds and aromas of the continent, and further developed a passion for the arts of Africa through my travels in Europe. Visits to European museums, exhibiting masterpieces collected from early "voyages" to the "colonies" of Africa, Oceania and the Americas, only reinforced my love and interest of non-Western art.

Together, Ned and I share our interest and intrigue surrounding the "life force" or "mana" that many of these works possess, which further spurs our exploration of their uses in their cultural context.

The current Foundation collection has been built over a ten-year period by acquisitions made directly in South Africa, as well as purchases made from auction houses and dealers in the United States and Europe, and the purchase of Charles Newberry's private Prynnsberg Museum collection in 1995. Ned and I felt a strong responsibility to preserve the contents of the Prynnsberg Museum and were willing to expend the time and energy necessary to provide the collection with the recognition it deserves. Future aspirations include securing a new permanent location to further promote the Foundation's work.

The opportunity to bring the Foundation goals to fruition presented itself after our making the acquaintance of Dr. Teri Sowell, curator and art historian. Teri's dedication to teaching and research in the field of non-Western art was quickly realized, and further discussions led to the proposal that we provide support to SDSU in a never-before-offered curatorial practices seminar for students in the School of Art, Design and Art History. We were delighted to offer our collection for the class curriculum, and through the additional support of John Gordon, former director of the School of Art, Design and Art History, and Professor Tina Yapelli, director of the University Art Gallery, the course was offered in the spring of 2004.

The openness of SDSU in encouraging its faculty to present new ideas, its support of the arts of Africa, Oceania, and the Americas, and its commitment to the completion of projects, has made the process of developing *Asking for Eyes* both smooth and enjoyable. The opportunity to support both a great institution and a talented professional curator and art historian has been a pleasure. The *Asking for Eyes* project has provided an invaluable opportunity for SDSU students to gain hands-on experience in their field of study, while further documenting the Edward M. Smith Family Art Foundation collection, and has given the community a chance to experience and enjoy the art and culture of Southeast Africa.

We would like to thank Dr. Teri Sowell for her vision, hard work and dedication, Kevin Walsh, who worked long hours, always with a smile on his face, to produce the majority of the beautiful images in this catalogue, and the students of the Spring 2004 Curatorial Practices Seminar, whose enthusiasm was contagious. We especially thank students Mary Axworthy, Ruth Broudy, Nancy El-Haddad, Adrian French, Nicole Newman and the others who continued to work behind the scenes on *Asking for Eyes* long after the semester was over. We would also like to acknowledge the support of Dr. Ida K. Rigby, director of School of Art, Design and Art History, and Michele Schlecht, director of development for the College of Professional Studies and Fine Arts. A special thanks also goes to Tim and Joan Hammond and to Nicki and Anthony Scheiderman, for without their friendship and support, acquiring the Prynnsberg Museum collection for the Foundation would not have been possible.

Wilhelmina Wilkie-Smith
Edward M. Smith Family Art Foundation

Acknowledgments

Teri L. Sowell

It is my pleasure to acknowledge the efforts of those who made *Asking for Eyes: The Visual Voice of Southeast Africa* possible. First and foremost, I would like to recognize the students from my Spring 2004 Curatorial Practices Seminar at San Diego State University who created the exhibition and its accompanying catalogue:

Mary Axworthy
Beth Baniadam
Suki Baz
Michael Boyd
Ruth Broudy
Kaitlin Cron
Nancy El-Haddad
Caroline Emmerson
Adrian French
Fadi Haddad
David Harris
Marilyn Jolley
Jayna Lee
Lindsay Magnuson
Sara Mandel
Rian Medlin
Nicole Newman
Nicole Rossi
Lisha Ryan

These talented students committed to producing an art exhibition, catalogue and educational materials, while managing all aspects of exhibition programming. After completing the course "The Art of sub-Saharan Africa" in Fall 2003, students were presented with the opportunity to enroll in my Spring 2004 seminar "Curatorial Practices" to develop an exhibition of African art. This seminar provided a unique opportunity for art, design and art history students to work together on a professional project that included research, exhibition development, exhibition design, graphic design and education, as well as development, fundraising, photography, marketing, public relations and community outreach. The success of *Asking for Eyes* is a direct result of their hard work and dedication.

I initiated and developed this project for the primary aim of providing students with professional experience relating to mounting an art exhibition and the production of a catalogue. While I had been formulating ideas for this project for years, it took the encouragement, support and generosity of Edward (Ned) and Wilhelmina (Mina) Smith to allow the project to unfold. Students realized what a singular opportunity this was and immediately immersed themselves into the project. The hardest work came long after the seminar was over, but the incredible dedication of a core group of students kept the project afloat. While all of the students in the seminar contributed greatly to the success of this exhibit and catalogue, I want to recognize those who continued to work on the project in a very professional manner, long after grades were in.

When push came to shove and I needed urgent help, Mary Axworthy came through graciously and without fail. I have never worked with a more "professional" student. In fact, her knowledge and dedication, combined with opportunities the seminar provided, allowed her to pursue a very serious professional goal, and today she is the registrar of the Edward M. Smith Family Art Foundation. Exhibition design fell squarely on the shoulders of Adrian French who took on the position with real bravado. Another true professional, he directed all elements of the exhibition's design and installation with impressive results. Ruth Broudy and Sara Mandel, meticulous researchers and writers, were always available when help was needed, jumping into any task with efficiency and good humor. Beth Baniadam directed the docent programming for the exhibition, and Nicole Rossi helped tremendously with both fundraising and the docent program. A heartfelt thanks also goes to Marilyn Jolley, our fundraising queen!

In the worst of times, she brought smiles to us all. The impressive work completed by the graphic design students speaks well of the program at SDSU, as evidenced by this catalogue and other exhibition related materials. The initial design of this catalogue was developed by Jayna Lee, and built upon by Nicole Newman, Nancy El-Haddad and Fadi Haddad. I would also like to acknowledge students who joined the project later on, especially Reylyn Buenaventura for creating a beautiful map of Southeast Africa, Nicholle Doll for assisting with public relations, Curtis Gannon for docent and installation assistance and Jayme Yahr for helping with the production of exhibition labels.

In addition to the students involved in the project, appreciation needs to be sent in so many directions, but most importantly to Edward Smith, Wilhemina Wilkie-Smith and the Edward M. Smith Family Art Foundation. Ned and Mina not only opened up their entire art collection to us, they also provided us with the resources to begin, and to complete, this massive undertaking. I am most profoundly indebted to Mina, who did whatever was necessary to get us what we needed when we needed it. She inspired us to continue when we felt overwhelmed, and encouraged us with unwavering support. To Ned and Mina, your generosity is deeply appreciated.

The exhibition and educational programs were realized with vital support from the San Diego State University Art Council and Africa and Beyond, Ethnic Art Gallery. Institutional sponsorship was provided by the School of Art, Design and Art History and the College of Professional Studies and Fine Arts. I would like to extend my gratitude to John S. Gordon, former director of the School of Art, Design and Art History, and the current director, Dr. Ida K. Rigby, for their commitment and leadership. From the College of Professional Studies and Fine Arts, Dean Joyce M. Gattas and Michele Schlecht were strong supporters from the beginning, cheerfully assisting and advising us along the way. I am also indebted to Professor Tina Yapelli, director of the University Art Gallery, who provided sound counseling throughout the process. Additional help came from David Camberg, Joyce Corpuz, Janice Minor and Lilla Sweatt.

I also want to extend a special appreciation to the San Diego Museum of Art, a wonderful partner in this multi-faceted project. Students made numerous visits to the museum to participate in roundtable discussions with the professional staff who provided real world advice and experience as it related to our project. These generous individuals include D. Scott Atkinson, Chief Curator and Curator of American Art; Dana K.M. Bottomley, Registrar for Collections; Maxine Gaiber, Director of Education; Cornelia Feye, Manager, Docent Programs; Brian Patterson, Manager, Community Programs; Jen Kendrik, Marketing and Promotions Coordinator; Chris Zook, Senior Public Relations Officer; Jessica Wood, Graphic Artist; and Keith Busby, Charge Artist/Preparator. This comprehensive experience provided students with competent guidance and allowed them an intimate glimpse into a range of professional worlds. The African Arts Committee of the San Diego Museum of Art also provided key support for this project, as did Mark Henderson at the Museum of Man. Dr. Barbara Blackmun, who introduced me to the art of Africa while I was an undergraduate at the University of California at San Diego, has always been a valued advisor. Her warmth, knowledge and friendship are gifts I will forever cherish.

I am greatly indebted to Lori Palmer, Graphic Designer, Instructional Technology Services, San Diego State University, who provided students with expert guidance throughout the project in all matters relating to graphic design. Her fingerprints can be found throughout this catalogue. Kevin Walsh, a wonderful photographer, worked closely with students, exuding a genuine concern for the quality of our project. I want to thank him and Joan Taylor, Spectrum Printing, for making this publication look beautiful. I also want to extend a warm appreciation to Sally Fall. At a time when we were struggling to find community interest and support, Sally provided both with grace and understatement. She also allowed us unrestricted access to her historic postcard collection, many images of which you will find reproduced within these pages. Mary Pat Hutt from Freese School offered us sage advice as we embarked into the local school districts to provide educational programs. Thank you, Mary Pat.

In terms of research, many scholars have been very generous of their time and expertise, including Bill Dewey, Sandra Klopper, Margaret Larlham, Peter Larlham and Marianna Visser. I would like to extend my gratitude to them and to Lynelle Gradwell and Hilary Prendini Toffoli for providing information and important contacts. I am grateful to Rayda Becker, Anitra Nettleton and Stan Schoeman for patiently answering questions and offering expertise and to Peter and Mara Baasch, Tim and Joan Hammond, and Paul and Betina Newberry for going above and beyond in willingly sharing their family history across the continents.

This project has proven to be a fruitful collaboration between all of the generous individuals and institutions mentioned above, and I want to express my sincere and profound appreciation to them all.

Teri L. Sowell, Ph.D.
Project Coordinator

Donors

Benefactors

Edward and Mina Smith

Patrons

San Diego State University Art Council

Spectrum Printing, Inc.

Tony Thomas

Sponsors

Africa and Beyond, Ethnic Art Gallery

Ridout Plastics

Supporters

Mrs. Ines Abadi

Bre Balthazar and Bill Medina for
the African Arts Committee,
San Diego Museum of Art

Barbara W. Blackmun, Ph.D.

Edwin and Sara Boniske

Dr. and Mrs. Abraham Broudy

Dr. Thomas Broudy and
Dr. Corrie Broudy
and Issac

Sam and Sandra Dimenstein

Nan and Bill Emmerson

Sally A. Fall

Frost Lumber

Mr. John S. Gordon

Mr. and Mrs. Jacques and
Brigitte Hautelet

Mr. Paul J. Hendricks

Jerry and Beverly Horton

James O. and Karen B. Hunt

S. Jenkins-Phelps, M.D.

KB Books

La Mesa Lumber and Hardware

Ms. Elizabeth A. Landen

Letty and Richard Lewis

Tom and Ynessa McElfresh
and Jakob

Fred Mooney

Elvi J. Olesen

P & P Bead and More

Mr. Oscar R. Padilla

Radisson Hotel Harbor View
San Diego

Edith Roach (Soft Safaris)

Dr. and Mrs. Gennaro Santangelo

Mr. and Mrs. Earl W. Saunders

Lilla A. Sweatt

Susan and Richard Ulevitch

Introduction

Ruth Broudy

This book and the exhibition it accompanies take their title from the Xhosa proverb *ucel amehlo*,[1] which translates as "he is asking for eyes (an audience)," referring to someone who seeks esteem and admiration. Because the artistic creativity of Southeast Africa reveals the cultural and spiritual aspirations of a people whose art has long been misunderstood and neglected, the exhibition and this publication, featuring the Southeast African collection of the Edward M. Smith Family Art Foundation, seeks admiration for the creative production of this aesthetically-rich region. It asks for an audience to open its eyes and minds, to experience the private and communal life of a people through their art, which is deeply rooted in sacred rituals and social traditions. Though often unnamed and therefore unrecognized individually, the collective efforts of the artists whose objects are presented in this exhibition reveal the work of an extraordinary people whose physical existence and spiritual sustenance are dependent upon their artistic achievements.

Unlike the established centers of culture in West and Central Africa, where peoples such as the Benin and Dogon have lived for great lengths of time in relatively fixed kingdoms and communities, the peoples of Southern and Eastern Africa, now inhabiting the areas extending throughout Zambia, Zimbabwe, Mozambique, Swaziland, Lesotho, and South Africa (figure 5), are cattle-owning pastoralists who, by their very nature, travel the land in search of newer pastures for their ever-growing herds.[2] Thus, their history is a complex one, which consists of series of migrations, rather than of settled societies. Their artwork, a reflection of this semi-nomadic lifestyle, tends to be small and modest because of the need to be portable and functional—a headrest rather than a bed, a food platter rather than a table.[3] Likewise, their colorful beadwork has a purpose far deeper than simple ornamentation, for, although it surely fulfills this intention, it is also the outward sign of a person's status within his or her community.[4]

The continuing importance of everyday objects, such as staffs, spoons, and milkpails, in the daily lives of the Southeast Africans cannot be over emphasized. A Zulu man, for example, never feels dressed if he goes out without one or two staffs, used both for walking and protection.[5] Among the Basotho of Lesotho, carved sticks are used for didactic purposes, recounting historical events and activities of the past. In Zulu society, beautifully fashioned wooden spoons are used in the ritual of eating, giving honor and respect to food, a gift provided by the ancestors. Snuff boxes, snuff spoons, and pipes, all used in the taking of tobacco, a highly valued and important act of sharing among the people of Southeast Africa, are also the ritualistic instruments that help keep the ancestral spirits in harmony with their living relations.[6] In the cattle-based culture of the Xhosa, where milk is the enduring staple sustenance, milkpails collect the daily milk of the cows, which is transferred into milksacks and served as *amasi*, the sacred curdled milk of the people.[7] Thus, these objects, meant for private use, are deeply imbued with personal meaning and spiritual beliefs. Es'kia Mphahlele refers to this aesthetic-spiritual fulfillment as African humanism, or "the organic unity between the spiritual forces, the material wants, the concrete materials used, temporal and spatial dimensions, reverence for life and for the creative act."[8] African humanism, as such, is an intensely spiritual experience inseparable from social relationships, whereas Western humanism is far more that of intellectual consciousness.

The general absence in Southeast African art of masking traditions like

1

those commonly found in West and Central Africa, together with the fact that carved ancestral figures are not customarily used as part of religious rituals, has further contributed to the neglect this region has received from experts in the field of African art. Lack of attention to historical detail and issues of migration has also led to incorrect attributions and classification of objects and, only recently, are art historians identifying styles with regions rather than with a fixed ethnic identity. Changes, which brought peoples together and then pulled them apart, have meant that identities which have subsequently been constructed as separate (for political reasons)—Zulu, Xhosa, Swazi, Sotho, Tsonga, for example—share so much in common, that in the examination of the art production from the Southeast African region, using these terms in an absolute sense is more misleading than useful.[9] Not only do ethnic attributions gloss over the complexity of historical relationships among the peoples of Southeast Africa, but it also dismisses the fact that an object stylistically attributable to a specific region may not necessarily have been created by an inhabitant of that area. For example, objects that correspond to the regional style of Zululand/Natal could possibly be the work of a migrant Tsonga-speaking carver, supplying the demands of the market or working for a Zulu patron.[10]

In presenting a selection of important works from Southeast Africa, *Asking for Eyes: The Visual Voice of Southeast Africa—Selections from the Edward M. Smith Family Art Foundation*, together with this more inclusive publication that documents the Foundation's complete Southeast African collection, provides viewers and readers with the opportunity for both admiration and appreciation. While it is truly a celebration of the art of a remarkable people, its deeper aim is towards a conceptual and cultural understanding. For the producers of these artistic creations, spiritual, political and social values are inherent within aesthetic values. It is therefore impossible to isolate the visual aesthetic from the conceptual meaning, for it is the complex values encoded in these objects that give rise to the form and, consequently, to the visual beauty of these marvelous works of art.

1   Zolile Calana and Patrick Holo, *Xhosa Proverbs and Metaphors* (Cape Town: Kwela Books, 2002), 33.

2   Karen Nel, "Consonant with Cattle-Culture: the Art of the Portable," in *The Art of Southeast Africa: from the Conru Collection*, ed. Annie Pérez 35 (Milan: 5 Continents Editions srl, 2002).

3   Nel, 14.

4   Aubrey Elliot, *Tribal Dress: Beadwork and other Decorative Arts* (Cape Town: Struik Publishers, 1986), 1.

5   J.W. Grosset, *Zulu Crafts* (Pietermaritzburg: Shuter and Shooter, 1976), 48.

6   Ann Wanless, "Public Pleasures: Smoking and Snuff-taking in Southern Africa," in *Art and Ambiguity: Perspectives on the Benhurst Collection of Southern African Art*, exh. cat. (Johannesburg: Johannesburg Art Gallery, 1991), 143.

7   Annie Pérez, ed., *The Art of Southeast Africa: from the Conru Collection* (Milan: 5 Continents Editions srl, 2002), 11.

8   Es'kia Mphahlele, "Introduction", in *Art and Ambiguity: Perspectives on the Benhurst Collection of Southern African Art*, exh. cat. (Johannesburg: Johannesburg Art Gallery, 1991), 9.

9   Agnes Havran, "Catalogue list," in *Art and Ambiguity: Perspectives on the Benhurst Collection of Southern African Art*, exh. cat. (Johannesburg: Johannesburg Art Gallery, 1991), 146.

10 Havran, 146.

Charles Newberry and the Prynnsberg Estate

Mary Axworthy

Figure 1. **Charles Newberry** (1841–1922), founder of the Prynnsberg Estate and Museum, Clocolan, Free State, South Africa. Photo courtesy of Peter Baasch.

Charles Newberry was a man with a vision, a hardworking man, a determined man and a man who appreciated the arts of southern Africa, long before African art became recognized as art versus craft or artifact.

While acquiring local black artists' work in South Africa, Charles could not have foreseen that, a century later, his treasured collection of southern African art would one day be made available to scholars, educators, students and the general public through the commendable efforts of the Edward M. Smith Family Art Foundation, which holds the entire inventory of Charles Newberry's African art collection. Of the three hundred plus Newberry objects that are extant, thirty-four are proudly showcased within this catalogue.

A significant portion of the Smith Foundation's Southeast African art collection originates from the former Prynnsberg Museum, the privately owned collection acquired by Charles Newberry, during the late nineteenth/early twentieth century. The Prynnsberg Museum was housed in the estate of Charles Newberry, located in the small town of Clocolan, in the Free State Province of South Africa, from its conception until the estate was sold in 1996. Edward and Mina Smith had the fortunate opportunity of purchasing the entire southern African art collection from the Prynnsberg Museum prior to Sotheby's public auction, which drew a crowd of eight thousand people from Cape Town, Gauteng, KwaZulu Natal and Lesotho, to bid on the contents of the estate in March 1996.[1] The Edward M. Smith Family Art Foundation's purchase of the Prynnsberg collection, in its entirety, ensured that the collection would remain intact for future generations.

Charles Newberry (1841–1922) was born in Brampton, in the County of Huntingtonshire, England (figure 1).[2] At about age fifteen, Charles left school to help his father with his surveying work and later joined a carpenter and builder's shop where he was employed for three years. Times being rough in England, Charles made the decision to immigrate to South Africa in 1864 to join his older brother John (1838–1928) in a carpentry business in Greytown. The slow voyage upon the small ship *Evangeline* took one hundred and three days to travel between London and Durban, and Charles spent six weeks of the journey suffering from sea-sickness.[3]

In 1873 the brothers moved to Kimberley to try their luck at the diamond fields, the "Diggings" as they were called, with their younger brother George joining them at Kimberley some years later. John and Charles worked their own claims, and through hard work and perseverance, they were able to accumulate enough holdings to participate in the formation of the Kimberley Central Mining Company, allowing them to withdraw from active mining. Kimberley Central Mining was later bought out by the De Beers Consolidated Mines (founded by Cecil John Rhodes), where John Newberry continued on as a Director.[4]

Charles had the foresight to know the shares he held in the De Beers Consolidated Mines would be fruitful. He states in a brief autobiography, dictated to his daughter Winifred in January of 1912, "we were often advised by those who thought they knew, to sell out... but these De Beers shares have been one of the best things known, and are likely to be even more profitable in the future."[5] But Charles' ingenuity did not stop with the diamond mines. A large boom in the grain trade followed the discovery of gold on the Witwatersrand, and both Charles and John used profits from the Kimberley diamond mines to invest in land.[6] In the 1890s, Charles Newberry alone owned more

Shaded pools, gardens, marble nymphs, a chapel, a tree plantation, and a game preserve for local antelope and imported black wildebeest, all surrounded the magnificent Newberry home.

than 127,000 acres of land in the Thaba Nchu district.[7] John Newberry built the largest grain mill of its kind in the Free State at Leeuwrivier in the early 1890s (figure 2).[8] Through hard work, diamond shareholdings and well-planned land speculation, by the age of thirty-seven, Charles Newberry was a wealthy man and ready to settle down. While vacationing in nearby Durban, Charles visited the family of an acquaintance, Thomas Daniel, son of the Reverend John Thomas Daniel and Mary Anne (Sephton) Daniel. Mary Anne was the granddaughter of William Prynn, who established a farm and the Prynnsberg trading station in Clocolan around 1836. It was at the Daniel residence that Charles met Elizabeth Mary Daniel, the fifth child of Reverend and Mrs. Daniel. Charles notes in his autobiography that he "soon saw that she [Elizabeth] was the sort of girl I admired and I quickly made up my mind

to ask her to marry me."[9] One year later, Charles and Elizabeth were married.[10]

During their honeymoon, Charles and Elizabeth searched for the perfect location to build their new home together. They traveled in a 4-horse Spider to Natal and through the garden route to Cape Town, but ended up returning home to select the family's Prynnsberg farm for their future home.[11]

Charles began construction on what became the Prynnsberg mansion in 1881. He commenced by making modifications and additions to the existing single story, dressed sandstone structure on the farm.[12] Charles and Elizabeth transformed the plain landscape into a spectacular twenty-room sandstone mansion, under a rock face in the veld (figure 3), filling it with Victorian antiques, ancient Egyptian treasures and a private museum housing over 300 indigenous works of art from southern Africa. Shaded pools, gardens, marble nymphs, a chapel, a tree plantation, and a game preserve for local antelope and imported black wildebeest, all surrounded the magnificent Newberry home.[13] The Newberrys entertained visiting dignitaries and celebrities at Prynnsberg, including President Steyn, the Duke of Connaught and famed author Rudyard Kipling.[14]

Charles and Elizabeth Newberry's six children were born at Prynnsberg: Winifred (1880–1959), Ernest (1883–1956), Ruby (1889–1948), Daniel and Amy (1894–1917/1922) and Charles Peter (1898–1971).[15] During the South African war between the Boers and the British troops (1899–1902), Charles moved his family back to his homeland, to live with his brother John in Whyteleafe, Surrey, England, until the conflict was over.[16] Lord Kitchener's strategy during the war was to destroy the countryside, relocating all inhabitants to sites along the railroad lines, which became known as concentration camps. "Lands were ravaged, farm

Figure 2. **Newberry Mill workers**, circa late nineteenth/early twentieth century. Charles Newberry sitting in profile with arms crossed, wearing a wide-brim hat and smoking a pipe. Photo courtesy of Peter Baasch.

Maintaining the estate intact, and in its pristine condition, was of great concern to Charles.

Figure 3. **Charles Newberry and family on the steps of the Prynnsberg mansion**, circa 1898. Photo courtesy of Peter Baasch.

buildings burned and livestock appropriated or destroyed...both black and white populations of the Orange River Colony were severely dislocated by his 'scorched earth' campaign."[17] Amazingly enough, the Prynnsberg estate was spared, as the British soldiers used it for their accommodations.[18] A rare anecdotal, etched staff from the Prynnsberg Museum depicts a scene of the British driving the fleeing Boers from the estate (figure 4).

After the war, Charles sold most of his South African land holdings to the new colonial government, in October 1901, for a very large profit.[19] These lands were then subdivided into small farms and settled by ex-British soldiers and others of "British stock."[20]

Upon returning to Prynnsberg after the Boers war, Charles and Elizabeth continued to spend a great deal of time and money creating a showplace of grand splendor. Maintaining the estate intact, and in its pristine condition, was of great concern to Charles. According to notes from Robin Newberry (Charles' grandson), Charles' will specifically stated, "we wish the property to be kept intact and developed further on the same lines, and we hope that our wish in this respect will be observed by our descendants."[21] In an effort to preserve Prynnsberg for future generations, Charles exercised the

inheritance law of fideicommissum (entrusted in faith) in 1911, willing the estate, and all its contents, to the eldest son of the fourth generation.[22] Under the fideicommissa of the time, a testator could bequeath property to successive generations indefinitely, with traditional wills reading that the property be left to sons (South Africa being a patriarchal society at that time).[23] In doing so, Charles thought he was ensuring future descendants the privilege of living at Prynnsberg, but preventing the estate from being sold or divided up. However, problems arose surrounding the fideicommissum laws when only daughters were left, or a son had no interest in the property, as well as issues involving "ruling from the grave," so the Removal or Modification of Restrictions Act 94/1965 was passed and came into operation in October 1965. This Act applied to fideicommissa created both before and after the commencement of the Act, limiting all fideicommissaries to two generations, which in turn granted

Trevor Newberry sole ownership of the Prynnsberg estate.[24]

Trevor Newberry, grandson of Charles' oldest son Ernest, was the last to live at Prynnsberg, in respect to Charles' original trust stipulations. Trevor, a suffering alcoholic, took little interest in the maintenance of the mansion, its contents and the surrounding estate. The overgrown gardens were neglected, wallpaper peeled from the walls, and an infestation of bees in a bedroom resulted in honey damage to the floorboards.[25]

Upon Trevor's death to cirrhosis of the liver in 1993, the entire estate went to his next-of-kin and the decision to sell Prynnsberg was made.[26] Tim and Joan Hammond (Joan being a granddaughter of Charles' eldest son Ernest and Trevor's cousin) were responsible for executing the liquidation of the estate, and resided at Prynnsberg from 1993–1995. The Hammonds found the mansion, its contents, and the grounds in a terrible state of decay.[27] The once exquisite interior was auctioned off, piece by piece, at "one of

Figure 4. **Lesotho etched walking staff** (detail). Catalogue number 598.

the most outrageous estate auctions witnessed in South Africa," bringing in R3,52-million (approximately $820,000).[28] The six farms on the estate, including the house, were sold separately to an asparagus farmer. Unfortunately, the magnificent sandstone mansion held no value in the farm sale, as farmland is assessed solely on its income-bearing potential and would merely have been listed as a domestic building, along with sheds and garages.[29] Surely, some of the Newberrys reflected that day on Charles' autobiographical words, as he emphatically tried to convey to his family:

> My aim has always been, and still is, to secure a good start and standing in the world for all my children and to save them from the anxious struggle I endured. I trust that they will understand that I only look for their loyalty and that I am not appealing to them for thanks or gratitude. In a greedy, grasping world a father does feel that he needs at least the whole-hearted loyalty of his family behind him.[30]

Sadly, at the close of the celebrated Sotheby's auction, Charles' expressed hopes for his descendants had been lost.

Since 1996, the Prynnsberg mansion and grounds has changed ownership three times. The farmer that purchased the estate at the Sotheby's auction in turn sold it to one of the director's of Sothebys in the United Kingdom, with the new owner visiting every now and then to ride horses. Prynnsberg was then sold to the current owner, who has plans to renovate the estate, turning it into a lodge.[31] Although the final outcome was not as Charles Newberry had planned, hopefully part of his legacy will live on in a future vacation resort at Prynnsberg, and through the continued efforts of the Edward M. Smith Family Art Foundation in bringing the Prynnsberg Museum's Southeast African art collection into public view.

1 Anthea Bristowe, "Going cuckoo at Clocolan," *Sunday Times*, 31 March 1996, sec. 2:17.
2 Paul Newberry, <penewberry@hotmail.com> "Newberry questions," 24 July 2004, personal email (25 July 2004).
3 Paul Newberry, facsimile to author, 29 July 2004. Includes Charles Newberry's dictated autobiography dated January 1912 and notes from Robin Newberry, grandson to Charles Newberry.
4 Tim Hammond, facsimile to author, 25 July 2004. Includes personal notes recorded by Robin Newberry, grandson of Charles Newberry.
5 Newberry, 29 July 2004.
6 Colin Murray, *Black Mountain: Land, Class and Power, in the Eastern Orange Free State, 1880s to 1980s* (Washington, D.C.: Smithsonian Institution Press, 1992), 48.
7 Murray, 280.
8 Murray, 49.
9 Newberry, 29 July 2004.
10 Hammond, 25 July 2004.
11 Hammond, 25 July 2004.
12 Hammond, 25 July 2004.
13 Hilary Prendini Toffoli, "The Curse of Clocolan," *Style*, October 1995, 87 and Murray, 49.
14 Toffoli, 90.
15 Newberry, 29 July 2004.
16 Murray, 59.
17 Murray, 53.
18 Newberry, 24 July 2004.
19 Murray, 265.
20 Murray, 281.
21 Newberry, 29 July 2004.
22 Toffoli, 92.
23 Carol Barry, <carolb@cmbarry.co.za> "Re: Fidea Commissum," 10 August 2004, personal email (11 August 2004). Fideacommissa inheritance law summary provided by Carol Barry, Attorney at Law.
24 Barry, 10 August 2004 and Toffoli, 92.
25 Toffoli, 90.
26 Toffoli, 92.
27 Hammond, 25 July 2004.
28 Bristowe, sec. 2:17.
29 Bristowe, sec. 2:17.
30 Newberry, 29 July 2004.
31 Peter Baasch, telephone interview, 29 July 2004.

Eyes of the Night: Headrests of Southeast Africa

Ruth Broudy

"Dreams are our eyes in the night."[1]
–Zulu Diviner

For the peoples of Southeast Africa, the headrest that travels with the bride to the homestead of her new husband is carried on a tide of emotion and faith as a link uniting intersecting values and aspirations.

Sleeping on a headrest signifies the young couple's change of status, for only married people customarily sleep with a headrest. The new standing of the bride and groom is also marked by the taking on of elaborate hairstyles, in which case the headrest is used for its protection.[2] More importantly, however, than being a declaration of status and protecting complex hairstyles during sleep, headrests are used in dreams, as a vehicle of communication between the living and the ancestors. Among African peoples, a very close bond exists between the departed and surviving family members, with ancestors continuing to play a significant role in the daily lives of the living.[3] The Shona and Zulu headrest, which forms part of the woman's dowry and is considered as a nuptial contract, seals the alliance between two families and connects the bride's husband with her father as a symbol of the continuity of the lineage.[4] Among the Zulu and Swazi, headrests reference cattle, suggesting that cattle are a major source of wealth, and it is through them that people maintain contact with their ancestors.[5] Thus, while headrests have varied functions among the peoples of Southeast Africa, they share a crucial role in uniting family members with the ancestors, allowing the living to continue to assume a very personal and devoted connection with those in the ancestral realm.

The study of Southeast African headrests appropriately must begin with a look at the map of Southeast Africa (figure 5) and a historical understanding of the various language-speaking groups who are responsible for their creation. Simplistically, Southeast African headrests can be divided into three major categories based on their design elements: 1) those of the Shona-speaking peoples living in eastern, central and north-central Zimbabwe and extending over the border into Mozambique, i.e. among the Manyika, Zezuru, Korekore, Ndau, Karanga and Kalanga sub-groups, 2) those of the Tsonga-speaking peoples living in Mozambique, Zimbabwe and the Transvaal, i.e. among the Thonga, Tonga, and Shangaan sub-groups, and 3) those of the Zulu- and Swazi-speaking peoples inhabiting the region extending from as far north as Transvaal into Swaziland to Port Shepstone in southern Natal (Northern Nguni).

The issue of classification, however, remains a debatable one due to the fact that classification of objects based on dislocation often ignores the fact that people journeyed, migrated, and married into other language and ethnic groups. Headrests were often commissioned from carvers by clients from another language or cultural group or even sold to or made for foreign travelers and buyers of curios.[6] Pieces also moved from one village to another and from region to region, as anyone traveling was accustomed to taking with them their sleeping mat and headrest. This is evidenced by headrests that have been found far from their area of origin—Shona headrests in KwaZulu-Natal, for example, and headrests of Tsonga origin in what is today modern-day Zimbabwe. Headrests were also used for trade or tribute. Historically, headrests formed part of the dowries of young Zulu-speaking brides who took them across the hills to the homesteads of their new husbands. They would have been commissioned by a bride's father from a carver in her home area. This explains, to some extent, why it is not uncommon to find various styles of headrests in a single polygamous Zulu homestead, having been brought there by the wives of the homestead's head, as well as by his sons, from carvers working near the brides' original homes.[7]

Figure 5. **Map of Southeast Africa** (illustration by Reylyn Buenaventura).

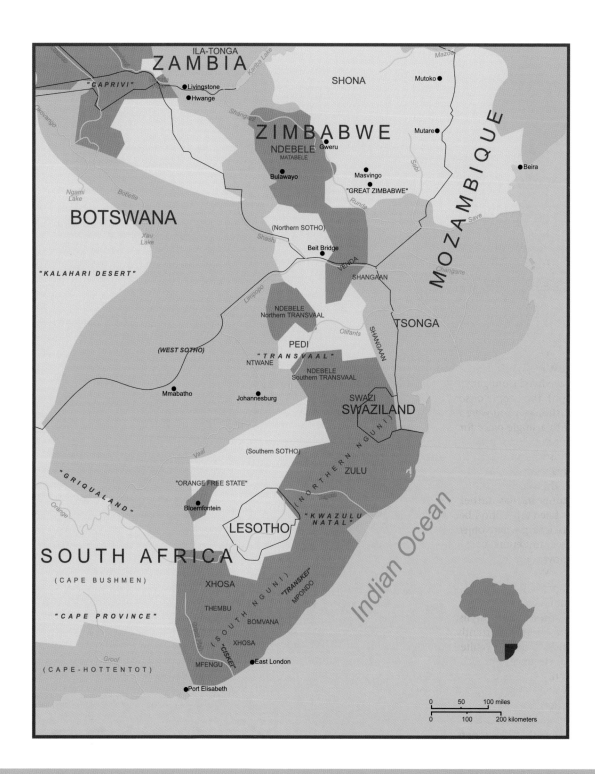

Apart from fulfilling an important practical function of protecting elaborate hairstyles, headrests afford the living an opportunity to communicate with the ancestors…

Unlike the fixed centers of culture in West and Central Africa (where peoples have lived from generation after generation), the people of southern Africa were pastoralists and were not associated with a single place for any great duration of time. The source of an object may consequently have been far from the area where it was ultimately collected.[8] In this regard, the collection history by Europeans has further obscured the issue of fixed attribution because, rather than disclosing where objects were carved and used, museums most often merely make known where items were collected.[9]

Keeping in mind the complications of provenance, we are nevertheless able to approach the study of Southeast African headrests from a stylistic point of view and, more importantly, from a conceptual understanding. While issues of color, patina, elegance, simplicity, delicate abstraction, and the like, are the concerns of Western cultures in a dialog of aesthetics, African cultures do not tend to compartmentalize conceptual categories to the degree that Westerners do. Therefore, an "aesthetic" discussion by an African will invariably reveal as much about religious, political, and social values as about what we in the West see as artistic values.[10]

Apart from fulfilling an important practical function of protecting elaborate hairstyles, headrests afford the living an opportunity to communicate with the ancestors and with *shave* spirits (benevolent or malevolent wandering spirits), serving as conduits to the spirit realm through dreams. The important role played by dreams in the culture of Southeast Africa cannot be over-emphasized. Without dreams, meaningful and uninterrupted living is not possible. Dreams are a channel of communication between survivors and the *shades* (ancestors). In his study of Zulu rituals, Alex-Ivar Berglund clarifies the use of the word *shade*, explaining that the Western concept of ancestor suggests ascendants who are dead; hence there is a distance between them and the living. In other words, a separateness is created between the living and the dead. The Zulu concept of ancestors differs greatly from this notion in that the Zulu assume a very close and personal relationship within the lineage between the departed and surviving family members. The idea that a deceased father is present and active is expressed by a Zulu man who states, "My father is departed, but he is."[11] Among the Shona and Tsonga peoples as well, ancestors are included in the family, and their influence and presence are felt so greatly among descendants that they are often referred to as "the living dead."[12] In the traditional religious beliefs of Southeast Africans, the notion of life after death does not exist, but people do feel the influence of the dead and continue to acknowledge their presence, performing rituals in their honor. The dead are ever present, caring for their families, and are consulted through dreams when problems arise.

In dreams the *shades* become very real, close and concrete. They enter the head of the dreamer through the mouth and visit the eyes so that they can be seen. Then they pass on to the ears so that they can be heard.[13] Diviners claim that they dream every night and even see things during the day. "We cannot work without dreams. The dreams are our eyes in the work."[14] Headrests serve in this essential function by inducing dreams, thus bringing together the departed and the living.

The Shona type headrest (*mutsago*) is thought to have existed since the twelfth century C.E. It was then that the remains of what appeared to be a headrest was discovered in a burial at the archeological site of Mapungubwe located in the Limpopo River Valley of present-day Zimbabwe.[15] There, the evidence of gold sheathing is believed to have adorned a long-disintegrated wooden headrest of a high-ranking individual. In his case study of Shona headrests, Dewey explains how people who held high status were often buried in caves "sleeping" on their headrests. Medium spirits, possessed by an ancestral spirit, might be called to the cave where the ancestor was buried to collect the headrest in order that it be used as a vehicle of continued communication with the departed ancestor, now living in the spiritual world. The spirit medium seen in figure 6, Sekuru Bwanya,

Headrests serve in this essential function by inducing dreams, thus bringing together the departed and the living.

9

maintains, for example, that the headrest resting beside him once belonged to the ancestral spirit that actually possesses him. Upon manifesting itself, the possessing spirit told people to go to the cave where he had been buried in order to collect his belongings.[16]

Headrests conventionally classified as "Shona" all vary to some extent in their composition, but the basic format of a curved upper platform, a flat bottom platform, and a supporting post between the two is common to most Shona headrests (figure 7). The upper platform that is rectangular in plan and section is the most consistent feature of all the Shona headrests, and is clearly distinct from the upper platforms of, for example, Zulu headrests which are thicker and often triangular in section. Appendages (curved flaps or rings found at the sides or underneath the upper platform) or lack of them, are one of the defining elements that differentiate the various Shona subtypes.[17] The central support between the upper platform and the base is most often slim and more narrow than the other two components. The various shapes and ornamental details found on this central support, which all vary somewhat in their makeup, also demonstrate the persistent use of certain motifs. These most often include two (in some cases, three or more) concentric circle designs sandwiched between two triangles, the upper triangle being inverted vertically over the lower. A rectangular element is often placed either horizontally between the two circles or vertically from base to platform.[18] Many of these headrests are ornamented with rows composed of chevron (v-shaped stripe) patterns along the upper edge of the short ends of their upper platforms (figure 7).

It has been argued by many art historians that headrests of this style seem to represent a human form with the upper platform being the shoulders, the vertical

support the torso, and the base serving as the lower limbs.[19] The designs on these headrests appear to have a semiotic multivalence. The concentric circle motifs, for example, have been interpreted by some to represent the female breast form, while others have identified the circle motifs as being a conus shell ornament known as *ndoro*. The conus shell is the outer shell of the marine mollusk often referred to as "marine snails." Because of their scarcity and beauty this shell is much sought after. The use of *ndoro* in Shona culture is associated with religious and political leadership or it is thought of as a prestige adornment, worn as a sign of status by adult Shona men and women.[20] In the mid-nineteenth century, conus shell discs were a sign of economic stability and high standing. For example, two cone shape discs could purchase a slave, whereas five bought an elephant's ivory tusk. In his account of Shona headrests, Dewey argues that the identification of the concentric circle motifs as *ndoro* ornaments rather than as female breasts is a more plausible explanation for their occurrence on headrests. Unlike breasts, *ndoro* can be worn in a variety of numerical combinations and on various parts of the body. This could be a possible explanation as to why concentric circles appear as a combination of two, three, four, or even six on various Shona headrests.

Ndoros have also been associated with spirit mediums or *shave* spirits and with the use of dreaming on the headrests in order to acquire specialized knowledge, such as judging court cases or enabling hunters to locate animals. All important knowledge is believed to come from spirits. A healing spirit, for example, reveals knowledge regarding herbs and medicines, often communicated through dreams. On the other hand, an important spirit of the land imparts knowledge about the history of the country and its beliefs and customs.[21] Whether it is done

Figure 6. **Sekuru Bwanya**, Shona spirit medium with the headrest belonging to the ancestor who possesses him.

Figure 7. **Shona headrest**.

on a headrest or not, dreaming is a very important way of acquiring knowledge for the Shona. Many musicians, in particular the *mbira* (thumb piano) players, believe they receive their musical inspiration from the ancestors through dreams.[22] Dewey interviewed a number of blacksmith-carvers who also assert to have received inspiration and instruction for their artistic efforts through dreams about the ancestors.[23] Thus, the insertion of the *ndoro* motif on the headrest is meant to enhance, as it did for those who wore real *ndoros*, communication with the spirit realm.[24]

Another reference suggested by the concentric circle motif is the association of the circles to the ripples in a pool after a pebble has been thrown into it, and, possibly by inference, to the eyes of a crocodile, especially where such motifs appear on Shona divining instruments (*hakata*).[25] Crocodiles are symbolically linked with chieftainship and wisdom, as well as the ancestral spirits by virtue of dwelling in deep pools. This association is further recognized because pools are known to be an important locus for many Shona groups as a means of alerting the ancestors that their attention is required. It is also possible that the image of the stone thrown into a pool is symbolic of the conception of a child and, therefore, the continuation of a lineage.[26] Dewey, however, points out that the linking of

All important knowledge is believed to come from spirits.

meaning of the motifs seen on Shona headrests with divination dice is a problematic one, due to the fact that historically divination dice have not been used by all Shona groups. Although today divination dice are almost universally acknowledged throughout the diverse Shona areas, many people reference the use of seed pods or bones for divination in their areas rather than *hakata*.[27]

It is also significant that the incised surfaced decorations on the Shona headrests are identified by many people as *nyora*, the same term that is used for human scarification. *Nyora* is commonly put into two classifications—those made for medical and magical purposes on both men and women, and those classified as beautification patterns, which are only made on women. These beautification patterns appear on headrests in the form of keloids (designs resembling an overgrowth of scar tissue), triangles, and chevrons, and correspond to the scarification designs found on a woman's shoulders, lumbar region, chest, abdomen, and around the pubis. The fact that this female type scarification is so prominently and consistently depicted on headrests from nearly all the Shona regions suggests it must have been conceived of being symbolic of the female gender.[28] That the female gender is referenced is further supported in that the bases of Shona headrests often consist of two lobes that adjoin in such a fashion as to form a small triangle between them, such as the female pubis lies between the legs. The same imagery occurs even when the base consists of three lobes. Among the Shona, headrests are only used by mature men. It is said that a husband places his headrest outside the dwelling of the wife with whom he wishes to sleep as a signal to her that she is to come to him.[29] When a man sleeps and dreams, he is said to be in the company of his ancestors, the source of knowledge and prosperity. The head-

rests as female figures without heads further intensify this ancestral association. The Shona believe that a woman's fertility is only on loan to the husband's family as is expressed in the Shona saying *Mukwasha chake mutimbi, musoro, ndowa-vatezvara* ("as for the son-in-law, his is her body, but her head, i.e. the seat of her ancestral 'being,' belongs always to her father").[30] This clearly refers to the fact that, among the Shona, a woman's fertility is merely on loan to her husband's lineage, of which she never becomes a part. Her "head," the seat of her ancestral soul, belongs to the group of ancestors of her own patrilineage, hence, the greater part of headrests do not have heads of their own. When a man sleeps on a headrest of this type, it is *his* head, *his* ancestral affiliation, which completes the human and specifically female image suggested by the headrest itself.[31]

Tsonga headrests (*xiqamelo*) resemble the Shona in structural composition and, like the Shona, are composed of three parts, a top and bottom horizontal plane joined by a vertical center support (figures 8a, 8b and 8c). The top plane is slightly curved to support the head and usually has the typical zigzag, diamonds or parallel lines ornamenting the upper ends. The base is most often elliptical or figure-eight shaped and usually rests flat on the ground. Similarities between Tsonga and Shona headrests, as well as differences found within each group, point clearly to style areas that overlap each other and do not necessarily coincide with ethnic boundaries. Such is the case in figure 9, where an Ndau (eastern Shona subgroup) man is holding what is considered a Tsonga-type headrest.[32]

The supporting vertical post of the Tsonga headrest is quite varied in composition and structure and, unlike the Shona and Zulu, it does not have a particular pattern or arrangement that is typical

Figures 8a, 8b and 8c. **Tsonga headrests**. (Left to right) Catalogue numbers 334, 336 and 340.

or canonical. This variety within a scheme has come to be regarded as a characteristic of the Tsonga group.[33] Rayda Becker, in her study of Tsonga headrests, suggests that the reasons for the stylistic variations in Tsonga headrests include more than experiences of mobility and migration among the carvers of Tsonga-speaking backgrounds. She points out that "the Tsonga" lacked a sense of shared ethnic identity before the twentieth century, making it difficult for them to develop or adopt symbols and styles that marked their own group identity.[34] The idea of the Tsonga as a unified ethnic grouping was first fostered by Swiss missionaries in search of a language that could be codified and delineated for use in Christian instruction.[35]

A distinctive feature of Tsonga headrests is the presence of small pendant pieces placed parallel to either of the main two axes of the headrest (figures 8a, 8b and 8c). These pieces are known as ears or lugs and take the form of a number of different shapes. They may be squared, semicircular or ring-like, closed or open, at right angles or parallel to the main axis of the headrest. The fact that lugs are almost always found on Tsonga headrests, however, does not automatically ensure its classification as being that of Tsonga. Lugs must be found in combina-

tion with other features to satisfy a Tsonga designation. For example, lugs have been found on headrests that have features that are more characteristic of Shona work, such as the raised bases seen on the headrest figure 8a or headrests with supports of concentric designs. This presents the possibility that the headrest in figure 8a is of a hybrid type, with elements of composition and design that are characteristic of both Shona and Tsonga work. Becker suggests that such headrests are part of a regional style, one that crosses cultural, language and political borders. It is a style that includes southeastern Zimbabwe, southern Mozambique, and the northeastern Transvaal. Waves of migration during the nineteenth century have made this region a culturally complex area with artworks that go beyond single ethnic categories.[36]

Although the basic form of the Tsonga headrest resembles that of the Shona, the female reference is much less clearly or extensively stated among the Tsonga headrests. Some art historians have pointed to certain features on Tsonga headrests that suggest female qualities, such as the lugs (representing earrings) or the central triangle found at the base (representing the pubes). It is possible to read a particular Tsonga headrest as female when forms like those of

the Shona are found at its base (figure 8c), even when the upper part is unlike the Shona type. However, as Becker points out, such associations cannot be made of headrests where no triangle exists at the base (figure 8a).[37] Among the Tsonga, it is customary for women to use headrests (unlike the Shona and Zulu, where headrests are used primarily by men). It would, therefore, be unlikely that women would sleep on female headrests (either metaphorical or representational).[38] Additionally, the central posts are generally less "figurative" in their overtones and rarely reference the scarification or breasts of a woman. Rather, the supports carry a range of different pat-

Figure 9. **Ndau** (eastern Shona subgroup) **man holding a Tsonga-type headrest**.

terns. Rectilinear pillars (single or double) with horizontal fluting are a common design (figure 10). Squared-off or rounded diagonal X-shapes are also seen, as are columns on dividing supports (figure 8b). Some Tsonga headrests carry complex circular and convoluted forms. The base of the Tsonga headrest is its most consistent feature—it is bi-lobed with smaller projecting triangles on either side placed centrally between the lobes (figure 8c and figure 10). The base is planar and unmodelled and differs from the raised, chamfered base of a typical Shona type. Some Tsonga headrests have open arches attached to the sides, while others have three-dimensional supports that have been hallowed out and converted into a container to be used as snuff boxes.[39]

The non-representational composition of the Tsonga headrest has made its interpretation more difficult than in the case of canonical Shona headrests. However, we do know that the headrest is an important part of the Tsonga man's possessions and that it is used, as among the Shona, in the important act of ritual. This fact has been attested to by Junod and Jaques, missionaries with the Swiss Mission, who lived among the Tsonga around the turn of the last century. Junod tells of how a man would make his first

sacrifice to his recently deceased father as ancestor by rubbing tobacco into his headrest in a ritual known as *mhamba*. Junod defines *mhamba* as "any object or act or even person which is used to establish a bond between the gods [ancestors] and their worshippers."[40] *Mhamba*, then, is a kind of vehicle that is used in communicating with and contacting the ancestor. It can function as a presence and, in physical form, can exist in any type of object, such as snuff boxes and beads, as well as headrests. What remains important is that the object should have belonged to the ancestor or be a replica of something once owned by him or her. Junod gives an example where the headrest is used as *mhamba*:

> The Tsongas have no sacerdotal caste but the right of officiating in religious ceremonies is strictly confined to the eldest brother…If, after the death of his parents, their son should happen to dream of them, he must offer worship to the deceased by pouring some ground tobacco on to his wooden pillow, this being the commencement of his religious functions.[41]

Headrests are constant companions of Tsonga men who carry them on their

travels. Many headrests have cords attached to facilitate carrying them around the neck or at the waist, in much the same way a Westerner would carry a bedroll. Some headrests include walking sticks which pass through the central support, while others include snuff boxes as part of the support. Jaques noted that the significance of a headrest rests in its use and its history. Headrests were essentially objects for private use and were rarely an item for use in public functions. The meaning of a headrest often changed over the owner's lifetime and acquired a new sense upon the owner's death. As the headrest became embedded with body oils and personal objects (headrests were often adorned with beads, shells, etc.) it became so much a part of the owner that it would often be buried with him upon his death.[42] Today, headrests remain important in Tsonga ancestor worship and are also used by traditional healers and diviners to facilitate their dreaming of the spirits. In rural areas, headrests are used as loci for connecting with spirits, a focus for offerings and as an aid to dreams.[43]

Among the Tsonga, both men and women use headrests, which accounts for the double (figure 10) and triple headrests that are sometimes seen. In most cases the two or three parts are carved from a single piece of wood and are identical, with a wooden chain connecting the headrests. The use and meaning of these double and triple headrests remains somewhat unclear, although they are said to have been used in the past by husband and wife (or wives).[44] Some art historians, such as G.I. Guy, argue that the double headrest was given to a well-off bride to be used as a double pillow and that the headrests, together with the connecting wooden chain, were painstakingly carved by the bridegroom from a single piece of wood. Others point to a Tsonga legend that refers to the chains being used to

Figure 10. **Tsonga double headrest**. Catalogue number 335.

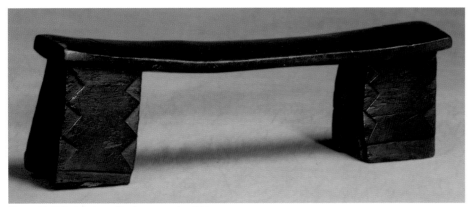

Figure 11. **Zulu headrest**. Catalogue number 344.

warn a sleeping partner of imminent danger by gently shaking the chain close to the sleeper's ear. When asked why double headrests were connected by a chain, the carver, Muraho Thully, explained that it was to "show cooperation of the wife and husband because in the old days there was full (mutual) love."[45] Most interpretations among the Tsonga, refer to double headrests as being used by married couples and take no account of the sleeping patterns of those who use them.[46]

One group of headrest type that is more difficult to distinguish between Shona and Tsonga examples are those with zoomorphic caryatids. Some of these animals are largely stylized, many have

Figure 12. **Zulu headrest**. Catalogue number 338.

rounded bodies and unarticulated cylindrical limbs, while others have a far greater rendering of detail. Headrests with animal caryatids have a wide distribution, having also been collected among the Shona, Zulu, and Swazi cultures. However, the greater number of these animal caryatids without bases has been classified as those originating in Tsonga areas.[47] Those with horns are said to represent a bovine creature, indicating the importance of cattle as the main economic means of exchange. Cattle-husbandry is as extensively followed by the Tsonga, as it is by the Shona and other southern and inland groups, however, cattle are not as central to the metaphysical and economic concerns of the Tsonga as they are among the Zulu and the Shona.[48] This presents the possibility that animals other than cattle are suggested from images found on Tsonga headrests. In Tsonga songs, for example, the antelope is often referred to as a metaphor for women,[49] and, while cattle is most commonly used in bride-wealth exchanges, goats are virtually the exclusive animal used in sacrifices to the ancestors.[50] It is possible, therefore, that the horned quadrupeds found on Tsonga headrests refer to these animals.

A final group of Tsonga headrests with representational components are those which include weapons or sticks through them. Although inclusions vary among each headrest, the forms of the headrests are of types found among Tsonga-speakers. Sticks found in this group of headrests include those with a head and headring at one end or others with faces carved in relief along the shaft. On some sticks, a European gun appears, while others have abstract circular ends, suggesting either a cross or the spokes of a wheel. Carving objects of varied functions, such as a headrest and weapon, is explained in a number of ways. Travel is often the reason given for a combination headrest. Often a bundle is tied to a stick while walking. The stick might well be used for protection, and the headrest used for sleeping on. Where the headrest is too small to function as a support during sleep, the stick becomes the object of primary function, with the headrest acting as a representation in its own right.[51]

The diversity of images found on the sticks of Tsonga headrests suggests various interpretations. The gun image, for example, became associated with status and power. It is said that the neighboring Pedi would bring home guns after working as migrant laborers in the gold and diamond fields further south. Guns, thus, not only represented prestige, but the safe return of workers. Equally, the headring motif found on a stick is associated with maturity and wisdom, which in some way represents the owner. Such interpretations of images found on the sticks of headrests allow one to regard headrests as suggestive of ideas beyond their function.[52]

The Zulu- and Swazi-language speaking groups are commonly grouped together under the broader category North Nguni and have distinctive headrest styles which are easily distinguishable from their Shona and Tsonga neighbors. While these latter groups commonly

Figure 13. **Zulu double headrest**. Catalogue number 345.

make headrests with a base, central support and upper platform, the Zulu and Swazi (figures 11, 12, 13 and 14) headrests are most often made without a base and have a series of legs (two to eight) supporting a longer horizontal upper platform. While there are numerous substyles, the commonest form of Zulu headrest is one in which two solid supports are placed at either end of the long horizontal rest section (figure 11), sometimes with a pendant knob placed at the center of the underside of this rest (figure 12). Generally, the legs are covered with relief ornamentation, either in the form of multiple projecting pyramids (figures 11, 12 and 13) or in the form of horizontal ridges. Zulu headrests (*izigqiki*) ordinarily have horizontal ridges or square designs carved onto the legs, while the Swazi ones mostly have vertical ridges. The raised square motifs found on Zulu headrests (figure 14) are known as *amasumpa* or "warts" and are also seen on Zulu beer pots, milk pails, meat trays, and cast brass prestige bracelets.[53] The *amasumpa* pattern is believed to have originated in central Zululand, or the area of the Valley of the Kings, and may once have been reserved for people belonging to the royal family, and to a number of groups related to the Zulu royal house. Sandra Klopper in her

study of Zulu headrests argues that, rather than being associated with particular ethnic or kinship groups, the *amasumpa* pattern functioned primarily as a symbol of royal patronage and power.[54] Given the dynamics of Zulu politics, such as the incorporation of other groups, gifts of prestige items to political allies of the Zulu, and possible copying by others to invoke Zulu associations, attempts to assign exact provenance to the *amasumpa* motif has proven to be difficult and unsuccessful. While groups may now share a common language, one cannot be sure that they always did, and "Zulu" is better understood as a political construct of many disparate groups incorporated into the military state of the first Zulu king, Shaka, who was assassinated in 1828. Even attempts to link styles to kingship groups or clans is problematic because of the fact that Shaka and his successors manipulated genealogical links in a deliberate effort to broaden the power base of the ruling elite.[55] On the other hand, to simply dismiss possible relations between style and descent groups altogether would be limiting and short-sighted.[56]

Numerous Zulu headrests are either literal representations of cattle or allude to cattle through subtle figurative refer-

ences and other aspects of design. These include headrests that have overt bovine features like heads, and more frequently, tails protruding from one or both ends; others with truncated legs or circular navels between two split legs, phallic in implication and suggesting associations with bulls; headrests with numerous tapering, parallel legs that look like horns; and ones with the *amasumpa* motif, referencing wealth in the form of large herds of cattle (figure 14).[57] Michael Conner makes clear the importance of the *amasumpa* motif to the Zulu peoples by pointing out that the Zulu also decorate their cattle with *amasumpa*-like patterns. This is done by lifting and tying the skin into nodules four to six inches long, thus covering a considerable portion of the animal.[58]

One design often seen on Zulu headrests that is uniquely associated with the ancestors and their traditional dwellings is an elaborate circular "beehive" pattern found in the area between the legs. The rounded dwelling of the Zulu and, in particular, the *umsamo* (the far back of the structure), is an important spiritual place that connects the living with their ancestral spirits. The *umsamo* of every dwelling is sacred, but the chief structure of the *kraal* is especially important for it is here that all the offerings to the spirits are made and that important guardian spirits

Figure 14. **Zulu headrest**. Catalogue number 337.

of the *kraal* reside. In his research on Zulu beliefs, Berglund cites an instance where a Zulu man suggested that the "shades" like the *umsamo* because it is cool and dark (with no windows) and has only one entrance, like the womb of a cow or a human.[59]

The Zulu have close ties with and astute observation of their cattle. For example, the Zulu have more than a hundred terms for various types of cattle. Each animal has its own unique color pattern and is given a name according to the patterns found in nature. For instance, an animal with black and white bands around its throat is named *iMezi* after the Mozambique spitting cobra which has the same coloring and markings. Similarly, a black cow with a white head and chest is called *iNkwazi* after the fish eagle of the same color. The spiritual bonding between the Zulu and their cattle is so strong that all males in the homestead know each cow by its name and can identify it on sight.[60] Among the Zulu, there is traditionally in every cattle herd, one particular animal associated with the ancestors, almost always a cow. The *eyamadlozi*, as it is known, is often the largest and most beautiful cow in the herd and is reserved for sacrifice in case of extreme necessity. Because this beast is specifically associated with the ancestors, it is never sold except in urgent need.[61]

Along with the crucial importance of cattle to the political economy of the Zulu kingdom and to communications between the living with their ancestors, the persistent reference to cattle found on Zulu headrests has recently brought to light yet another interpretation. Klopper points out that numerous historical and contemporary accounts also give evidence to the possibility that bulls, in particular, are powerful symbols of masculinity.[62] Throughout Southeast Africa they have thus become likened with such male attributes as strength, independence, and virility. Klopper cites the example of when a missionary to the court of the second Zulu king, Dingane, mentioned the exchange of a bull between two leaders of two groups south of the kingdom, he noted that "in the usual symbolic style, well understood in those countries," this implied "a consciousness of power and an independence of action."[63] Equally, the third Zulu king, Mpande, referenced himself and his two predecessors and half-brothers, Shaka and Dingane, to bulls when he exclaimed, "The sons of Senzangakhona are mad bulls."[64] Given the fact that, among the Zulu, women give headrests to the bridegrooms as part of their dowries, it is understandable why contemporary Zulus often refer, not only to ancestral spirits, but also to the notion of masculinity when explaining the regularity with which the bull metaphor appears in diverse types of headrests.

While there may be some lack of consistency among the Zulu regarding the interpretation of motifs found on Zulu headrests, there is much evidence that points to variations in style having been associated with both political allegiances and social inequalities in nineteenth century Zululand-Natal. Likewise, Zulu headrest styles and motifs have been linked with and still invoke

Through dreams, the ancestors reveal themselves, allowing those living on earth to carry on life, uninterrupted, within their presence.

widely-held religious beliefs, even pointing to the idea of male virility and thus to the power of the ancestors. Klopper points out that, according to Zulu belief, it is the ancestors that regulate and control human and animal fertility.[65]

Among the Zulu, all material objects trace relationships, both those between the living and the spirits of the ancestors. The headrest is often created and put to use at the beginning of a marriage, being commissioned by the bride's father, especially for the bridegroom, or being handed down to a daughter, who, in the future, will give it to her husband. Such a gift unites clans and generations, and connects the bride's husband with her father as a symbol of the continuity of the lineage. The headrest, with its overt allusion to cattle, serves as an exchange with the bridegroom's family that will have given the bride's family a gift of cattle in recognition of her worth and in gratitude for their generosity. This gift, called *lobola*, is considered, primarily, as a nuptial contract that seals the alliance between the two families and, at the same time, compensates the father of the bride for his contribution to her upbringing and the loss of her presence to the family unit. The cattle involved in the exchange are regarded as "the knot of relationship and marriage, therefore when a girl goes to one *kraal*, something is to go from that *kraal* to the father of the girl, so that each family should possess something."[66] The importance of cattle in the union of two families is further suggested by the ritual among the Zulu of slaughtering cattle at the time of the wedding. Upon leaving her home and settling in the homestead of her husband, a bride is accompanied by cattle from her paternal home which will be used by her to maintain communion with the ancestors of her lineage. Traditionally, she is given three beasts, of which two are slaughtered at the wedding, symbolizing the meeting of the ancestors of the uniting families. The third animal is slaughtered ritually by the bride's family, once she has settled in her new home. When the animal is killed, the ancestors are called upon "to work nicely with her in giving birth so that there be no disturbances."[67] This ritual suggests that the ancestors of the woman's lineage supply the blood with which the ancestors of the male, in the male fluid, fashion the child in the womb.[68]

Without the formality of the gift of cattle, and the ensuing rituals, the marriage is not considered legal and women regard the marriage as incomplete and themselves as vulnerable.[69] The headrest, with its allusion of the bride-wealth cattle that have united the two families, symbolically refers to that union. It also looks both ahead into the future, at the children that will be born from this union, and ultimately backward to the ancestors from whom the couple came.[70]

If a headrest is not buried with its owner, it is used as a means of accessing the *amadlozi* (guardian spirits) or the *idlozi*, the spirit of the particular ancestor. This is achieved through the dream state, using the headrest as a vehicle of communication. For the Zulu, it is essential to dream in order to continue living with the ancestors in the spiritual realm. Through dreams, the ancestors reveal themselves, allowing those living on earth to carry on life, uninterrupted, within their presence. Among the Zulu, there is cause for anxiety if one does not dream. Not being able to dream could be a sign that something bad is about to happen or it could indicate a lack of interest on the part of the ancestors. Because the Zulu continue to be guided in everyday life by their ancestors in the spiritual world, dreamless nights leave one in a state of inactivity, not knowing what action to take.[71] One Zulu compared not being able to dream to sitting in

prison, not knowing when the court case will take place or what the verdict will be.[72]

The important function of headrests during the dream state is pointed out by Nettleton when she puts forth the idea that, among many Southeast African groups, including the Zulu, sleep is considered analogous to death.[73] Because in this "death state" one is unable to support his head, this function is taken over by the headrest. Furthermore, because a corpse is said to cast no shadow, a body lying flat on its back would cast very little shadow, thus resembling a dead body. The headrest, therefore, is used to elevate the head above the ground, allowing the person sleeping on the headrest to cast sufficient shadow to demonstrate himself to be a "live body."[74] As an important instrument of mediation, allowing communication, through dreams, between the living and their ancestors, the headrest acts as the "support of dreams"[75] which in its material form, manifests this interdependence.

The Swazi headrest (*izicamelo*) is very similar in form and design to that of the Zulu. Cattle are also tremendously important in the economic, political and cosmological systems of the Swazi peoples. Their headrests appear to reference cattle even more consistently than their southern neighbors the Zulu. Among the Swazi headrests, one finds a regular pattern of a horizontal cross-bar supported by two legs with a lug pendant from the center of the underside of the crossbar. The legs are almost always fluted with vertical grooves, and in some cases, tails and leg-like forms are attached at the short ends of the headrest, the design as a whole, referencing the bovine form.[76] There is no specific research known to have been done on Swazi headrest symbolism and usage. It is, therefore, generally assumed that the Swazi follow a model similar to their southern neighbors, the Zulu, with

Because the Zulu continue to be guided in everyday life by their ancestors in the spiritual world, dreamless nights leave one in a state of inactivity, not knowing what action to take.

whom they share many cultural patterns.[77] There has, however, been further research done on the headrests of other related Nguni-speaking groups such as the Ngoni. During the time of intense war that engulfed much of southern Africa during the 1800s, this group, originally from the Swaziland Transvaal region, left the area led by the African king, Zwangendaba. They moved northward through Mozambique and Zimbabwe to ultimately inhabit areas in present-day southern Tanzania, Malawi, and eastern Zambia. Headrests that are very similar to the Swazi ones are found among both the Tanzania Ngoni and the Malawi Ngoni.[78] Michael Conner's studies on the Ngoni of Malawi reveal that several known headrest styles in this area relate to where a man and his ancestors lived before being assimilated into the Ngoni.[79] This would account for the complications of ethnicity and style interaction, where a single ethnic group use headrests of various styles; one being "Swazi-like," another lakeside Tonga in form (Tsonga), and a third an adaptation of a northeastern Shona style.

Since the twelfth century C.E., when the remains of the first known headrest was discovered in a burial at the archeological site of Mapungubwe in present-day Zimbabwe, headrests have played a significant role in the practical and spiritual lives of the peoples of Southeast Africa.[80] Not only are headrests utilitarian, protecting elaborate hairstyles and indicating the married status of a man and woman, but they are, more importantly, the vehicle used to induce dreams, thereby bringing together the departed and the living through contact with the ancestors. Because cattle are the life blood of Southeast Africa and are regarded as the most essential source of wealth, headrests, particularly among the Zulu and Swazi, often reference them. It is also through cattle that people maintain communication with the ancestral spirits, the headrest being the instrument that allows for this connection. The semi-nomadic lifestyle of the peoples of Southeast Africa accounts for the hybrid styles of headrests which often allow for a regional classification rather than fixed ethnic attributions.[81] Thus, by relating the correlations of style to group migrations and acknowledging the value placed upon the identification with and the attachment to the ancestral, we are better able to understand and appreciate the confluences of social, cultural, and geographical tendencies characterized in each particular and personal headrest.

1   Axel-Ivar Berglund, *Zulu Thought-Patterns and Symbolism* (London: C. Hurst and Company, 1976), 98.

2   Karel Nel, "Headrests and Hairpins Signifying More Than Status," in *Hair in African Art and Culture*, eds. Roy Sieber and Franck Herreman 151–153 (New York: The Museum for African Art, 2000).

3   Berglund, 29.

4   N. Mostert, *Frontiers* (London: Pimlico, 1992), 963–64. Cited in Roy Sieber and Franck Herreman, *Hair in African Art and Culture* (New York: The Museum for African Art, 2000),154.

5   Sandra Klopper, "'Zulu' Headrests and Figurative Carvings: the Benthurst Collection and the Art of South-east Africa," in *Art and Ambiguity: Perspectives on the Benthurst Collection of Southern African Art*, exh. cat. (Johannesburg: Johannesburg Art gallery, 1991), 86.

6   Rayda Becker, "Headrests: Tsonga Types and Variations," in *Art and Ambiguity: Perspectives on the Brenthurst Collection of Southern Africa*, exh. cat. (Johannesburg: Johannesburg Art Gallery, 1991), 58–59.

7   Lindsay Hooper, "Domestic Arts: Carved Wooden Objects in the Home," in *Zulu Treasures: of Kings and Commoners*, exh. cat. (KwaZulu: KwaZulu Cultural Museum and the Local History Museum, 1996), 76.

8   Annie Pérez, ed., *The Art of Southeast Africa: from the Conru Collection* (Milan: 5 Continents Editions srl, 2002), 35.

9   William Dewey, *Sleeping Beauties: The Jerome L. Joss Collection of African Headrests at UCLA* (Los Angeles: Fowler Museum of Cultural History, 1991), 105.

10   Dewey, 24.

11   Berglund, 29.

12   Michael F. C. Bourdillon, "Social and Religious Life in Traditional Zimbabwe," in *Legacies of Stone: Zimbabwe Past and Present*, Vol. I, ed. William Dewey, 118 (Tervuren: Royal Museum for Central Africa, 1997).

13   Berglund, 98.

14   Berglund, 97–98.

15   Dewey, 98.

16   Dewey, 100-101. This information was obtained from an interview between William Dewey and Sekuru Bwanya, Shamva, 30 June 1984.

17   Dewey, 107.

18   Anitra Nettleton, "'Dream Machines': Southern African Headrests," *South African Journal of Art and Architectural History* 1, no.4 (1990): 147–54.

19   Tom Phillips, ed., *Africa: The Art of a Continent* (New York: Prestel Verlag, 1999), 204. The identification of Shona headrests with the human figure is discussed in William J. Dewey, *Sleeping Beauties: The Jerome L. Joss Collection of African Headrests at UCLA* (Los Angeles: Fowler Museum of Cultural History, 1993),116–132, and Anitra Nettleton, "'Dream Machines': Southern African Headrests," *South African Journal of Art and Architectural History* 1, no.4 (1990):147–54.

20   Dewey, 120–125.

21   Bourdillon, 126.

22   Paul F. Berliner, *The Soul of Mbira* (Berkeley and Los Angeles: University of California Press, 1978), 136–8.

23   Dewey, 102.

24   Dewey, 125.

25   Nettleton, 147–54.

26   Nettleton, 147–54.

27   Dewey, 118–119.

28   Dewey, 124.

29   Dewey, 101. Revealed in an interview with a carver on the various uses of headrests.

30   Anitra Nettleton, *The Traditional Figurative Woodcarving of the Shona and Venda*, diss. (Johannesburg: University of the Witwatersrand, 1984), 141, quoting Hodza and Fortune 1979: 324.

31   Phillips, 204.

32   Dewey, 106.

33   Becker, 59.

34   Perez, 49. For a more extensive discussion of Tsonga ethnic identity, see Becker, Rayda. *Tsonga Headrests: the Making of an History Category*. Ph.D. diss. Johannesburg: University of the Witwatersrand, 1999. This subject is also discussed in Anderson, B. *Imagined Communities*. London: Verso, 1983.

35   Perez, 49. For a greater discussion of the role of Swiss missionaries and their role in establishing Tsonga identity see Harries, P. "The Roots of Ethnicity, Discourse and the Politics of Language Construction in South-East Africa." *African Affairs* 87, no. 346 (1988): 25–52.

36   Becker, 60.

37   Becker, 72.

38   Nettleton, 150.

39   Becker, 64.

40   Cited in Dewey, William. *Sleeping Beauties: The Jerome L. Joss Collection of African Headrests at UCLA*. Los Angeles: Fowler Museum of Cultural History, 1993.

41   Cited in Dewey, 81.

42   Becker, 74. Jaques, in a lecture on Tsonga headrests (ca. 1930), recorded that a headrest would often be buried with its owner upon his death, putting forward the idea of a close identification between a man and his headrest.

43   Nettleton, 151.

44   William Dewey, ed., *Legacies of Stone: Zimbabwe Past and Present*, vol. 1 (Tervuren: Royal Museum for Central Africa, 1997), 259.

45   Dewey, 132.

46   Becker, 68.

47   Nettleton, 151.

48   Nettleton, 151.

49   Nettleton, 151. Referenced in Johnston, F.T. "The Music of the Shangana-Tsonga." Unpublished Ph.D. diss., University of the Witwatersrand, Johannesburg, 1971, and Junod, H.A. *The Life of a South African Tribe*, vol. 2, 2nd ed. London: Macmillan, 1927.

50   Nettleton, 151, cited in H. A. Junod, *The Life of a South African Tribe*, vol. 2, 2nd ed. (London: MacMillan, 1927), 50. Junod further maintains that the animals sacrificed at the chief's capital were always sheep.

51   Becker, 70.

52   Becker, 72.

53   Michael W. Conner and Diane Pelrine, *The Geometric Vision: Arts of the Zulu* (West Lafayette: Purdue University Galleries, 1983). Several examples are illustrated in this work.

54   Klopper, 86.

55   C. Hamilton, "Ideology, Oral Tradition and the Struggle for Power in the Early Zulu Kingdom" (master's thesis, University of the Witwatersrand, 1985). Cited in Klopper, 84.

56   Klopper, 84.

57   Klopper, 88.

58   Michael Conner, personal communication with William Dewey, July 1992. Cited in Dewey, *Sleeping Beauties*, 82.

59   Berglund, 102.

60   Barbara Tyrrell and Peter Jurgens, *African Heritage* (Johannesburg: McMillian South Africa Publishers, 1983), 203.

61   Berglund, 199.

62   Klopper, 89.

63   A.F. Gardiner, *Narrative of a Journey through the Zoolu Country* (London: William Crofts, 1836). Cited in Klopper, 89.

64   J.B. Wright and R. Edgecombe, "Mpande Senzangakhona, c. 1798–1872" in *Black Leaders in Southern African History*, ed. C. Saunders, (London: Heinemann, 1979). Cited in Klopper, 89.

65   Klopper, 89.

66   Roy Sieber and Franck Herreman, *Hair in African Art and Culture* (New York: The Museum for African Art, 2000), 154.

67   Berglund, 206–7.

68   Berglund, 207.

69   Mostert, 963–64. Cited in Sieber, 154.

70   Sieber, 154.

71   Berglund, 97–8.

72   Berglund, 96.

73   Nettleton, 153.

74   Nettleton, 153.

75   Christiane Falgayrettes, *Support de Rêves* (Paris: Editions Dapper, 1989).

76   Nettleton, 152.

77   Dewey, 83.

78   Kurt Krieger, *Ostafrikanische Plastik* (Berlin: Museum für Völkerkunde, 1990). Cited in Tom Phillips, *Africa: The Art of a Continent*, 208.

79   Michael W. Conner, "The Art of the Jere and Maseko Ngoni of Malawi, 1818–1964" (Ph.D. diss., Indiana University, 1991). Cited in Dewey, *Sleeping Beauties*, 83.

80   William Dewey, *Sleeping Beauties: The Jerome L. Joss Collection of African Headrests at UCLA*, (Los Angeles: Fowler Museum of Cultural History, 1991) 105.

81   Becker, 58–59.

Not Just for Play: Southeast African Dolls and the Hope for Children

Mary Axworthy

"Ithemba alidanisi."
"Hope does not disappoint."
Xhosa Proverb[1]

There is little of more importance in a southern African woman's life than the hope for children. Women are taught from an early age the great value of children, and the idea is reinforced throughout adolescence and adulthood. The pressure to become a mother is enormous, as a childless woman cannot move to the highest level of knowledge within the community because most high ritual positions must be held by mothers. Children also assume the critical responsibility of insuring their parents' proper burial after death.[2] Without a proper burial, an individual cannot join their ancestors, a process that keeps the lines of communication and continuity firmly established within their culture. Therefore, remaining childless can be a disastrous fate in an African woman's life.[3] Thus, the issue of fertility has been a driving force among young southern African women, and the use of fertility dolls a major element in a woman's life. This essay addresses the importance of fertility dolls among several Southeast African societies, including the functions, materials and styles of these intriguing figures.

There is little noted research on fertility dolls, also referred to as child figures, prior to the 1950s, and the early history of these figures was often hampered by poor documentation or misleading assumptions.[4] A private and secretive nature surrounding African rituals associated with fertility exists, and much of the information regarding the associated dolls is seldom made available to collectors or researchers.[5] Therefore, dolls among African communities have largely been misunderstood. Additionally, the generally accepted Western view of dolls has been rather narrow and focused primarily

Figures 15a and 15b. **Ndebele child figures**. Catalogue numbers 236 (left) and 269.

**African child figures
are more than just
toys; they function as
mediating devices that
connect the visible
and invisible worlds.**

on play among children.[6] But African child figures are more than just toys; they function as mediating devices that connect the visible and invisible worlds.[7] The fertility doll acts as a spirit medium and link with the ancestors. The figure possesses its own identity, which is recognized by the ancestors as their own.[8] These dolls are created to ensure the fertility of some women, while restoring it to others. When a girl reaches childbearing age, dolls are used to protect and celebrate her fertility, and after she marries, they enhance her ability to conceive. Child figures are also used to treat infertility among barren women.[9] Some figures serve as manifestations of wished-for children and others function as tools of instruction to young women during initiation rites.[10] In regards to African dolls, Elisabeth Cameron emphasizes, "these objects and the properties assigned them speak volumes about an individual's and a culture's beliefs and values."[11]

The materials used in the construction of early Southeast African child figures are varied, but not arbitrary. All the construction materials contain spiritual significance related to fertility. Grass and reeds, used to form the base or core of a doll, are associated with a common origin myth that evolves around a pool of water, reeds and mud. Reeds, being the carriers of water, serve as a metaphor for semen. According to oral history, the conception of humankind resulted from the penetration of reeds into the earth. Many early fertility figures were constructed by inserting a bundle of reeds into a hole made in a calabash (gourd), the calabash representing a woman's womb. The union of the reeds and calabash supports the interpretation that the fertility doll represents the procreative act that will hopefully result in the birth of a child.[12]

The use of clay in the construction of dolls is a long-standing tradition. In southern Africa, women are almost always the exclusive workers of clay vessels. They dig, process and shape the clay, creating a phallic-like core for the fertility figure. This process is thought to evoke the male presence, willing him to come to the woman.[13]

In some regions, an inner wooden core, representing the male element, supports the fertility doll. In many cases, the wood was probably carved by a man, which is a significant exception to the usual female-only construction of fertility figures. The wood core, however, would be turned over to a woman of the community for the addition of embellishments (cloth, beads, etc.) to transform it into a child figure.[14]

As mentioned above, calabashes were sometimes used to form a simplified human body as the base of a fertility doll. The gourd's role, a vessel with seeds, clearly parallels that of the womb. In some examples, a bottle replaces the gourd, contrasting the curvaceous female form of the calabash with a more conical, phallic male base. The bottle forms were then wrapped with cloth and beaded, to complete the child figure.[15]

The use of cloth on fertility dolls further enforces the connection of the child figure to the female realm, and beads are often used as embellishment. Glass beads are highly valued in southern Africa and were once a sign of status and wealth. The inclusion of beads in the production of dolls serves to emphasize their importance and value among their culture.[16]

Ndebele Dolls

Ndebele beaded fertility dolls, called *umtwana wa madlozi* (figures 15a and 15b), are given to young girls when they attend initiation school. The doll is cared for and cherished until the woman's first pregnancy. According to custom, the child figure must be given away, sold, or destroyed after the birth of the third child, because it is thought unwise to keep the doll any longer. The Ndebele child figure symbolizes both fertility and the hope for a woman to have a beautiful baby.[17]

Traditional Ndebele child figures can vary in size and shape, and old beads taken from a young girl's apron may be

Figures 16a and 16b. **Ntwane child figures**. Catalogue numbers 260 (left) and 248.

incorporated into the hoops encircling the body of the doll. The body is constructed of tightly wrapped rags, covered with a layer of beads. Covered grass hoops, made of predominantly white beads with splashes of blue, red, green, and orange, are added to create a tiered appearance. The faces of the figures are usually pink and the hair consistently black.[18] The circular beaded hoops of grass around the dolls are identical, except in size, to the *isigolwane* beaded hoops worn around the neck, legs, arms and waist of young Ndebele women after their initiation.[19]

Beaded dolls also play a significant role in courtship among the Ndebele people. A doll is placed outside the home of a prospective bride by her suitor, indicating his intentions of a marriage proposal. They are also symbolically used to establish a bridal price (*lobolo*) between the father and the groom. If the bride-to-be is not a virgin, the groom may offer the father an armless doll, suggesting that he intends to pay a lower price than requested.

Ntwane Dolls

The strong emphasis on the Ntwane woman's primary role as wife and mother is established at a very young age. The most visible form of this important role is found in the Ntwane fertility doll, called a *gimwane* or *popenyane* (figures 16a and 16b). These dolls are constructed from plaited grass, wool and beads, and the intricate skills used in producing these beautiful dolls are passed down from mother to daughter.[20]

Gimwane dolls are used in a "game" played by young Ntwane girls and boys, before they are initiated. The boys and girls contract "marriages" with each other with the dolls functioning as their "children." The dolls are given names and treated like real children, with the young girls preparing meals for them and their "husbands."[21]

The lower part of the conical *gimwane* figure is covered by beaded cylindrical waistbands that mimic those worn by initiated and married Ntwane women.[22] These beaded waistbands are usually arranged in traditional colored pattern, composed of two white bands on top, followed by one red, one blue, one pink and sometimes one white band on the bottom. White, red and blue/black colors are commonly used among the Ntwane because of their association with different soil types found in similar hues. These special soils are believed to possess spiritual healing powers.[23]

The upper part of the *gimwane* doll is enclosed in grass rings, much like those worn by young Ntwane girls, and strings of beads in colors worn by older women are added for embellishment.[24] Another adornment often found on a *gimwane* figure is a *sehlora*, a rosettelike motif placed on the side of the head. The *sehlora* (squirrel's tail) appears to have great significance among the Ntwane because it reoccurs on most of their traditional regalia, however, its meaning is unclear.[25] The long strings of clay encased woolen "hair" finishing the dolls resembles the hairstyles traditionally worn by female Ntwane healer/diviners.[26]

Another type of doll found among the Ntwane is made of wood, and sometimes clay (figure 17). This figure usually represents a Ntwane woman, evident by her distinguishing bicycle seat, helmetlike hairstyle (*tlhotshwana*). This rigid, stylized hairstyle is accomplished by rubbing in a mixture of fat and red ochre into the hair and is traditionally worn by Ntwane women on their wedding day. This type of doll usually sports traditional Ntwane costume, but its function among the community is uncertain. It is possible that these dolls were produced primarily for commercial purposes.[27]

Figure 17. **Ntwane trade doll**. Catalogue number 261.

21

South Sotho Dolls

Child figures among the South Sotho, living in and around Lesotho, serve two main functions. They were used by women in the past, during wedding ceremonies, to demonstrate to their future husbands the desire for children, and are still used to treat infertility in barren women.[28]

"Bride dolls" were made and given to South Sotho women, just before their marriage, by a grandmother or another mature women from the bride's family. The bride carried her doll at her wedding, as a sign that she wished to present her husband with many children. The doll was kept by the bride, as her most precious possession, until the birth of her first child. The carrying of bride dolls was once universal among the South Sotho, but by the early 1920s, the practice was rarely observed.[29]

The South Sotho myth surrounding child figures, used to treat infertility in women, was documented as early as 1903

Figure 18. **Lesotho child figure**. Catalogue number 239.

by Minnie Martin.[30] Martin noted that oral tradition recounts a piece of swampy ground, called "*Khapong*," at Butha-Buthe, which is sacred and inhabited by the Spirit of Maternity. Barren women offer gifts of beadwork, money, food and dolls in the hope that the spirit will answer their prayers for children. In order to prove to the spirit how earnestly they desire a child, women will make a wooden or clay fertility doll, which they carry on their backs, as they would a living child, for at least six months. At the end of the six-month period, a woman lays her doll in the *Khapong* as an offering to the spirit, along with any other bangles, beads, or ornaments she can collect. If a child is not born after this period, it is interpreted as a sign that the woman has not found favor with the spirit yet, and the doll is removed from the *Khapong* to repeat the process.[31]

The cores of South Sotho fertility dolls are made from a wide variety of materials that can include calabashes, reeds, clay, wood, bottles and amaryllis bulbs. The torso of the doll may be adorned with strings of beads, bead and/or grass ornaments such as necklaces and belts, and in some cases, bits of clothing may be added to represent a *thethana* (fiber-fringed pubic apron). Wood became the preferred foundation for South Sotho child figures in the early twentieth century, and dolls are usually shaped into slightly tapering cones or cylinders. A groove carved into the circular base, just above the bottom edge, serves to anchor the lower band of beadwork on the doll. The wooden core is often covered with cloth before being beaded, and the beadwork sheath is typically comprised of elaborate designs of triangles, parallelograms or diamonds, usually outlined in white or black (figure 18). These dolls frequently have arms made of beadwork strips, three to five beads wide, typically ending in five tiny

Figure 19. **Tsonga child figure**. Catalogue number 257.

fingers, often tipped with a single red bead representing nails. Hair is most commonly represented by short strands of beads, but fiber can also be substituted, and facial features are most often depicted by a single round brass stud-button.[32]

Tsonga Dolls

Tsonga beaded dolls (figure 19), called *nwana* (child), are made by pubescent girls after attending initiation school, and are taken along with the girls to their new homes when they marry. The dolls are used during a ceremonial courtship dance in which each doll is balanced on the palm of their maiden's hand during the dance, and then offered to a man of her choice. Acceptance of the doll constitutes a formal betrothal.[33]

The *nwana* doll consists of two parts, a simple cylindrical base and a fabric skirt. The cylinder is completely covered in beads, matching the colors and designs found in other Tsonga beadwork, and consists primarily of white with orange, red, blue, green and sometimes pink accents, patterned in horizontal stripes, chevrons, diamonds or rectangles. The base of the figure is surrounded by a replication of the large traditional skirt, the *xitlekutana/xibelani*, or the shorter dancing skirt, *xigejo*, worn by Tsonga women. The fabric used to construct the skirts is usually salempore (a cotton cloth), and embellishments to enhance the doll can include a beaded waist piece, strings of plastic and glass beads, colored hair ornaments, *xitura* (a locally made circular ornament) and occasionally a metal piece, *nxanga*, that represents the ritualistic *nxanga*, a metal bracelet or object enclosed in a beaded belt, prepared after a Tsonga girl's first menstruation.[34]

Early Tsonga *nwana* figures had no indication of facial features, but recent dolls include buttons and beads to signify a nose, eyes and mouth. Ready-made tins commonly replace the traditional wood torso of earlier dolls, which was longer and thinner and more phallic in shape. The components of the Tsonga fertility doll, the male torso and the female skirt, symbolizes the union of the two elements required to produce the hoped for child (the bones given by the father and the flesh from the mother).[35] After the birth of the couple's first daughter, some of the beads that decorated the *nwana* figure are removed and used as ornaments for the baby. As the young girl grows, the mother may continue to remove beads from the doll to incorporate them into the girl's skirts, reinforcing a strong generational link between women within the culture.[36]

Zulu Dolls

Early traditional Zulu beaded dolls are rare and many examples in museums and private collections are erroneously labeled Zulu, when in fact, they are actually South Sotho dolls. Differentiating dolls between these neighboring cultures can be difficult, but variations in bead-work patterns and colors, as well as different methods of construction, may help towards correct identification. Documentation of early Zulu child figures is sparse, and how these dolls were used is unclear.[37]

Early Zulu child figures are cylindrical in form, with the core usually made of wood, cut flat at both the base and the top. The figure is wrapped in a layer of cloth and adorned by wrapping a long string of beads round and round the core, changing colors periodically to create horizontal stripes. The most common bead colors found on these dolls are red, black, green and white, followed by pink and then blue. A mop of fiber hair is often embellished with various beads, small coins or metal rings. Facial features are typically represented by beads for eyes and a bead, or small row of beads, for the nose or mouth. Earrings are always found on these dolls and are represented by small loops or clusters of beads. Arms are typically present in the form of a single string of beads, ending in four tiny beaded fingers and a thumb.[38]

Although the nature of these early dolls is unclear, a possible connection to fertility does exist. A loop of beads, usually double and twisted, hanging from the vicinity of the naval, is present on all early Zulu child figures. This beaded addition was thought in the past to represent a waist ornament or male sex organ, the later unlikely, as all dolls would then be depicted as males. The alternate theory, suggesting a link to fertility, is that the beaded string references the umbilical cord.[39]

A more contemporary Zulu child figure is found in the Msinga region, and is made by older girls in connection with local courtship customs. The dolls are comprised of a string of beads, wound over a tightly compacted cylinder of cloth that is moistened during the bead winding process, to ensure a snug fit when dry.[40] Heads appear to either be an extension of the body, wrapped with additional cloth to build them up, or a separate ball of cloth. The beaded body creates a pattern of horizontal stripes, chevrons or occasionally other designs. A finishing

edge is added to the base of the body, just below the wrapped beads, by sewing short strings of beads in a vertical row. In some cases, a fringed girdle (*udidla*) and/or a beaded apron/pubic covering (*isigege*) is added. A variety of beaded necklaces sometimes adorn the upper body, and the face is outlined by a circular arc of white beads between one and four beads wide. Facial features (eyes, mouth) are not represented on the dolls, and the hair is dressed in the *umyeko* (mop) style, worn by girls during their *umemulo* (coming-of-age) ceremony. The girls actually wear wigs during the *umemulo* ceremony, and the doll's long strands of black silken fiber or cord, with red and light blue beads strung along the scalp line, realistically mimic the wigs.[41]

In the past, when a young Zulu girl reached marriageable age, she would seek permission from the older women in her family to begin the courtship process. When she found a man who interested her, she would present him with a doll, telling him the doll's name. If the gentleman shared her interest, he would publicly display the doll by wearing it on a string over his shoulder or hanging it inside his house.[42] These child figures were also hung around the maker's neck, hidden from view by her *ibayi* (shawl or shoulder covering). Anyone wishing to see the doll was required to pay for the privilege. Young men, during the courtship process, could request a doll to be made for them. This child figure would then symbolize that the man had a steady girlfriend. The young man would take the doll to his home, announcing that he had brought home a "baby" and members of the household would be invited to see the "baby," but had to pay for the privilege. When the young man wore the doll on special occasions, a fee for viewing was again charged. After the couple married, the doll would be given to their first-born daughter.[43]

Dolls in the 20th Century

Traditional Southeast African dolls, full of symbolism and meaning, experienced a new transformation of purpose in the twentieth century. These dolls, once rich in ritual and the promise of human fertility, found themselves rich in ritual and the promise of economic fertility, as they became commodities of the Western world.[44]

Commercial forces, cross-cultural aesthetic influence, and economic need resulted in Ndebele dolls becoming increasingly more representational and decreasingly symbolic.[45] Today the market place is filled with contemporary dolls dressed in traditional Ndebele fashion (figures 20a and 20b), as well as Western-style dolls embellished with Ndebele beadworking. Ntwane *gimwane* dolls have suffered a similar fate. Traditional doll styles are being altered, with their details changing in such a way as to make them unacceptable for use in traditional contexts.[46] Some Zulu Msinga dolls have retained most of their original form, but others have acquired faces, arms and even legs. Other modern trade figures have completely broken away from tradition and have adopted a Western doll protocol, dressed in local Msinga costume (figure 21). The meaning of these dolls have also changed, as they no longer speak of courtship, fertility and children, but speak instead to the tourist seeking an ethnic memento.[47]

Museums and collectors have developed interest in traditional fertility figures, and visitors eagerly purchase "tourist" dolls, miniature versions of traditionally costumed African women, as tokens of their travels. Adaptation to changing times have resulted in women producing dolls for both an internal (traditional fertility dolls) and an external (tourist dolls) market (figures 22a and 22b).[48]

Figures 20a and 20b. **Ndebele trade dolls**. Catalogue numbers 245 (left) and 237.

Every beautifully formed fertility doll has its own story and identity, each filled with the promise and blessing of children.

Figures 22a and 22b. **Zulu trade dolls**.
Catalogue numbers 241 (left) and 242.

Unlike the Western doll, a mass-produced child's toy manufactured for entertainment purposes, traditional Southeast African dolls are individually crafted by loving hands, filled with dreams and expectations for the maker or recipient. Every beautifully formed fertility doll has its own story and identity, each filled with the promise and blessing of children. Their story is definitely one worth hearing, as it speaks of the hope of past, present and future generations of Southeast African women. Each new day renews a hope for children, and each fertility doll is a testament to the Southeast African woman's undying faith, as the proverb of her culture states, "Hope does not kill; I shall live in hope of getting what I seek another day."[49]

Figure 21. **Zulu Sangoma trade doll**.
Catalogue number 247.

1 Zolile Calana and Patrick Holo, *Xhosa Proverbs and Metaphors* (Cape Town: Kwela Books, 2002), 45.

2 Elisabeth L. Cameron, "In Search of Children: Dolls and Agency in Africa," *African Arts* 30, no. 2 (1997): 23.

3 Margaret Carey, *Beads and Beadwork of East and South Africa* (Aylesbury: Shire Publications, 1986), 57.

4 Elizabeth Dell, ed., *Evocations of the Child: Fertility Figures of the Southern African Region* (Cape Town: Human & Rousseau, 1998), 12.

5 Veliswa Gwintsa, "Double Talk," *Evocations of the Child: Fertility Figures of the Southern African Region* (Cape Town: Human & Rousseau, 1998), 29.

6 Elisabeth L. Cameron, *Isn't S/he a Doll?: Play and Ritual in African Sculpture* (Los Angeles: UCLA Fowler Museum of Cultural History, 1996), 19.

7 Cameron, *Isn't S/he a Doll?*, 20.

8 Gwintsa, 31.

9 Carey, 57 and Cameron, "In Search of Children," 29.

10 Dell, 11.

11 Cameron, *Isn't S/he a Doll?*, 19.

12 Karel Nel and Nessa Leibhammer, "Evocations of the Child," *Evocations of the Child: Fertility Figures of the Southern African Region* (Cape Town: Human & Rousseau, 1998), 221.

13 Nel and Leibhammer, 223.

14 Nel and Leibhammer, 223.

15 Nel and Leibhammer, 225.

16 Nel and Leibhammer, 227.

17 Rhoda Levinsohn, *Art and Craft of Southern Africa: Treasures in Transition* (Craighall: Delta Books, 1984), 120.

18 Levinsohn, 121.

19 Nel and Leibhammer, 225.

20 Hazel Friedman, "Ntwane Gimwane: Ntwane Grass Figures," *Evocations of the Child: Fertility Figures of the Southern African Region* (Cape Town: Human & Rousseau, 1998), 131.

21 Anitra Nettleton and David Hammond-Tooke, "Art of the Pedi and Ntwane," in *Catalogue: Ten Years of Collecting (1979–1989)*, eds. David Hammond-Tooke and Anitra Nettleton (Johannesburg: University of the Witwatersrand, 1989), 21.

22 Nettleton and Hammond-Tooke, 20 and Friedman, 131.

23 Friedman, 131 & 135.

24 Nettleton and Hammond-Tooke, 20.

25 Friedman, 135.

26 Nettleton and Hammond-Tooke, 21.

27 Friedman, 135–137.

28 Marilee Wood, "The Sorghum Child: Nguana Modula: South Sotho Child Figures," *Evocations of the Child: Fertility Figures of the Southern African Region* (Cape Town: Human & Rousseau, 1998), 35.

29 Wood, "The Sorghum Child," 35.

30 Wood, "The Sorghum Child," 39.

31 Cameron, *Isn't S/he a Doll?*, 104.

32 Wood, "The Sorghum Child," 41–45.

33 Rayda Becker, "Ku Veleka Vukosi...To Bear Children is Wealth...: Tsonga Figures," *Evocations of the Child: Fertility Figures of the Southern African Region* (Cape Town: Human & Rousseau, 1998), 123.

34 Becker, 119 and Rayda Becker and Anitra Nettleton, "Tsonga-Shangana Beadwork and Figures," in *Catalogue: Ten Years of Collecting (1979–1989)*, eds. David Hammond-Tooke and Anitra Nettleton (Johannesburg: University of the Witwatersrand, 1989), 10.

35 Becker, 121.

36 Becker and Nettleton, 11.

37 Marilee Wood, "The Girl Who Ran Away," in *Evocations of the Child: Fertility Figures of the Southern African Region* (Cape Town: Human & Rousseau, 1998), 77.

38 Wood, "The Girl Who Ran Away," 79.

39 Wood, "The Girl Who Ran Away," 79.

40 Frank Jolles, "Contemporary Zulu Dolls from Kwalatha," *African Arts* 27, no. 2 (1994): 60–61.

41 Wood, "The Girl Who Ran Away," 85.

42 Cameron, *Isn't S/he a Doll?*, 114.

43 Wood, "The Girl Who Ran Away," 83–85.

44 Cameron, *Isn't S/he a Doll?*, 41.

45 Ivor Powell, *Ndebele: A People and Their Art* (Cape Town: Struik Publishers, 1995), 121.

46 Nettleton and Hammond-Tooke, 21.

47 Jean Morris and Eleanor Preston-Whyte, *Speaking with Beads: Zulu Arts from Southern Africa* (New York: Thames and Hudson, 1994), 54.

48 Dell, 12.

49 "South African Proverbs," *Creative Proverbs from Around the World* <http://creativeproverbs.com/sf04.htm> (8 March 2004).

Attraction and Meaning in Courtship Beadwork Panels

Sara Mandel

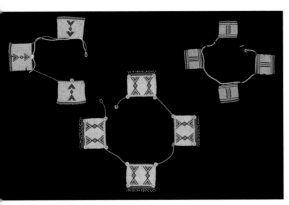

Figures 23a, 23b and 23c. **Xhosa necklaces**. The unique combinations of color and design elements (diamonds, chevrons, and stripes) on these ornaments likely contain a message sent by the artist to her lover. While the symbolism may have been more standardized a century ago, changes due to migration, availability of bead colors, and Western influence have made a definitive "reading" of these ornaments impossible by anyone other than the artist. Catalogue numbers 424, 423 and 422.

In Southeast Africa, beadwork is a visual form of artistic expression that serves to amplify the voice of both the artist and the wearer. Many Southeast Africans incorporate beadwork into their daily and ornamental attire to aesthetically enhance their physical appearance. Among the Zulu and Xhosa people,[1] one of the most personal forms of visual expression is courtship neck ornaments (figures 23a, 23b and 23c), crucial tokens of affection, created and given by young women to young men during sophisticated rituals of courtship. Beaded neck ornaments are a public form of personal expression within Zulu and Xhosa societies. Women use beadwork to express their personal feelings, hopes, and concerns about a relationship, while men accumulate beadwork in order to create a public perception about themselves. The basic function of courtship beadwork is to attract attention, or "ask for eyes," either in the creation of these objects by women to attract the attention of the men they desire, the adornment of beadwork by men to attract the attention of the community by making a statement about their sexual desirability, or, when made for the art market, to appeal to outside audiences and consumers. While researchers have utilized a diversity of approaches in their attempts to understand the meaning of bead ornaments in Zulu and Xhosa society,[2] this essay explores the cultural significance of Zulu and Xhosa sentimental beaded panels from a more individualized and indigenous perspective, with a focus on formal characteristic variation (historical and regional), etymological interpretation, and audience-based levels of meaning.

Formal Characteristics

Forms of courtship beadwork vary among the individual cultures of

Figure 24. **Zulu man**. This young Zulu man, photographed in approximately 1886, wears many of the common beaded courtship regalia found among Zulu youth. The coiled rope-like headpiece and neckpiece shown, called *imigingqo*, can be worn interchangeably. This gentleman also dons multiple beaded panel neckpieces (*amaqabane*), a single beaded panel neckpiece (hanging lowest on the chest), called a *umphapheni*, and a beaded rolled waistband (*umutsha*). The beadwork may have been given to him by different young women to communicate something about their potential relationship. The more beadwork a young man wears the more desirable he appears to be. Appendix A-1.

Southeast Africa, as well as within each ethnic group. While Xhosa courtship beadwork can take a variety of forms, such as three white beaded headbands or a beaded tapestry panel on a safety pin, Zulu courtship ornaments are traditionally a necklace with three or more beaded flaps. The young Zulu man in figure 24 wears an assortment of beaded neck ornaments with panels, the form of courtship beadwork this essay will concentrate on.

The main strand of a courtship necklace in both Xhosa and Zulu is called an *ucu* and can be made of either all white or a variety of colored beads, including

Women use beadwork to express their personal feelings, hopes, and concerns about a relationship, while men accumulate beadwork in order to create a public perception about themselves.

white, black, red, yellow, pink, green, and blue. The rectangular projections extending from the Xhosa *ucu*, sometimes called "keeper of the heart,"[3] is considered the expressive element of the courtship beadwork and contains combinations of different shapes such as diamonds, chevrons, zigzags, dots, stripes, and a simplified human form wearing a large triangular skirt. The geometric shapes refer to the Xhosa woman's relationship status (single, engaged, married[4]), age (young, old), state of fertility (virgin, pregnant, number of children), and *lobolo* or bride price,[5] while variations in the anatomy of the human form express the beadworker's character ("very hard working," "glamorous," "gossip," "beautiful dancer,") and/or diligence (hardworking, lazy).[6]

However, the ideas expressed in the colors and designs of Xhosa beadwork may vary depending on region and context. An assortment of colors, shades,

designs, textures, and sizes of beads, depending on availability regionally and historically, and the beadworker's aesthetic preference, allow for a broad spectrum of forms.[7] Every design is individual and only those involved in the process of creating these objects can fully understand the personalized meaning of each piece. Women beadworkers utilize an extraordinary and ever-changing vocabulary created within the micro-social system of bead artists, making a reliable lexicon unfeasible.

There is great disparity between different forms of Xhosa courtship beadwork resulting from variation within the society.[8] In some Xhosa groups, the *ucu* is made of only white beads and tends to be roughly six to ten feet long. One is worn around the neck of each young woman and her fiancé upon betrothal. When the *ucu* is doubled and twisted into a rope, it announces that the second day of engagement has passed. A regional modification on the Xhosa *ucu* may include tassels on the end signifying that marriage negotiations are in process.[9] Another indication of Xhosa engagement occurs when a young man accepts and wears three white beaded headbands made and gifted from an interested young woman.[10] Though formally different from beaded panels, the headbands or neckropes are also social indicators that help to define personal and social status.

The formal variations in Xhosa beadwork do not apply to Zulu beadwork since the Zulu courtship beaded neck ornament is more standardized, basically consisting of the *ucu* and a number of rectangular panels. Also, the designs in the Zulu beaded panel do not represent the character of the beadworker as do the shapes in the Xhosa "keeper of the heart," but instead function as a tool to express a young woman's interest in a young man or to communicate an emotion or concern regarding the state and future of their relationship.

In 1907, Father Mayr was among the first to publish literature addressing Zulu courtship beadwork worn by young men as gifts from interested young women who were expressing "her feelings towards her sweetheart."[11] He described how the colors of Zulu beadwork each refer to a different emotion or concept such as purity, sorrow, poverty, or desire, for example, and the order of the colors in relation to each other literally articulate concepts such as confessions of the girl's affection, concerns regarding the genuine intentions of a lover, or fear that he may not be able to afford the *lobolo*. For example, Mayr translates a single strand of pink and white beads to mean, "Here is my letter to you, my heart is white (full of love) in the long weary days; but you have no cattle to buy me."[12] Unfortunately, Mayr's translation may not be completely accurate. As discourse has concentrated on describing and decoding the formal characteristics of Zulu and Xhosa courtship beadwork ornaments, accurate interpretations have become increasingly problematic because variation is so widespread.

Linguistic and Etymological Interpretations

Interpreting Zulu and Xhosa beadwork by simply translating colors to mean specific concepts over simplifies the significance and expression of courtship beadwork panels. It is impossible to ascribe a definitive meaning to a bead color not only because it varies regionally, but also because a color may mean something different when juxtaposed with another color, or may not even exist in the beadworker's vocabulary due to historical and regional availability. Context is crucial when attempting to interpret messages. Individuals knowledgeable in the "specific local origin" and the "colour code native to it" may be capable of an accurate translation; however, there is variation in interpretations that can be attributed to the "ingenuity" of the beadworkers who develop each their own "individual idiolect,"[13] meaning that each individual beadworker may depend on their own concept of what a color or combination of colors may mean to them. Furthermore, not all colors or styles of beads have been available throughout history, allowing for continuous changes that deter any possibility of common symbolism or stylistic standards through time. Despite attempts to compile a comprehensive dictionary, only white is generally accepted to mean love and purity.[14]

According to Mayr, beaded necklaces were equivalent to a form of correspondence sent by the young woman to her prospective lover with the hopes of receiving some kind of a reply acknowledging her appeal and responding to it. Mayr translates the Bantu word *inCwadi* to mean "letter" in English. Following that, *incwadi yokuthanda* has been translated as a "letter or book of love."[15] Another local term for beaded courtship ornaments includes *ubala abuyise*, translated to mean "she writes, that he should answer,"[16] or "one writes in order that the other should reply."[17] Thus, the origin for the Western interpretation of the beaded panels as "love letters" may stem from an etymological interpretation.[18] Barbara Tyrrell goes further stating that the beaded panels are "sent by the hand of a friend" to the young man of interest,[19] creating a scenario that supports the interpretation of courtship beadwork panels as objects that are equivalent to Western modes of written correspondence, i.e. that they are "love letters."

However, in calling them "love letters," courtship beadwork panels have come to be understood as an alternate form of written communication equivalent to Western modes of correspondence, an interpretation stemming from attempts to understand an indigenous form of visual expression through Western sensibilities. The word "letter" can mean a variety of things, from items of correspondence to a symbol within a phonetic system.[20] The use of the word "letter" probably seemed appropriate when initially translating the indigenous term. However, courtship beadwork panels are not love notes written for exchange, nor are they cryptographic symbols expressing amorous intentions. The pervasiveness and history of the term "love letter" does not preclude that interpretation from being questioned for its accuracy.

According to the Zulu-English dictionary, *Ncwadi* refers to a mark or sign that can be either on a dwelling, indicating the owner's absence, or on one's person for a variety of reasons.[21] *Ncwadi* is also translated as "paper, letter, book." However, the latter definitions are "not native...but have been formed by corruption from the English or Dutch languages, or have been coined by Missionaries and are now in common use [sic] among people of this colony."[22] The definition of *Ncwadi* as "paper, letter, book" and the subsequent note on linguistic corruption demonstrate that while beadwork panels are a form of visual communication, the classification of these objects as correspondence is exaggerated. The word "letter" has been misappropriated by outsiders who consider this complex form of expression in beadwork to correspond with Western conventions of communication.

These linguistic fallacies have contributed to later misinterpretations and misunderstandings of courtship regalia and indigenous practices in academic and non-academic discourse. In some literature, the term *ucu* has even been translated to mean "love letter" even though an *ucu* is a line of beads.[23] Interestingly, the second indigenous term, *ubala abuyise*, corresponds with the Zulu language in the same manner. The root of the term *ubala abuyise* is translated into "mark or scratch, as with the nails," with the potential context of reading and writing and a reference to the same note regarding corruption as above.[24] Scholars have characterized the iconography in Zulu and Xhosa beadwork as a simplified and universal form of written communication, assuming that the use of marks and scratches stems from illiteracy,[25] refusing to accept this artwork as a medium for individual expression by concentrating on analyzing its visual form instead of its social role. The propensity in research to translate colors and designs literally is probably a consequence of the historical mistranslation of the indigenous term for courtship beadwork panels.

Audience and Communication

Understanding the significance of Zulu and Xhosa beadwork is most effectively investigated by exploring its use within and outside the local communities, and how individuals create and use beadwork as a medium for expression. Men and women use beadwork in different ways to communicate gender specific concepts about themselves. Xhosa women use the beadwork panels to articulate their perceptions of self and Zulu women express feelings regarding romantic involvements. Men in both cultures often accumulate beadwork in order to create a positive public perception about themselves. Furthermore, courtship beaded panels are increasingly being created for an outside art market for purchase by visitors to Southeast Africa.

Young women create beadwork ornaments to give to specific young men as part of the courtship process. The gift of beadwork by a young woman can express an interest in the young man,

Afraid of being derided as unattractive, young men may commission their female relatives to make "courtship" beadwork for them to wear, thus creating a socially distorted indicator of desirability.

initiate a relationship, or communicate an emotion or concern regarding the state and future of their relationship. Women tend to bead in groups, discussing their relationships and their beading patterns while they work, which helps them develop imagery and symbolic meaning that may be encoded within the beaded panels. Since the expression within the beadwork is not necessarily known within the wider community, the gift of a beaded object is an opportunity for the young woman to privately, as well as publicly, communicate with her lover. This gift invites the man to ask the woman for an explanation of what she has expressed in a more intimate setting after the exchange has been witnessed by the community. This process allows the young woman to express herself, but do so "without loss of maidenly pride or modesty."[26]

Young men at the age of courting will wear a variety of beadwork that is presumably made by several young women (figure 24). This collection implies that the man has a large number of lovers or wives and suggests wealth and status, because, according to Zulu and Xhosa cultures, the accumulation of beadwork is a gauge of a man's sexual appeal.[27] Afraid of being derided as unattractive, young men may commission their female relatives to make "courtship" beadwork for them to wear, thus creating a socially distorted indicator of desirability.[28] Therefore, it is not just the creators of courtship beadwork who determine their significance, but the men who wear beadwork can also use these objects to convey a self-image, whether real or invented.

Beadwork is also a popular form of art produced by the local community for visitors to purchase as souvenirs. New motifs added into the indigenous beadwork vernacular have expanded the artist's visual vocabulary.[29] In the past few decades, Zulu beadwork has begun to display designs beyond long-established motifs, including heart shapes and Roman alphabetic characters. The popularity of written words has been incorporated into beadwork designs, probably developed from the growing market for tourist art, as visitors to the region may seek to purchase "love letters" to take home. While outsiders often have a distorted or romanticized understanding of this art form, the growing demand has provided enormous financial support to many beadworkers and their families.

Whether created by women for the men they desire, worn by men as a display of their desirability, or made to satisfy the demands of an external market, courtship panels are created, worn, and given meaning by individuals and meaning varies by intent, context, and audience variation. In the creation and use of courtship beadwork, individuals are requesting the attention of a particular group of people to communicate a wide range of ideas, sentiments, and aesthetic visions.

Conclusion

Among the Xhosa and Zulu, courtship beadwork is a highly visible form of artistry that fosters personal expression and invites attention, intimately, publicly, and economically. Courtship beadwork neck ornaments are part of a complex system of communication dependent on individual expression, personal image, and public perception, drawing from a complex iconographic vocabulary that has developed over geography and time, but remains individually specific. Western concepts regarding the form and role of beaded panels probably stem from linguistic misinterpretations and regional differences, but an indigenous perspective allows us to better understand the significance of this art form. Essential to courtship, beadwork serves as a form of expression for both women, in creating and presenting it, and men, in choosing to wear it. Furthermore, outside patronage has created alternative versions of courtship beadwork for tourist purchase, and this practice has in turn influenced local conventions. While colors and designs may have general associations, they are not intended to be "read" as much as they trigger a range of related conceptual meanings that are ultimately defined by individual context. Similar to interpretations of proverbs and proverbial statements, beadworkers and their local audiences interpret the meaning of beaded panels based on a shared social experience, yet actual meaning ultimately resides in individual perception, interpretation, and understanding.

1   Zulu and Xhosa are two societies within the Nguni ethnic group of the Bantu-speaking people of southern Africa.

2   Gary van Wyk compares messages created through color and design to a language embodying a "semiotic system" of interpretation. (Gary van

Wyk, "Illuminated Signs: Style and Meaning in the Beadwork of the Xhosa- and Zulu-speaking Peoples," *African Arts* 36.4 (Winter 2003): 12–33, 93–94.) Sandra Klopper's work is a more focused historical account of artistic expression in Zululand. She asserts concern for the "reductive approach to colour symbolism" that has dominated the majority of scholarship on Zulu beadwork used in courtship rituals. (Sandra Klopper, "The Art of Zulu-Speakers in Northern Natal-Zululand. An Investigation of the History of Beadwork, Carving and Dress from Shaka to Inkatha," diss. (University of the Witwatersrand, Johannesburg, 1992), 84.) Eleanor Preston-Whyte concentrates on changes in Zulu beadwork resulting from the influence of the Western art market, as beadworkers adjust their styles to accommodate a growing demand outside the local community for these objects. (Eleanor Preston-Whyte and Jean Morris, *Speaking with Beads* (New York: Thames & Hudson, 1994). Eleanor Preston-Whyte and Jo Thorpe, "Ways of Seeing, Ways of Buying; Images of Tourist Art and Culture Expression in Contemporary Beadwork," in *African Art in Southern Africa: From Tradition to Township*, eds. Anitra Nettleton and David Hammond-Tooke (Johannesburg: AD Donker, 1989), 123–51.) While these approaches are helpful in attempting to understand specific messages that may be articulated in personalized beaded panels, this body of literature has failed to address the fundamental role of these objects in the elaborate social system of partnership and self-expression.

3   Joan A. Broster, *Red Blanket Valley* (Johannesburg: H. Keartland, 1967), 65. Broster has done the most extensive research on Xhosa beadwork, specifically on the Thembu society with whom she lived in the Engcobo district in the Transkei. This may be problematic, however, because her research has focused on a very specific group and generalizations are often misleading.

4   Xhosa women in some groups continue to make beaded neck ornaments after marriage to publicly communicate to their husbands. Broster 1967.

5   The bride price or *lobolo* is what a young Nguni man offers, often in cattle, to a father in order to marry his daughter. The *lobolo* is a culturally significant element in the negotiations of courtship and marriage.

6   Broster.

7   Van Wyk and Broster. Both scholars discuss the value of beads in commerce and their role in the local economy throughout history. As beads became more available, they became less expensive; however, they were initially very costly.

8   Martin West and Jean Morris, *Abantu: An Introduction to the Black People of South Africa* (Cape Town: C. Struik Publishers, 1976). Xhosa people were relocated several times and they were subjected to cultural exchanges due to contact and warfare among Nguni ethnic groups, as well as colonial encroachment. The Xhosa-speaking people were crammed between Shaka and the Zulu kingdom in the north and the Cape Colony in the south. Furthermore, their heritage was influenced by intermarriage with the Khoi and multiple migrations, and the Xhosa were among the first in Southeast Africa to be exposed to white explorers and travelers, missionaries, and colonial settlers. Although somewhat antiquated in terminology and ideology, West and Morris's text offers the most user-friendly introduction into the various ethnic groups in the region. They provide a broad and mostly accurate account of the historical background of the different ethnic groups and express how they are similar, different, and generally and historically interrelated. Also van Wyk, 93, note 4.

9   Margaret Carey, *Beads and Beadwork of East and South Africa* (Princes Risborough: Shire, 1986), 57.

10   Carey, 47–48. Carey differentiates between Xhosa and Zulu courtship beadwork by saying that the Xhosa create "love tokens" in a variety of forms throughout the courting process, whereas Zulu gifts of courtship generally maintain the form of beaded panels for communicating sentiments in encoded messages. The first gift from a young Xhosa woman to a young Xhosa man is a group of three headbands. However, throughout courtship, the Xhosa woman continues to create beaded objects for the man of her interest, including necklaces, ankle bands, arm bands, and beaded panels. Zulus primarily exchange neck ornaments, not the variety of objects that Xhosa exchange. Also see Broster, 24–25. Broster discusses the three beaded headbands that young Xhosa women make for the objects of their affection, explaining that the initial gifts are presented to the chosen male the afternoon before a dance. If he accepts the beads, he will wear them to the dance as a public statement that he has become romantically linked or in the early stage of courtship with the maker of his headbands.

11   Father Mayr, "The Zulu Kafirs of Natal," *Anthropos 2* (1907): 633–45, p. 641.

12   Mayr, 642.

13   Rhoda Levinsohn, *Art and Craft of Southern Africa: Treasures in Transition* (Johannesburg: Delta, 1984), 84.

14   Preston-Whyte and Morris, 58; Preston-Whyte and Thorpe, 129; Carey, 55; Barbara Tyrrell, *Tribal People of Southern Africa* (CapeTown: Books of Africa, 1968), 116; John W. Grossert, *Zulu Crafts* (Pietermaritzburg: Shuter & Shooter, 1978), 53; Regine Twala, "Beads As Regulating the Social Life of the Zulu and Swazi," *African Studies 10*, (Johannesburg: Whitwatersrand University Press, 1951), 115. While the multitude of researchers admit to the difficulty in attributing absolute definitions to specific colors and sequences, they still seem to insist on defining a common denominator of meaning in color.

15   Preston-Whyte and Thorpe, 130.

16   Mayr, 641.

17   Levinsohn, 84. She sites Walter Battis, *The Art of Africa* (Pietermaritzburg: Shuter and Shooter, 1958), 137.

18   The term in *Cwadi* is also found in other literature. Eileen Jensen Krige, *The Social System of the Zulus* (Pietermartizburg: Shuter & Shooter, 1950), 118. It is written as *iNcwadi* in A.T. Bryant's text, *The Zulu People: As They Were Before the White Man Came* (New York: Negro Universities Press, 1948), 535.

19   Tyrrell, 116.

20   Victoria Neufeldt, ed., *Webster's New World Dictionary*, (New York: Prentice, 1988).

21   John William Colenso, *Zulu-English Dictionary* (Farnborough, Gregg, 4th edition, 1967), 371. The "other reasons" were not specified.

22   Colenson, viii.

23   Colenson, 84.

24   Colenson, 16.

25   It is interesting to note that *Buyisana* was translated as a verb, "bring or send back mutually, withdraw mutually bad words," Colenson, 64.

26   Tyrrell, 116.

27   Levinsohn 1984:84.

28   Michael Stevenson and Michael Graham-Stewart, ed., *South East African Beadwork 1850–1910, from Adornment to Artifact to Art* (London: Farmwood Press, 2000), 38.

29   Morris and Preston-Whyte, 58.

A Visual Voice: Revealing Southeast African Beadwork

Mary Axworthy

"Kuhlwile pambile, kusile emuva."
The past we know; the future is hidden.
   Zulu Proverb[1]

Whether it is past, present or future, beads have, and probably always will, play a very important role in the lives of southern Africans; they invoke "a sense of belonging to a people, to a place, and to a chain of tradition."[2] Aside from their pleasing aesthetic value, the various beadwork articles produced in southern Africa serve to mark significant transitions in a person's life. The detailed beadwork of this region visually communicates ethnic identity within southern African groups, clearly establishing the individual's status within one's specific culture. Distinct personal identity and character is also apparent through the innovation of creative and diverse designs, as the implementation of unusual or recycled items are artistically incorporated into inspiring beaded works. Focusing on the Ndebele, Zulu and Xhosa regions of Southeast Africa, this essay provides an overview of the history of African beads, the critical role beads play in society and how beads "speak" to the people who use and wear them, conveying important information about their cultural beliefs, experience and identity.[3]

When viewing Southeast African beadwork, it is important to keep in mind these beautiful objects were made to be worn. Beads, together with the human body, form a complete work of art. Viewed alone, the aesthetic appeal of each intricate piece can be admired, but it is merely a part of the whole experience.[4] Joan Broster noted from her extensive fieldwork among the Tembu that "words and photographs cannot adequately describe the brilliance of the beads, the clarity of the colours, or their sparkling effect on the dark skin of the wearer."[5]

Beads can be crafted from various materials into many different shapes and sizes. African beadworkers have handcrafted beads, for thousands of years, from natural and manufactured materials.[6] Indigenous materials include metals (brass, copper, gold, silver and iron), stones (gneiss, agates and jasper), clay, copal amber, wood, seeds, coconut shells, seashells, snail shells and glass.[7] The earliest known African beads were made from ostrich shells and date back to 10,000 BCE.[8] The first imported glass beads introduced in Africa were thought to have been brought from India by Arab merchants around 200 BCE, and were probably only available in small quantities. Before European contact, bead colors found in Africa were limited to blue, green, yellow, red and black.[9] The Portuguese were the first to introduce larger quantities of Venetian glass seed beads in the 1400s in exchange for gold, ivory and slaves.[10] Until the nineteenth century, glass beads were still relatively

> When viewing Southeast African beadwork, it is important to keep in mind these beautiful objects were made to be worn. These beads, together with the human body, form a complete work of art.

Most of the traditional beadwork produced in Southeast Africa is worn by women, and their appropriate forms record the development of a woman's entire life, from birth through childhood, pubescence, adulthood, marriage, childbearing and maturity.

thetic preferences developed.[14] Southeast African beadworkers were found to be very discriminate. On his first visit to the Colony of Natal in 1854, Bishop Colenso documented, "the Natives…are as capricious in their taste for beads, as any English lady in the choice of her bonnet. The same pattern will only suit them for a season or two; and they are at all times difficult to please."[15]

Beadwork in its simplest form can be a single string of beads, even a single bead, worn on any part of the body or added to a carved figure as decoration or an offering. More elaborate beadwork can be strung into complex ropes, sewn into panels resembling fabric, applied as a covering to figures, clothing and masks, or used to enhance everyday items.[16] Openwork beading may be done by creating strands of beads linked together by space bars and strung in a netted trellis pattern or picot edging. Applied beadwork incorporates beads that have been sewn individually in a prepared medallion and attached to a base material. Applique is also accomplished by using a "lazy stitch" to attach a string of up to twelve beads at a time and securing them with a small stitch through the base cloth.[17]

Dating beadwork has been problematic because of inadequate or contradictory oral evidence, little existing written documentation and beads from older beadwork pieces sometimes being re-used in new pieces. The symbolic significance of colors and styles often seem confusing and sometimes contradictory for the same reasons.[18] However, methods of beadworking and the materials used in the stringing process can give some indication of date. The early traditional method of stringing beads was usually accomplished by twisting a thread of vegetable fiber or animal sinew or using a thin leather strip, and pieces of beadwork exhibiting this method are likely to have

Figures 25a and 25b. **Ndebele young girl's aprons.** Catalogue numbers 10 (left) and 9.

been produced prior to 1945.[19] Among the Ndebele people, oral histories imply that beadworking is a tradition that has been passed down for more generations than anyone can remember, yet there is no physical evidence of Ndebele beadwork prior to the nineteenth century. This could be attributed to a past tradition of burying beadwork along with its owner. At some unknown point, this tradition changed and women began passing beadwork down to their daughters or other relatives.[20]

Women are the exclusive makers of beadwork among the Ndebele, Zulu, and Xhosa peoples of Southeast Africa.[21] Although these three groups observe different customs, they share a common heritage with related languages and they all base their livelihoods on farming and herding.[22] The beadwork made by these groups is distinctly different in style and color, but it serves the same purpose, to celebrate ethnicity and identify the social status of the wearer. Most of the traditional beadwork produced in Southeast Africa is worn by women, and their appropriate forms record the development of a woman's entire life, from birth through childhood, pubescence, adulthood, marriage, childbearing and maturity.[23] The clearly defined levels of status are recognized by changes in ornamentation, including beadwork, and

rare and valuable in Africa, making them a symbol of wealth and status.[11]

The growing availability of beads by the mid-nineteenth century increased the opportunity for women to develop their creative skills, and beadwork production began to flourish throughout southern Africa. At one point during the nineteenth century, South Africa was the largest market for beads in the world.[12] Although beads were no longer used as a valuable item of exchange, beadwork continued to be a significant symbolic means of communicating social relationships among rural traditionalists.[13] By the mid-nineteenth century, an estimated four hundred different varieties of trade beads were being manufactured, but each African cultural group might only accept five to ten colors, sizes or shapes as aesin clothes. These important levels give stability to the social structure because associated with each level come specific responsibilities, obligations and privileges. Beadwork is so influential in southern African society that it can serve as a legal document in traditional court cases such as breach of promise or adultery.[24]

The Transvaal Ndebele (also known as the Southern Ndebele or Nguni of the Interior) demonstrate a distinct style of beadwork that differs from the Zimbabwean Ndebele. This essay concentrates on the Transvaal Ndebele with the oldest existing examples of their beadwork probably dating back to the late nineteenth century.[25] Beadwork for the Ndebele is "a visible means of emphasizing group values and identity as well as communicating status and the passing of rites of passage to the community."[26]

The *umucu* celebrates the birth of a Ndebele child and consists of a single strand of beads worn around the waist. The *umucu* signifies the child's first induction into society and is thought to encourage a favorable destiny.[27] A four- to five-day-old infant is also adorned with a *khetsa*, a small beaded collar, during a ceremony in which grandparents traditionally select the baby's name.

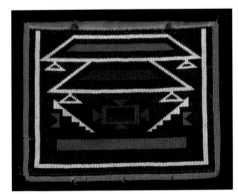

Figure 26. **Ndebele initiated girl's apron.** Catalogue number 11.

The *khetsa* is worn for about two years before being passed on to another child.[28]

The *lebeshu* and *lighabi* (or *ghabi*) are the next items in the bead cycle and are worn by little boys and girls respectively. The *lebeshu* for young boys is a beaded loincloth made of leather. The *lighabi* (figures 25a and 25b) is a beaded loincloth with the frontal skirt having a border of beads at the top with strands of twisted sisal (a strong, durable white fiber derived from hemp), trimmed with beading, hanging from it. The *lighabi* is usually made by the maternal grandmother and is worn by girls from the age of four months to twelve years.[29]

Puberty marks a young girl's initiation and seclusion, called *iqhude*, where she learns the responsibilities of adulthood and the important aspects of Ndebele culture including beadwork and mural painting.[30] The *isiphephethu* (figure 26) marks the passage from youth to adulthood and the girl's new prospect of marriage. The *isiphephethu* is made by the girl's mother or grandmother, and is a stiff, rectangular-shaped apron panel made from hide or canvas and decorated with geometric beaded patterns.[31] In addition to the *isiphephethu*, young women often wear the *isithimba*, a backskirt typically made from a semi-circular piece of leather that is sometimes rudimentarily beaded. The leather of the skirt is often suspended from a bead-covered roll of grass and a row of brass rings can be attached for decorative purposes.[32]

For important ceremonies, such as female initiations, young women also wear *isigolwane*, wide beaded arm and leg rings made by stringing beads around a thick pad of grass. The rings are thought to mimic the rolls of fat appreciated in a prosperous adult woman.[33] The *isigolwane* accentuates the maiden's beauty and charm to interested male observers and may help to increase the chance of a marriage proposal.[34]

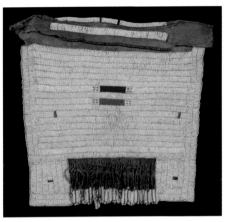

Figure 27. **Ndebele married woman's apron.** Catalogue number 12.

The *liphotu* (also known as a *mapoto*) is the first apron worn by married women (figure 27). Usually described as an everyday apron, the *liphotu* actually serves a very different purpose from the other married woman's apron, the *ijogolo*. The Ndebele marriage process is divided into phases. The first phase includes complicated negotiations between the two families wherein the bridal price (*lobolo*) is set. At the ceremony celebrating this step of the marriage, the bride will wear the beaded *liphotu* apron for the first time. The *liphotu* is easily identified by its two side flaps and beaded tassels hanging in a row between them. The two side flaps are said to represent the bride and groom and the center tassels the expectation of their children.[35]

The second beaded apron worn in the marriage process is the *ijogolo* (figure 28). In contrast to the *liphotu*, the *ijogolo* has five front finger-type panels cut from leather or canvas that is then beaded. According to researcher Diane Levy, the center panel represents a mother and the panels on either side of the center symbolize her children. The *ijogolo* is worn for the final marriage ceremony that takes place only after the bride has born her first child. Under Ndebele tradition,

33

if the bride does not produce children, she can be returned to her parents and the bridal price must be refunded.[36]

Other traditional Ndebele wedding items that may be worn are the *nyoga*, *linaga* and *isiyaya*. The *nyoga* (snake) is a long beaded train, entirely woven from beads with no backing, which hangs down the back of the bride and trails along the ground (figures 29 and 30). The *nyoga* is sometimes worn during a special dance that expresses the bride's willingness to have many children. The *linaga* is a beaded cape of goatskin and the *isiyaya* is a beaded veil that covers the bride's face as a sign of respect to her future husband and his family. Both the *linaga* and *isiyaya* are rarely worn nowadays and have been replaced by the *nguba*, a marriage blanket worn draped over the shoulders, that is comprised of brightly colored vertical bands of red, blue, green, yellow and brown, often with beaded panels applied to the surface.[37]

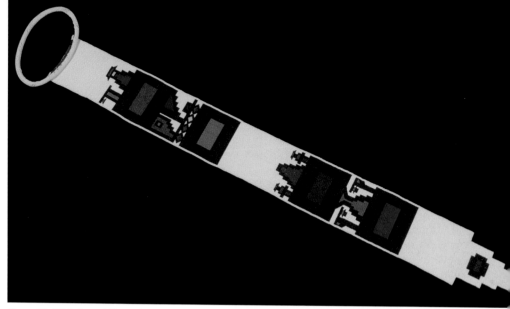

Figure 29. **Ndebele wedding train**. Catalogue number 197.

One of the most unusual pieces of Ndebele beadwork is the *linga koba*, or "long tears," which signifies a very special event in a mother's life. The *linga koba* is made from two narrow strips of woven beading with each strip hanging down either side of the woman's head connected by a narrow headband. The *linga koba* is worn on the occasion of a mother's son returning from his long initiation seclusion in the mountains. The "tears" represent both the mother's joy at her son's attainment of manhood and her sorrow at losing him, as well as mark her arrival at the next level of maturity.[38]

Beadwork among the Zulu, also known as the North Nguni, plays a major role in dress and expression of personal style. There are more than fifty names of beadwork articles existing among the Zulu people, but many are difficult to distinguish accurately and some are only known in isolated areas.[39] Although new and modern designs, referred to as *isimodeni*, are apparent in contemporary Zulu beadwork, older color combinations and distinctive patterns of traditional beadwork styles have survived.[40]

Figure 30. **Ndebele wedding train**. Catalogue number 198.

The elevated role of beads among the Zulu was explored in 1824 by Henry Francis Fynn, one of the first white men to travel extensively in southern Africa. Through Fynn's observations, and the research of others, it is clear to social anthropologist, Eleanor Preston-Whyte that beads to the Zulu have consistently been

far more than mere ornaments, for they had come to have cultural and symbolic meaning. The varieties and the colours of the beads that people wore (and were permitted to wear) immediately indicated their general social position, as well as any extraordinary personal achievements. Thus particular styles of beaded ornament characterized male as opposed to female dress and distin-

Figure 28. **Ndebele married woman's apron**. Catalogue number 45.

guished the young from the old, the married from the unmarried, commoners from royals and lords from their servants.[41]

Zulu children wear a single string of beads worn around the waist in infancy, to which beads are added as the child grows.[42] Little boys wear an *ibeshu nesinene*, a skin loin covering comprised of a front and back panel. Little girls progress to various loindresses (figure 31) which include: the *isigege* (figures 32a and 32b), a small square or rectangular panel of beadwork attached to a fiber fringe with a few beads, or a beaded fringe on a bead cord; the *umayidika* which is similar to the *isigege* but with dangling bead strings instead of the beadwork panel; and the *isiheshe*, a short skirt made of beaded strings.[43] Unmarried women and girls of marriageable age commonly wear skirts that touch the knees (figure 33), while very young girls often wear

tightly bound cloths that show most of their legs.[44]

In some regions, on her marriage day, a bride wears a brightly colored Ngwane wedding cape called an *isikoti* or *isibheklane* (figure 34).[45] The cape is constructed of multiple beaded strips of varying ages. The bride's older female relatives make bands of beading in the "old style" (beading done in a white field), while her younger generation female relatives complete beaded bands in the contemporary style (in black fields). Two strands of multiple white bead tails on an *isikoti* would indicate that the bride was a virgin.[46]

Married women can easily be identified by their *isidwaba* (figure 35), a knee-length skirt made of goatskin or oxhide that is cut into strips and stitched back together to give the appearance of pleating. The *isidwaba* is traditionally rubbed with fat, blackened with charcoal, and scented with a powder made from the branches and leaves of pleasant

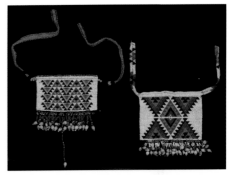

Figures 32a and 32b. **Zulu Ceza-Nongoma pubic aprons**. Catalogue numbers 36 (left) and 35.

Figure 33. **Unmarried Zulu women**. These young Zulu women are shown in full traditional beaded costume. Their beaded regalia includes hair beads, various neck ornaments, belts, bracelets, anklets and rolled waistbands with small apron panels over their short, beaded cotton skirts. This photograph was taken around 1900. Appendix A-2.

Figure 31. **Zulu loindress and belt**. Catalogue number 44.

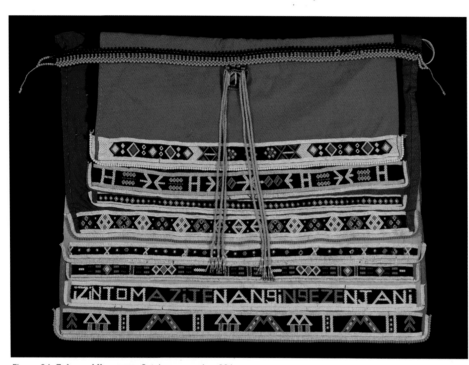

Figure 34. **Zulu wedding cape.** Catalogue number 231.

Figure 35. **Zulu married woman's skirt.** Catalogue number 28.

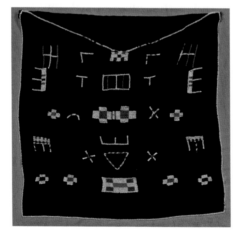

Figure 36. **Zulu Msinga skirt.** Catalogue number 68.

smelling trees and plants.[47] Even when covered with a scarf or hidden by a cloth, the *isidwaba* still indicates the married status of the wearer by the unmistakable silhouette and gait produced when wearing it.[48] The Zulu *isidwaba* was sometimes constructed using long fringed strips of hide attached to a beaded waistband. Strips of hide were used in place of solid hides during periods when hides were scarce and animals were reserved for religious purposes.[49] Skirts (figure 36), cloaks and breast coverings (figure 37) are often adorned with beaded edgings or bead "lace" (figures 38a and 38b) and various types of beaded belts and aprons are worn over a skirt.[50]

Another unique, distinguishing Zulu article of apparel is the flared headdress, worn strictly by married women, which somewhat resembles a beehive. Beadwork attached to the headdress conveys a multitude of messages pertaining to the woman's virginity before marriage, her feelings toward her in-laws, whether or not she has borne children and the type of marriage in which she is involved.[51]

Zulu men usually wear European clothing, but will wear beadwork for special occasions. The traditional men's rear apron (*ibeshu*) was made of soft calfskin with the furry side worn towards the outside.[52] A more contemporary version of the *ibeshu* can be made of leather decorated with metal studs (figure 39). Young men's beadwork during courtship includes "love letter" necklaces, received from admiring young women, and a large number of necklets, bandoliers, loin belts, and ankle and arm ornaments (figure 24).[53] The beaded, crossed shoulder belt can only be worn by Zulu men and unmarried women.[54]

Zulu women wear a special apron during pregnancy, an *umbodiya* (figure 40), that is traditionally made of the hide of a cow sacrificed to her husband's ancestors for the protection of her

Figure 37. **Zulu woman**. This married Zulu woman, photographed in approximately 1900, wears a beaded breast covering (probably cotton) over her knee-length hide skirt (*isidwaba*). The *isidwaba* is traditionally rubbed with fat, blackened with charcoal and scented with a pleasant smelling powder. The woman holds an *imbiza*, a hand-built, pit-fired vessel used for the storage of liquids and other materials. Appendix A-3.

unborn baby. The apron is also thought to provide prosperity and good health for the child.[55] Pregnancy aprons were often studded with brass beads made by indigenous metalsmiths from imported ingots.[56] These metal studs probably represented the Zulu motif called *amasumpa* (warts) that symbolized herds of cattle and was used to emphasize the role of cattle in marriage and procreation.[57] After delivery, new mothers use long strips of beadwork, *ixhama*, as stomach binders

to reduce the bulge experienced after childbirth. These long strips are rarely sold, but may be handed down from mother to daughter, or between sisters.[58]

The independent black church of the Nazareth Baptists has created its own distinct style of beadwork that changes approximately every decade. The church, founded in 1910, blends an unorthodox charismatic/messianic Christianity with Zulu dance, custom and dress, and followers express their culture through dance uniforms of four major age/sex groups, all with their own ensemble of beadwork including headbands, hatbands, wristbands and anklets, blouse-hems and lap-covers.[59]

The Xhosa-speaking people, also known as the Cape Nguni or South Nguni, can be broken down further into nine cultural groups including the Mpondo, Bomvana, Bhaca/Ntlangwini, Thembu, Mpondomise, Xesibe, Mfengu, Hlubi/Sotho and Xhosa.[60] The major artistic expression of these people is exhibited in their clothing and beadwork.[61] Contemporary Xhosa clothing consists of blankets and heavy cotton baize (also described as "Kaffir sheeting"), which is typically white or dyed black. The blankets and often the cotton baize are colored with red ochre that varies in shade depending on the Xhosa cultural group. Xhosa beadwork can often be identified by the pinkish stain of the red ochre from the clothing that is considered the "blood of the earth" and used in honoring the ancestors.[62] The wearing of beads signifies well-being, purity and revelation among the Xhosa and is symbolic of illumination received from the ancestors.[63]

The traditional beadwork transitions of the Xhosa begin shortly after birth. During the ritual of introducing a new baby to the ancestors, the baby's father gives each guest two white beads which they return to him while saying "*Camagu*," which translates loosely to,

Figures 38a and 38b. **Zulu skirts**. Catalogue numbers 64 (top) and 62.

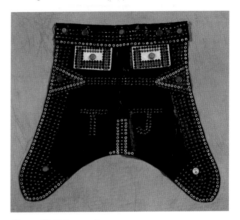

Figure 39. **Zulu men's rear apron**. Catalogue number 51.

The wearing of beads signifies well-being, purity and revelation among the Xhosa and is symbolic of illumination received from the ancestors.

37

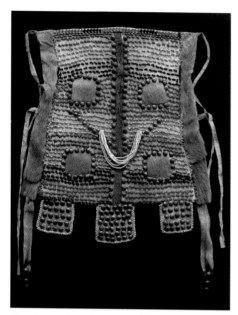

Figure 40. **Zulu Msinga pregnancy apron.** Catalogue number 39.

"We give thanks to the ancestors for blessings received." "*Camagu*" not only thanks the ancestors for blessing them with the baby, but also requests that they care for the child in the future. The mother immediately strings the white beads into a necklace for her baby.[64]

Until about age five, young children wear a simple string of large beads around the waist called an *amaso*, which is enlarged as the child grows. Any color of beads may be used for the *amaso* but white is preferred. A tiny beaded cloth purse (*isipaji somntwana*) is also tied around the child's neck and holds protective medicine obtained by herbalists or diviners.[65]

The amount of beaded regalia among the Xhosa increases dramatically at puberty. During a girl's initiation seclusion, she makes a beaded fringe pubic covering called an *inkciyo* (figure 41), which is predominantly made from white beads, and the young woman will wear this for the rest of her life.[66] After a Xhosa girl completes her initiation, she wears a short skirt decorated with strips of narrowly torn black cotton fabric, stitched on by hand, with her *inkciyo* worn over the skirt.[67] Additional beadwork can include headbands with long beaded fringe, hoop earrings linked by bead strings which loop over the face and head, various types of neckbands, necklets and collars, waist girdles and rear girdles. Throughout the courtship process, a girl makes headbands, arm and leg bands, belts, waistcoats and various types of neck ornaments for her boyfriend, as well as covering purses, safety pins, mirrors, snuffboxes and whistles with beads as gifts for her beloved.[68] Beaded love-tokens worn as a single square panel on a necklet are generally referred to as *izigcina-ntliziyo*, the "keepers of the heart," and often incorporate a geometric female figure into the beaded pattern.[69]

A young man's first gift to his bride-to-be is a string of beads or an *assegai* (spear), which is left outside her hut, and during the bride's pre-marriage seclusion she works on the wedding beadwork. Formal beaded wedding attire is worn by both Xhosa men and women. The bridegroom wears headbands, long fringed necklaces, a body harness, armbands and neckbands. Everything he carries is also beaded and can include bags, an umbrella and a handkerchief.[70]

Married women and women of marriageable age wear a long wrap-around braided skirt, an *umbhaco*, made from cotton sheeting or a blanket with a black stripe woven into it (figure 42a). The number of black braided rows at the bottom of the skirt indicates the woman's status in her household. Married women wear considerably less beadwork and a

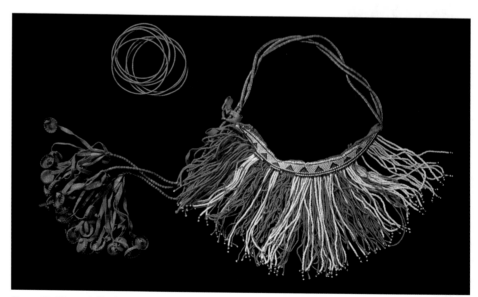

Figure 41. **Xhosa girdle**. Catalogue number 14.

Figures 42a and 42b (opposite page). **Xhosa woman's** (left, Catalogue numbers 30, 227, 386, 409, 411, 416, 448, 449 and 533) **and man's costumes**. Catalogue numbers 15, 139, 233, 384, 385, 387, 407, 408 and 419.

narrow bib-like apron, an *incebetha*, is worn tied above her breasts and hangs down to the braiding on her skirt. Xhosa women also wear a lightly braided cotton sheeting *ibhayi* (shawl) that is worn over the shoulders or tied under the arms when working. The *ibhayi* is also used to secure a baby on its mother's back.[71]

Married men and mature women are entitled to wear intricately beaded wide flared collars (figures 42a and 42b) and both men and women smoke beaded pipes (figure 43).[72] The shape and size of Xhosa pipes are different for each status

Figure 43. **Xhosa pipe**. Catalogue number 518.

level. Older men typically carry a short stemmed pipe, young people sport a slim pipe of medium length, and older women smoke pipes with stems up to thirty centimeters (11.8 inches) in length. Tobacco bags are a part of both men's and women's daily attire. Women's pouches are generally made of cotton sheeting decorated with beadwork, braiding and possibly a few wool tassels (figure 42a). Men's bags are made from either cotton sheeting or the hide of goat with the body shape still intact.[73]

For special occasions, married men may wear an impressive ensemble of beadwork that can consist of up to seventy pieces and must be donned in correct sequence. Because of the heavy weight of such a costume, the full ensemble is only worn to celebrations such as beer-drinks (*intlombe*) or weddings that are held at his own home or in close proximity. Many ornate beaded collars are worn, layered on top of one another, with the widest on the bottom, and a variety of neck ornaments are displayed, some of which include long streamers of beads that hang to the knees (figure 42b).[74]

On special occasions during the nineteenth century, Xhosa women commonly wore beautiful beaded breast coverings that reached their knees. Most of these exquisite breast coverings were made from long strands of large white beads, as opposed to the woven tapestries demonstrated in their beaded aprons. It is speculated that the breast covers were designed with dance in mind, as the kinetic visual effect created by the loose beaded-strand movement would be quite stunning.[75]

Beadwork also holds spiritual significance among southern African cultures. Unlike many African cultures, the Zulu and Xhosa are iconoclastic societies without the customary spiritual figures used to contact the ancestors. The Zulu and Xhosa therefore needed different channels through which they could

accomplish this important communication with their deceased relatives. As a result, their spiritual art found existence in abstract forms and in beadwork.[76]

The spiritual diviner in Southeast Africa interprets the wishes and requests of the ancestors and easily can be recognized by the large quantity of white beads worn. The diviner is consulted for sickness or in times of trouble since the underlying cause is usually thought to be supernatural.[77] Diviners can be either male or female and are usually called to service through dreams. Spiritual diviners combine herbal medicine and divination and are important links to the wisdom of the ancestors. The white beads of the diviner are the most significant element of their costume as white represents purity and the ancestral spirits.[78]

Zulu diviners are distinguished by their traditional beaded costume that includes a flowing wig made of white beads, crossed breast bands of animal skin, and beaded necklaces, anklets and wristbands.[79] Xhosa diviners are expert in herbal medicine and provide protective amulets for all occasions. During celebrations, the Xhosa diviner's costume includes a white beaded skirt (short for a male, long for a female), white bodice or beaded waistcoat, headbands, anklets and cascading white beads that fall over the chest, cover the eyes, drape down the back and wind around the wrist. In addition to the beaded clothing, Xhosa diviners also don amulets, animal-skin headdresses and beaded regalia including flywhisks, staffs, tobacco pipes, medicine gourds and horns.[80]

Color, pattern and technique of Southeast African beadwork vary considerably from culture to culture. Author Duncan Clarke notes,

It is clear that although the Ndebele, Cape Nguni, and Zulu are culturally and linguistically related peoples, living in the same nation-state, in broadly similar economic and social circumstances, they appear to have developed their shared esthetic of beadwork body decoration in different directions, taking in both different color ranges and, it would appear, very different ideas about the communicative possibilities of colors.[81]

In the Ndebele culture, the color of beads once held distinctive meanings relating to the stages of development in a person's life. They also often reflected the mood of the maker. But over time, largely due to contact with urban societies, bead color connotations gradually changed and have mostly dwindled into obscurity. Some traditional color associations in the past included white as a symbol of goodness, purity, love, protection and transition. Greens and yellows generally had "good" connotations and were associated with the growth in spring, abundance in summer and the harvest in autumn. Blues were "powerful" colors and linked with the sea and sky, while reds tended to suggest times of trouble. Black represented sorcery, death and widowhood, and pink was a sign of authority.[82] Researchers have been unable to identify any underlying symbolic code in the colors and patterns of contemporary Ndebele beadwork, but that does not necessarily mean one does not exist. Significant meanings may be privately known, passed down from mothers to daughters, and not meant to be revealed to outsiders.[83]

Early Ndebele beadwork was executed on capes, aprons, and skirts made of sheepskins.[84] These clothing articles were adorned with predominantly white beads, with small geometric design motifs worked in a limited palette of colors, usually red, green, blue and orange (figure 44). It is unclear whether the choice of white beaded backgrounds was

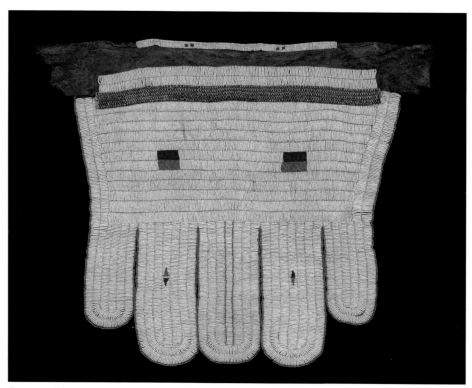

Figure 44. **Ndebele married woman's apron.** Catalogue number 13.

due to white beads being the most plentiful and inexpensive beads supplied by early traders, or if it was related to the older ideas about white being a marker of transitions.[85] The holes in these small beads were too small to allow the use of a needle, so stiff sinew thread was used without the use of any other threading tool. This traditional style of beadwork probably continued until about the 1940s. By the late 1940s and early 1950s, a wider variety of bead color and sizes became available allowing the use of needles and machine-made thread and bolder, more inventive designs soon followed. Colors then included red, pink, orange, yellow, green, blue (light and dark), black and white, with many of the colors being transparent.[86] The new emergence of modern designs included

pitched-roof houses, car license plates, razor blades, telephone poles, electric lights and airplanes.[87] These new designs reflected women's aspirations of things they wanted to possess rather than the truth of their existence, as most Ndebele dwellings are without electricity and other modern conveniences.[88] In approximately 1970–1971 Ndebele beadwork exhibits a shift towards the preference of opaque beads in mostly green, blue, purple, brown and black, with a white beads. The backing material for aprons also changed from the traditional animal skins to leather backed with canvas or just canvas alone.[89]

Techniques found in Ndebele craft demonstrate several variations of herringbone stitch, particularly tubular herringbone, in their beadwork style. In using

41

the herringbone stitch, the beads are set opposite each other in pairs at a 45-degree angle. The pattern that results is linear and diagonal, with each seem ingly straight line having a slightly zigzag effect. The herringbone stitch is only seen in Ndebele and some Zulu beadwork.[90]

Zulu beadwork draws from a wide range of colors and is made by the young women of the community, but worn by children and adults of both sexes. In each region, "there are widely accepted groups of color combinations and certain, quite specific, meanings associated with each color of bead, allowing messages that range from general greetings to quite intimate and detailed communications between lovers to be conveyed."[91] The beadwork from this region has long been thought to incorporate a system of non-verbal communication and has been surrounded by the mystery associated with "the language of beads."[92]

The range of Zulu beadwork patterns includes lozenges, triangles and small rectangles in solid blocks of color, or horizontal or zigzag bands, often divided

Figure 45. **Zulu loindress**. Catalogue number 31.

by lines of black beads creating vivid contrast (figure 45).[93] The shield motif, commonly found in Zulu design, is said to symbolize protection and security from attack.[94] Modern patterns may incorporate letters that can either form words or simply be used to create a decorative design.[95]

Various techniques are used to create Zulu beadwork, and can include the herringbone stitch, netting and the brick stitch, the most common form found. In the brick stitch method, beads are placed in staggered rows and as each new bead is threaded, the thread is passed under a loop of thread on the previous row and back through the bead. This looping technique gives the Zulu beadwork its characteristic strength.[96]

Zulu beadwork form falls into four main divisions: 1) a single string of beads worn around the neck, waist, arm or ankle; 2) flat beadwork worked into rectangular panels; 3) round beadwork (beads strung onto a continuous thread and wound onto a roll of fabric or fiber); 4) bead-covered objects.[97]

The single string of beads can be worn as a single strand, doubled over several times and twisted, and can also support a bead panel worn as a necklet or a small girl's apron. Single strings of beads can also be combined to create beaded fringe for veils and aprons. Flat beadwork can be incorporated into *ulimi* (tongues) worn by men on the chest, "bandoliers" worn by men and unmarried girls over the chest and one shoulder, headdress adornment, neck and chest ornaments and aprons. Round beadwork rolls can be formed into arm, neck, chest, waist or loin ornaments, and bead-covered objects can include snuff containers, staffs, fertility dolls and medicine containers.[98]

Four distinct color combinations were characteristic of Zulu beadwork made prior to 1960. This old style of beadwork made use of a restricted color

palette of somewhat somber colors in an ordered sequence.[99] The color schemes making up the old style included:

isishunka (seven colors)—white, light blue, dark green, pale yellow, pink, red and black;

isitembu (five colors)—light blue, grass green, bright yellow, red and black;

umzansi (four colors)—white, dark blue, grass green and red;

isinyolovane—a combination of any colors not consistent with the other schemes.

After the 1960s, fashion began to influence beadwork style and greater individuality surfaced. New colors were added to the traditional color schemes and small designs became popular.[100] Zulu color symbolism is linked with an understanding of Zulu cosmology and the cycle of life.

White is associated with the ancestors, concepts of purity, calm, and good intentions, and light and divine enlightenment. In some contexts, black represents darkness, evil, death, and defilement. In other contexts, black is linked to the ancestors and carries positive connotations—it evokes the dark rain clouds necessary for the sustenance of life…the leather skirt of marriage [is] blackened to please the ancestors. Red is the color of blood, menstruation, and fertility, and red ochre is strongly associated with the earth and women and their fertility.[101]

Pink beads generally signify poverty when worn by a commoner, while yellow beads are thought to represent wealth.[102]

A number of factors still come into play in interpreting the "meanings" of beads as color alone does not tell the whole story. The size of the beads and how they are placed in relationship to adjacent beads can alter the meaning of the beadwork. The material the beads are made from—glass or plastic—can also influence the message.[103] Even the property of a specific color (light or dark, opaque or transparent) can affect the meaning, and most colors have both a favorable and unfavorable connotation depending on the other variables present.[104] Reading beads can be very complicated and when messages are involved, the code tends to be locally specific.[105]

Among the Xhosa culture, another very significant color association is present, in addition to bead colors. Red ochre is rubbed into textiles, as well as applied to the body, as a visible sign that the individual is partaking in the everyday life of the community.[106] Red ochre symbolizes the blood of the earth and the Xhosa believe its color to be beloved by the ancestors.[107] Individuals in a transition period prior to acquiring a new status—women who have just given birth and are breastfeeding or young people in seclusion during initiation periods—use white clay to cover their bodies.[108] White is also generally the preferred color for ceremonial and festive occasions.[109] The significance of these red and white colors is reflected in the colors of beads worn—red being the prominent color associated with chiefs and white worn by diviners and healers.[110]

Bead colors characteristic of all Xhosa groups are blue, pink, red and white, with each group exhibiting color variations within this spectrum plus additional colors according to local custom.[111] Some colors found in Xhosa beadwork have symbolic meaning: yellow for fertility, green for new life, dark turquoise blue for youth and white for purity.

Green and yellow beads are worn strictly by men, and older women's headbands are made only from navy, pink and white beads. Xhosa beadwork patterns are usually simple, including lozenges, chevrons, zigzags and horizontal or diagonal lines against a white background.[112] Strips of fabric and cord are also included into the designs for additional creative expression, and individuality can further be achieved with the addition of mother-of-pearl buttons.[113]

In many African cultures today, traditional beadwork is dying out and is found only in remote areas, relatively untouched by Western influence, or reserved for ceremonies and social events, often as a sign of respect for ancestors.[114] Some older, traditional Ndebele women confess to hiding a special piece of beadwork from peers, collectors and researchers for the specific purpose of communicating with the ancestors. These women explain that the ancestors do not recognize the modern "party style" beads. They only understand the old styles.[115] Increasing economic difficulties have forced many Southeast African women to sell rare and precious beadwork articles such as initiation attire, married women's aprons and capes, belts, necklaces and fertility dolls used in traditional rituals. Beadwork that would normally be passed down from generation to generation as a treasured possession is being dispersed, threatening a valuable cultural heritage.[116]

Traditional beaded costume has largely been replaced by contemporary Western dress in most African communities. However, in an attempt to reclaim their past, many proud southern Africans have been framing traditional beadwork pieces behind glass, and they can be seen on countless walls of politicians and business executives, transforming them into "works of art." Their new status would surely have been unimaginable to their original makers and owners.[117]

Southeast African beadwork is "asking for eyes." It is a visual voice professing its pride of heritage and its commanding identity.

There does exist an upside to this new trend of beadwork in today's environment. It allows women to become viable wage earners by making beadwork articles for sale to tourists, galleries and fashion markets, and by wearing large quantities of personal beadwork while posing for fee based photographs.[118] The women of the Nazareth Baptist Church also make beadwork for sale at festivals for tourists and locals in need of traditional garb for special occasions.[119] The tourist trade and fashion world have enabled formerly housebound African women a chance at financial independence and a new sense of contributing to the family income.[120] The downside of the situation is some women no longer make beadwork for themselves, focusing instead on commercial markets and threatening a disappearance of the traditional social meanings associated with beadwork.[121]

The art of beadwork, with each carefully strung bead and intricate detail, speaks volumes about the Southeast African woman who makes and wears it. Beadwork offers a glimpse into her soul, a peak into her heart and more than just a hint of her individuality. Beads express her hopes, her fears, her joys and her sorrows. They have a story to tell. They speak of a woman's past, present and future. Southeast African beadwork is "asking for eyes." It is a visual voice professing its pride of heritage and its commanding identity. It wants to be seen, heard and preserved for future generations. Southeast African beadwork is a beautiful, expressive form of communication, rich with a meaning that speaks to all levels of humanity.

1 Robert Robertson, *Zulu Izaga*, Christison Rare Books <http://www.anti-quarian.co.za/Zulu%20Proverbs.htm> (24 October 2004).

2 Gary Van Wyk , "Illuminated Signs: Style and Meaning in The Beadwork of the Xhosa- and Zulu-speaking Peoples," *African Arts* 36, no. 3 (2003): 12.

3 *African Beads* (New York: The Metropolitan Museum of Art and Simon & Schuster, 1999), 4.

4 Emma Bedford, "Exploring Meanings and Identities: Beadwork from the Eastern Cape in the South African National Gallery," in *Ezakwantu: Beadwork from the Eastern Cape* (South African National Gallery, 1993), 13.

5 Joan A. Broster, *The Tembu: Their Beadwork, Songs and Dances* (Cape Town: Purnell, 1976), 33.

6 *African Beads*, 7.

7 Duncan Clarke, *Colors of Africa* (San Diego: Thunder Bay Press, 2000), 94.

8 Henry John Drewal and John Mason, *Beads Body and Soul: Art and Light in the Yoruba Universe* (Los Angeles: UCLA Fowler Museum of Cultural History, 1998), 34.

9 Caroline Crabtree and Pam Stallebrass, *Beadwork: A World Guide* (New York: Rizzoli, 2002), 33.

10 *African Beads*, 7–8.

11 *African Beads*, 40.

12 John Gillow, *African Textiles* (San Francisco: Chronicle Books, 2003), 222.

13 Sandra Klopper, "From Adornment to Artefact to Art: Historical Perspectives on South-east African Beadwork," in *South East African Beadwork: 1850–1910. From Adornment to Artefact to Art*, eds. Michael Stevenson and Michael Graham-Stewart (Vlaeberg: Fernwood Press, 2000), 39.

14 Margret Carey, *Beads and Beadwork of East and South Africa* (Aylesbury: Shire Publications, 1986), 12.

15 Klopper, 31.

16 Margret Carey, "Gender in African Beadwork: An Overview," in *Beads and Bead Makers: Gender, Material Culture and Meaning*, eds. Lidia D. Sciama and Joanne B. Eicher (Oxford/New York: Berg, 1998), 83.

17 Carey, *Beads and Beadwork*, 14.

18 Klopper, 29.

19 Carey, *Beads and Beadwork*, 14.

20 Ivor Powell, *Ndebele: A People and Their Art* (Cape Town: Struik Publishers, 1995), 110–113.

21 *African Beads*, 36.

22 *African Beads*, 39.

23 Powell, 126.

24 Dawn Costello, *Not Only for Its Beauty: Beadwork and Its Cultural Significance Among the Xhosa-Speaking Peoples* (Pretoria: University of South Africa, 1990), 13.

25 Carey, *Beads and Beadwork*, 36.

26 Crabtree and Stallebrass, 50.

27 Powell, 126.

28 Rhoda Levinsohn, *Art and Craft of Southern Africa: Treasures in Transition* (Craighall: Delta Books, 1984), 113.

29 Levinsohn, 116.

30 Clarke, 112.

31 Crabtree and Stallebrass, 52.

32 Powell, 130.

33 Clarke, 112.

34 Crabtree and Stallebrass, 52.

35 Powell, 134.

36 Powell, 134.

37 Ernst Wasmuth Verlag Tubingen, *AmaNdebele: Signals of Color from South Africa* (Berlin: Haus der Kulturen der Welt, 1991), 64 and Powell, 135.

38 Powell, 135.

39 J.W. Grossert, *Zulu Crafts* (Pietermaritzburg: Shuter & Shooter, 1978), 57.

40 Jean Morris and Eleanor Preston-Whyte, *Speaking with Beads: Zulu Arts from Southern Africa* (New York: Thames and Hudson, 1994), 6.

41 Morris and Preston-Whyte, 15.

42 Carey, Beads and Beadwork, 54.

43 Carolee Kennedy, *The Art and Material Culture of the Zulu-Speaking Peoples* (Los Angeles: UCLA Museum of Cultural History, 1978), 13 and Carey, 54.

44 Morris and Preston-Whyte, 25.

45 The Zulu phrase incorporated into the cape in Figure 34 (SA-309), *izinto mazinjena ngingenzenjani*, translates to "things are like this, what should we do?" Translation courtesy of Marianna Visser, Head of African Languages of the University of Stellenbosch, South Africa.

46 *Zulu Treasures: of Kings and Commoners* (KwaZulu Cultural Museum and Local History Museums: 1996), 167.

47 Kennedy, 13.

48 Morris and Preston-Whyte, 25.

49 H.S. Schoeman, <stan@marques.co.za > "Re: Zulu Leather and Beaded Skirt," 11 March 2004, personal email (12 March 2004). Information based on Dr. Schoeman's field research in the region of KwaZulu-Natal during 1964–1968.

50 Carey, Beads and Beadwork, 54.

51 Levinsohn, 88.

52 Kennedy, 13.

53 Carey, *Beads and Beadwork*, 55.

54 Morris and Preston-Whyte, 31.

55 Morris and Preston-Whyte, 41.

56 Klopper, 12.

57 Monica Blackmun Visona et al., *A History of Art in Africa* (New York: Harry N. Abrams, 2001), 489.

58 Carey, "Gender in African Beadwork," 90.

59 Crabtree and Stallebrass, 49.

60 Costello, 1.

61 Crabtree and Stallebrass, 38.

62 Carey, *Beads and Beadwork*, 45.

63 Costello, 18.

64 Costello, 27.

65 Costello, 23.

66 Crabtree and Stallebrass, 45.

67 Costello, 6.

68 Carey, *Beads and Beadwork*, 47.

69 Anitra Nettleton, Sipho Ndabambi and Daivd Hammond-Tooke, "The Beadwork of the Cape Nguni," in *Catalogue: Ten Years of Collecting (1979–1989)*, eds. David Hammond-Tooke and Anitra Nettleton (Johannesburg: University of the Witwatersrand, 1989), 42.

70 Crabtree and Stallebrass, 45.

71 Costello, 6.

72 Carey, *Beads and Beadwork*, 47.

73 Costello, 11.

74 Costello, 26.

75 Klopper, 8.

76 Van Wyk, 14.

77 Costello, 33.

78 Carey, "Gender in African Beadwork," 90.

79 Morris and Preston-Whyte, 41.

80 Carey, *Beads and Beadwork*, 47.

81 Clarke, 112.

82 Peter Becker, *Inland Tribes of Southern Africa* (London: Granada Publishing, 1979), 76.

83 Diane Levy, "Ndebele Beadwork," in *Catalogue: Ten Years of Collecting (1979–1989)*, eds. David Hammond-Tooke and Anitra Nettleton (Johannesburg: University of the Witwatersrand, 1989), 29.

84 Carey, *Beads and Beadwork*, 36.

85 Clarke, 112.

86 Carey, *Beads and Beadwork*, 36.

87 Crabtree and Stallebrass, 50.

88 Powell, 117.

89 Carey, *Beads and Beadwork*, 36-37.

90 Gillow, 221.

91 Clarke, 102.

92 Morris and Preston-Whyte, 44.

93 Carey, *Beads and Beadwork*, 50.

94 Morris and Preston-Whyte, 29.

95 Morris and Preston-Whyte, 58.

96 Gillow, 216.

97 Carey, *Beads and Beadwork*, 53-54.

98 Carey, *Beads and Beadwork*, 54.

99 Morris and Preston-Whyte, 44.

100 Morris and Preston-Whyte, 45.

101 Van Wyk, 27.

102 Kennedy, 12.

103 Morris and Preston-Whyte, 55.

104 Kennedy, 12.

105 Morris and Preston-Whyte, 55.

106 Crabtree and Stallebrass, 40.

107 Costello, 8.

108 Crabtree and Stallebrass, 40 and Costello, 8.

109 Costello, 8.

110 Crabtree and Stallebrass, 40.

111 Costello, 17.

112 Carey, *Beads and Beadwork*, 48.

113 Costello, 20.

114 *African Beads*, 43.

115 Powell, 126.

116 Levinsohn, 121.

117 Klopper, 43.

118 Carey, "Gender in African Beadwork," 91.

119 Crabtree and Stallebrass, 49.

120 Carey, "Gender in African Beadwork," 91.

121 Tubingen, 65.

Among the Zulu of South Africa, food is recognized as a gift bestowed upon the living by benevolent ancestors. Because of this belief in the power of ancestors over food, utilitarian items related to eating,

primarily spoons, beer pots, and cooking pots, are considered very special objects. Such items are thoughtfully created and cared for, and used with profound respect according to communal practices and cultural values. Ancestors provide continuing strength and support to their families, and communion between humans and their ancestors often occurs through ritualized eating and drinking. Gender roles and patriarchal social organization help to define ancestral ties. As family and community leaders, men are responsible for public ancestral offerings, while women are able to participate in more private offerings within the home. This essay serves to document how the creation, storage and ritualized use of utilitarian items reinforce ancestral relations and the social construction of Zulu power.

Ancestral Gifts of Food and the Power of Zulu Utilitarian Objects

Beth Baniadam
and Marilyn Jolley

Kraals

Rural Zulu society is organized into patrilineal groups living in circular homesteads called *kraals*. Each *kraal* is home to an insular patriarch and his wife or wives, and their children. *Kraals* contain circular beehive housing structures, with separate dwellings for each wife and her children (figure 46), surrounding a central circular cattle pen (also referred to as a cattle fold). As wealth is measured in cattle, the cattle fold is viewed as a source of earthly prosperity, and a display of social power in the public realm. Cattle are not only owned by the patriarch of the *kraal*, but are also considered the property of his entire male lineage of ancestors.[1] Consequently, the ancestral wealth of the central cattle pen is a place of intense spiritual power, as well as social power.

For the Zulu, the spiritual sphere and the human sphere are entwined. Ancestors, referred to as *shades*, actively participate in human affairs and maintain a permanent presence in the *kraal*. The lineage of male ancestors is thought to reside not only in the cattle fold, an area restricted to women, but also in the interior of domestic dwellings. Initiated adult men of the *kraal*, relatives, and invited local community members use the sacred

Figure 46. **Zulu girls dressing hair**. Rural Zulu society is organized into patrilineal groups living in circular homesteads called *kraals*. The women in this photograph, taken around 1900, are dressing their hair in front of a typical beehive shaped dwelling inside the *kraal*. On the ground next to them lies a pot called an *imbiza*, a hand-built, pit-fired vessel used for the storage of liquids and other materials. Appendix A-4.

cattle fold together, as a place to communicate with ancestors during the ritual consumption of beer and meat.[2] The sharing of food, drink and snuff occurs among men in the cattle pen to solidify their alignment with ancestors and to reinforce their status as overseers of their respective family units (figure 47). Access to the cattle pen is a primary source of social authority, as men tend to discuss important community matters under the watchful eyes of ancestors.[3]

The cattle pen is not the only place in the *kraal* where ancestral presence exists. Contrasting with the more public cattle area used by men, there is a private area inside each dwelling reserved for ancestral contact.[4] Located behind a central hearth, the *umsamo* is delineated by a semicircular, oval shaped raised border, and no one may enter the area, except under special circumstances.[5] Both the patriarch and the women of the dwelling may reach in, to place or retrieve objects,

but rarely does anyone physically enter the space. Like the cattle fold, the *umsamo* is a dwelling place of the ancestors, but a more private and restrictive location, where personal offerings of beer and meat are made to honor and nourish the ancestors by family members. Ancestors prefer to work in darkness and feel comfortable in the cool, dim atmosphere of the *umsamo*. The one-door floor plan of the circular Zulu home creates a womb-like atmosphere, especially in the back of the structure where the *umsamo* is located.[6] Because ancestors expect and appreciate gifts of prepared food and drink served to them, small offerings are placed in the *umsamo* after each meal.[7] Food and beer offerings are made by the female head of the household or her husband, the patriarch male, to honor the presence of the ancestors.

Another important use of the *umsamo* is for the storage of utilitarian items related to the cooking and serving

of food, such as bowls, spoons, pots, lids, and other items of monetary or emotional value in each household. To make certain ancestors understand they are being considered and cared for by the living, objects familiar to departed family members are kept within the *umsamo*, to strengthen the ancestors' ties to the home and to aid in the protection of important household objects.[8] The act of "sharing" utilitarian items with the ancestors (objects in the *umsamo* are considered belongings of the ancestors, as well as the living inhabitants) adds an additional layer of spiritual significance to the objects. Since women do the cooking in Zulu society, they are near the *umsamo*, which is located behind the central hearth, throughout the day. Through the act of retrieving and replacing vessels and utensils stored in the *umsamo*, and through the act of preparing and offering food as gifts to the ancestors, women privately interact with the ancestors in a domestic, rather than a public, setting, to help ensure the prosperity and protection of the entire family.

The *umsamo* in the dwelling of the patriarch, as opposed to the *umsamo* in the dwelling of his wife or wives, is the most important in the *kraal*, since those offerings are made to honor and nourish the ancestors and guardians of the entire *kraal*.[9] These private offerings guarantee the male head of the household a powerful and close link with the spiritual world, as he attempts to gain favor from his ancestors to assure prosperous crops and safety for his family. The *umsamo* of the patriarch is also used to store clothes, money, meat, beer, and snuff the night before those items appear in more public rituals held in the *kraal*. Thus, the private *umsamo* of the patriarch is utilized to spiritually "prepare" items for public consumption, and to ensure the ancestors are made aware that an event will be happening the next day.[10]

Figure 47. **Zulu men taking snuff**. Appendix A-5.

Spoons are treasured by the Zulu for their spiritual significance and their utilitarian necessity.

The Zulu homestead, or *kraal*, is organized for the benefit of everyone within the patriarchal construct. Ancestors are given attention through offerings of food, beer, comfortable architectural spaces, and familiar utilitarian and ritual objects placed in their dwelling area (*umsamo*). The living benefit from the ancestors' special powers that provide food and protection for all family members. Men are given access to both public (cattle pen) and private (*umsamo*) ancestral spaces, and maintain their patriarchal leadership and influence over society, the *kraal*, their wives and children. Women, who are responsible for running their individual households and providing food and drink for guests, have access to ancestral power through the interior *umsamo* of their home. Thus, all adults in the *kraal* are provided areas of ancestral access, creating strong and lasting links between the Zulu and their ancestors.

Spoons

Spoons are treasured by the Zulu for their spiritual significance and their utilitarian necessity. Only a few basic types of spoons are necessary for cooking and beer making. Deep-bowled wooden spoons or ladles (*isixembe*) are used to pour water and beer (figure 48),[11] while

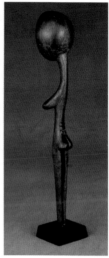

Figure 48. **Female figured spoon**, front and back view. Catalogue number 541.

smaller wooden spoons (*izinkezo*) are used for individual eating, cooking, and the serving of food (figures 49a, 49b, 49c and 49d). The power contained within a spoon originates from the wood used to create it. Potent spirits inhabit the trees used to make spoons, and various patterns carved into spoons further enhance their potency. While some patterns relate to personal aesthetics, others relate to ancestors, important leaders, personal lineages and/or geographic areas, references that increase the spoon's prestige. When not in use, personal spoons are carefully and safely stored in the womblike darkness favored by the ancestors in the *umsamo* (ancestral resting place within the home), to protect them and possibly to empower them.

Each family member (male and female) has their own individual spoon made for them, and cared for by them. Over time, when the spoon is handled, oils from the owner's body darken and smooth the surface, as the wood is slowly filled with the individual spirit of the

Figures 49a, 49b, 49c and 49d. **Zulu Spoons.** Smaller wooden spoons are used for individual eating, cooking and the serving of food. When not in use, personal spoons are carefully stored in the *umsamo* (a place of ancestral offering), linking the objects to the power of ancestors and the ancestral ability to provide food for the family. (Left to right) Catalogue numbers 542, 543, 567 and 568.

47

To demonstrate gratitude to the ancestral powers that have bestowed gifts of food on the living, eating among the Zulu is governed by strict rules of etiquette.

owner. Personal spoons are not shared, but serving spoons can be shared among cooks in a *kraal*. Eventually, it is possible for a personal spoon owned and used by a male to build up enough individualized spiritual power to function as an ancestral relic, and thus a point of continued contact, when kept by living descendents in the *umsamo*.[12] The original owner of the relic spoon, once an ancestor, will

recognize his utensil in the *umsamo* and know that he is home.

Spoons can be made from leaves as well as wood. Large grass or palm leaf strainers (*isikhetho*) are used for skimming or straining beer during the brewing process (figure 50). Beer-making is an activity usually shared by the women of the *kraal* homestead. *Isikhetho* are made from the center ribs of *ilala* palm folioles (one of the leaflets, or fingers, of a palm leaf). Once the leaves are stripped off, the remaining strong center ribs are chain woven into the shape of a spoon. *Ilala* palms have a waxy coating, giving objects made from this material, such as sifters, spoons and baskets, a waterproof quality. Beer sifters made with the palm may have a delicate lace-like appearance, but they are extremely durable and long lasting. Skimmers and strainers are kept in the domestic ancestral dwelling place (*umsamo*), along with the other utilitarian items.

To demonstrate gratitude to the ancestral powers that have bestowed gifts of food on the living, eating among the Zulu is governed by strict rules of etiquette. For example, women serve food

to honor guests, while guests honor the host's ancestors by receiving the gift with both hands. When women kneel to serve elders and guests in high-ranking positions, the server honors and reaffirms the power, social position and lineage of the guest through ritual action. This serving ritual, which takes place for the two main meals of the day, also requires the proper placement of utensils. Spoons, for example, are placed around the communal food dish, and are not left standing in the food, or sitting in a pot.[13] Special observances govern all aspects of cooking, serving and eating among the Zulu, as the ritual of food functions to unite the living with their ancestors.

Changing Role of Artists

Social changes over the last two centuries have disrupted many of the long-standing cultural traditions and practices in Zulu life, including carving. In the late nineteenth century, men began to leave the *kraal* homestead for long periods of time to work in the cities and the gold mines. After WWII, transportation became more readily available from rural areas to cities, further increasing the number of men traveling to the city for work. The male head of a *kraal* would traditionally carve spoons for the household, but when men began to work away from the *kraal*, spoon carving became an area of expertise for men who remained,[14] for carvers who returned home after years of employment as migrant laborers, and sometimes for women.[15] Because men were staying away from home in greater numbers and for longer lengths of time, women began to take on some of the men's traditional labor duties, and traditional provider roles began to change. As people began to pay specialized carvers to create spoons and other household utensils, a monetary exchange system was encouraged to develop. Spurred by the potential promise

Figure 50. **Zulu spoon/beer strainer**. Large grass or palm leaf strainers are used for skimming or straining beer during the brewing process. Beer making is an activity usually shared by women of the *kraal* homestead. Catalogue number 183.

of monetary gain, and for practical and cultural needs, the art of carving has survived and is now a part of the curriculum in many local schools.[16]

Beer

Another utilitarian item used to honor ancestors is clay beer pots. Sorghum and millet beer, the Zulu's most important beverage, provides sustenance with essential amino acids, vitamins and minerals, and helps to unite the community through shared social and religious gatherings and communal rituals. Important social and cultural occasions usually include the brewing, sharing, and consumption of beer. Beer is not only a libation for social celebration and hospitality, but also an important part of many spiritual ceremonies in which the community seeks to appease and give sustenance to the ancestors. In recent years, honoring ancestors through beer ceremonies has become more popular than animal sacrifices, due in part to the general reduction of cattle herd sizes as a result of their poor economic value.

Beer figures prominently in important ceremonial events, such as in marriage, when the bride's family provides beer for the grooms' family. Circumcisions are another important ceremony for which beer is made and

Important social and cultural occasions usually include the brewing, sharing, and consumption of beer.

served. After the cutting ritual, all of the "new" men dress in their best clothing with their families and friends, and everyone sings, dances, and drinks beer.[17] Beer is used for blessings, protection, and giving thanks, especially after the harvest season, which occurs the first week of June. Josiah Tyler, a missionary living among the Zulu between 1849 and 1889, observed that women would take turns throwing parties for up to 40 or 50 men after the harvest was in and grain was milled.[18] In addition to harvest celebrations, beer can be used during the mediation of disagreements, used as a trade good in exchange for various types of labor, or simply given as a gift, tribute, or reward for hard work.

Since the production of beer is time consuming and labor intensive, the complex art of creating a good brew is highly valued. Providing beer to guests enhances social prestige through the display and sharing of wealth (grain), and results in a higher status and increased social power for the host. When a family's *kraal* holds a beer drinking party, the entire community is invited to attend. While all are invited to participate, other *kraals* are expected to host as well. However, this system of cooperative sharing and reciprocity, highly esteemed by all, has started to change due to population pressures on the land. The expense and time required to provide large beer drinks for all neighbors is economically prohibitive to most Zulu now. More often, beer is sold instead of given away, as the etiquette of hospitality continues to change.

While a strict division of labor is followed in the production of beer, all adults take part, at some point, in the creation of this important resource. In the past, men would clear and tend the sorghum and maize crops used for beer production. Today, women primarily perform this intensive agricultural labor

Figures 51a and 51b. **Zulu beer pot and cover.** When guests arrive, beer is poured into smaller clay pots called *ukhamba* and served to each person visiting. The smooth black finish is achieved by using two firings and a rubbing of animal fat and gooseberry leaves on the surface. Catalogue numbers 482 (left) and 211.

since men are commonly absent from the homestead due to migrant labor practices. Women traditionally harvest the crops, ferment, and serve the beer. The initial processing of beer includes several steps prior to fermenting. First, millet grains are bagged and set in a stream, then the bag is removed and the soaked grains are sprouted in a large, reddish clay pot called *imbiza*, and dried.[19] Throughout the winter months, when the harvest is in and there is no pending agricultural work, young girls grind the grains together at each *kraal* homestead.

The actual brewing process begins by covering the prepared grains with warm water, and leaving them to sit and ferment in an *imbiza* pot. When the beer is finished fermenting, it is strained through long, narrow, woven grass basketry strainers, as it is poured into another *imbiza* for storage until serving. When guests arrive, the beer is poured into smaller clay pots called *ukhamba* or gourds for individual use (figure 51a). A special basketry spoon (*isikhetho*) is used for shooing flies and scraping off the foam (figure 50).[20] The pots in which

49

Figure 52. **Zulu beer pot and covers**. The small-necked *uphiso*, used mainly for transporting beer, usually has a flat bottom so it may be placed on top of a grass or cloth ring and carried on the head. Catalogue numbers 457 (pot), 215 (cover on left) and 207 (cover on top of pot).

Zulu beer is brewed, stored, and served are created and maintained with a significant sense of pride by the individual owner (figure 37). While some of these pots have largely been replaced by enamel, metal and plastic products purchased from the market, the ritual of beer ceremonies remains intact.[21] At a beer ceremony, the earthly power of the community, combined with the spiritual power of the present ancestors, reminds people they are only partially responsible for their providence, and that the ancestors ultimately have control over their lives.

Beer Pots

For each stage of storing and serving beer, Zulu women utilize a specific pot of which there are four basic types. A large, unpolished, two foot high *imbiza* can hold anywhere from 30 to 200 gallons and is used for brewing large amounts of beer for special ceremonies and celebrations. The *imbiza* is also used for storage of water and beer. The smaller *iphangela*, also used in the production and storage of beer, is black and highly polished, often with raised or incised surface decorations and comes in various circular shapes such as oval, round, or squat. When beer is offered to guests at both

informal meals or at large gatherings, it is often served in the most widely used pot, a round, finely decorated black clay pot called *ukhamba* (figure 51a). The small-necked *uphiso* (figure 52), used mainly for transporting beer, usually has a flat bottom so it may be placed on top of a grass or cloth ring and carried on the head (figure 53). Sometimes, a smaller pot called *umancishane* is served to a guest. This pot has a special meaning that the guest being served will readily understand: either there is not much beer left in the host's supply, or the guest should make the visit short by drinking the beer and then going on his or her way.[22] The *umancishane* is also employed to honor ancestors with an offering of beer when placed in the *umsamo* (domestic dwelling place of ancestors). Ancestors are thought to recognize the *umancishane* and will be aware of it, or any item, they are familiar with from their lifetime. The use of a traditional form of pot allows ancestors to find the offering and enables them to enjoy it by licking or tasting the inside of the clay pot.[23]

Although pottery making is on the decline, Zulu potters continue to create vessels based on traditional models with innumerable variations. The pottery process begins by locating the correct clay, then drying and milling it to a fine powder on a grinding stone. This fine clay is then mixed with water and raw clay to create the desired consistency. Smaller blackened pots are created with large amounts of fine powdered clay, while larger pots use much less powder, more raw clay, and are sometimes tempered with pieces of potsherds to add strength. To begin construction, the potter rolls handfuls of clay between her palms, creating cylinders of finger-size thickness. The first clay coil is placed on a round flattened disc of clay, which makes up the bottom of the pot. The coil is smoothed where the ends and the sides touch the subsequent layers to ready for the next layer of coiled cylinder. The whole coiling process is repeated as circles of clay rolls are joined together until the pot is built up to the desired form. Then a gourd, piece of metal or stone is used to smooth the exterior surfaces. Roundness, smoothness and thickness are valued in the finished vessel.

After the pot's exterior is smooth, surface decoration and motifs may be added.

Figure 53. **Zulu woman**. This Zulu woman is carrying an *uphiso* vessel on her head. She has previously gone through the *Qhumbuza* ear piercing ceremony and wears a reed in each earlobe. The diameter of her ear piecing can continue to be enlarged, to eventually accommodate large decorative earplugs, by gradually increasing the size of the reeds inserted into the holes. This photograph was taken around 1900. Appendix A-6.

Ornamentation on Zulu pots vary, but most serving and drinking vessels display traditional patterns consisting of incised geometric motifs. Such designs are created by gouging a stick into the clay, or by placing additional clay pieces on the outer surface to produce raised relief motifs. Oftentimes, hundreds of small balls of clay, each a uniform size, are placed on the sides of the pot and secured with a slip (clay mixed with water to the consistency of cream) which acts as a glue. These small raised bumps, called "warts" or *amasumpa*, can be rounded, square, or pyriform (pear shaped).[24] *Amasumpa* are used in multiple or single rows and are placed around a pot in bands or used to create a variety of patterns including zigzags (referring to ancestors and/or Shaka, the nineteenth-century warrior king), circles (which relate to rains or good news), diamonds (a feminine symbol), triangles (a male symbol), or other very basic shapes such as semi-circles and squares. Because of the time required to create them, *amasumpa* are rarely made today. Instead, *amasumpa*-like designs (figure 51a) are created by carving into the clay, resulting in a design similar to the older technique, but in much lower relief. These incised "wart-like" designs are similar to those found on carved wood utensils. Historically, Zulu women were beautified with scarification on their torsos and arms, with markings similar to *amasumpa*. The meanings of *amasumpa* are not fully understood, but they remain a core Zulu design aesthetic, and are used in several types of visual art.

Once the exterior surface design has been applied, the pot sits inside the house for twenty-four hours to dry, after which the undecorated surfaces are rubbed with a special family-owned pebble to further smooth and compact the surface. When the undecorated surfaces are perfectly smooth, the pot is placed in

Figure 54. **Lesotho beer pot**. Grains are sprouted for beer production in this type of large clay pot. Catalogue number 456.

Figures 55a and 55b. **Zulu beer pot covers**. Shaped like a shallow dish, these beer pot covers are woven from various plant fibers, with beading generally added. These lids enhance the pot with color, design, and individuality, but they also protect the beer from dust, insects and other impurities. The Zulu believe that izimbenge lend pride, dignity and warmth to a home. Brides customarily give a series of beer lids and beer pots to in-laws during matrimonial ceremonies. Catalogue numbers 207 (left) and 215.

Brides customarily give a series of beer lids and beer pots to in-laws during matrimonial ceremonies.

a shallow open pit and covered with wood for firing. This technique creates a pottery piece with black splotches (figure 54).

If the potter is creating black serving vessels, a second firing occurs, in which the pot is covered with dry grass or cow dung. This material is lit to blacken the whole surface with carbon, creating a hard, glossy, impermeable finish. After it is taken off the fire and still hot, animal fat and gooseberry leaves are rubbed into the surface and a pebble is again used for smoothing, creating a black, lustrous finish (figure 52). The dark, rich black is considered pleasing to the ancestors, as the color mimics their revered interior resting and eating area by the hearth, the *umsamo*.[25] After completion, all pots are given a useful embellishment called an *imbenge* (pl. *izimbenge*), a small basketry lid.

Beer Pot Lids

Shaped like a shallow dish, *izimbenge* (figures 51b, 52, 55 and 56) are woven from various fibers, including the *ilala* palm leaf, with beading generally added. The woven coil technique, most often employed for this type of basket, begins by wrapping stalks of grass or strips of palm around a core of grass to create a long continuous coil. While this coil is formed into a spiral, an awl is used to open tiny holes along the edge of the coil, which are sewn and bound tightly together with another piece of palm. This technique produces a basket with a strong structure and a convex spiral with a dip in the middle like a saucer. While variations in the weaving and dyeing of wrapping materials create distinctive patterns,[26] most *izimbenge* also contain design motifs created from a variety of colored beads. Overall, white is the most popular bead choice, due primarily to its associations with purity and ancestors.[27] These woven, and often beaded, lids aesthetically enhance the pot with color, design, and individuality, but they also protect the beer from dust, insects and other impurities. The Zulu believe that *izimbenge* lend pride, dignity and warmth to a home. Brides customarily give a series of beer lids and beer pots to in-laws during matrimonial ceremonies. Beer lids can also be used as a serving plate for dry food and as a spoon rest for the skimmer, stirrer, and gourd, all of which are used for serving beer. Each family owns several lids; they are cared for and considered very special. Every husband has his own *imbenge*, which is presented to him by his wife during the wedding ceremony.[28] Beer lids serve many practical purposes.

Figure 56. **Zulu beer pot covers**. (Clockwise from left) Catalogue numbers 211, 214, 213 and 212.

They protect food, they may be used as holders for utensils and snacks, and they are an important part of marriage gift exchanges.

Conclusion

The economic, social, and spiritual structure of Zulu society is based on the benevolence of ancestors, beings who are integral to the daily life of all people. For the Zulu, food is a crucial gift bestowed upon the living by generous ancestors. The receiving, preparation and serving of food is ritually performed to recognize and honor the gift. Utilitarian items related to eating, spoons, beer pots, and cooking pots, receive special consideration in the ceremonial process, and are attentively cared for by their owners. Not only are cooking and eating utensils beautifully created according to Zulu aesthetic systems, they are also infused with the power of ancestors through ritual storage and use in each Zulu home. The creation and ritualized use of special utensils reinforce the social construction of Zulu power, influence and belief structures.

1   Axel-Ivar Berglund, *Zulu Thought-Patterns and Symbolism* (London: C. Hurst & Co., 1976), 110.

2   Joan Broster, *Red Blanket Valley* (Johannesburg: Hugh Keartland Publishers, 1967), 60.

3   Berglund, 200.

4   Lindsay Hooper, "Domestic Arts: Carved Wooden Objects in the Home," in *Zulu Treasures: of Kings and Commoners* (KwaZulu Cultural Museum and the Local History Museums, 1996), 74.

5   Berglund, 102.

6   Berglund, 110.

7   Berglund, 214.

8   Berglund, 102, 106.

9   Berglund, 102.

10 Berglund, 103.

11 J.W. Grossert, *Zulu Crafts* (South Africa: Shuter and Shooter, 1978), 389.

12 Sandra Klopper and Karel Nel. *The Art of Southeast Africa* (Milan: 5 Continents Editions, 2002), 45.

13 E. Jensen Krige, and J.D. Krige, *The Realm of a Rain Queen* (London: Oxford University Press, 1943), 49.

14 W.D. Hammond-Tooke, *The Bantu Speaking Peoples of Southern Africa* (London: Routledge & Kegan Paul, 1937), 199–120.

15 Klopper, 41.

16 Hammond-Tooke, 130.

17 Broster, 128–136.

18 Josiah Tyler, *Forty Years Among the Zulus* (Boston: Congregational Sunday School and Publishing Society, 1891), 121.

19 A.T. Bryant, *The Zulu People; As They Were Before the White Man Came* (New York: Negro Universities Press, 1970), 274.

20 Hammond-Tooke, 100.

21 Berglund, 102.

22 Rhonda Levinsohn, *Art and Craft of Southern Africa; Treasures in Transition* (Cleveland: Delta Books, 1984), 80.

23 Berglund, 103.

24 Bryant, 399–401.

25 Berglund, 176.

26 Grossert, 19.

27 Gary Van Wyk, "Illuminated Signs: Style and Meaning in the Beadwork of the Xhosa- and Bantu-speaking Peoples," *African Arts* 36, no. 3 (2003): 19.

28 Berglund, 102.

Selected Objects: Adornment

Mary Axworthy
and Ruth Broudy

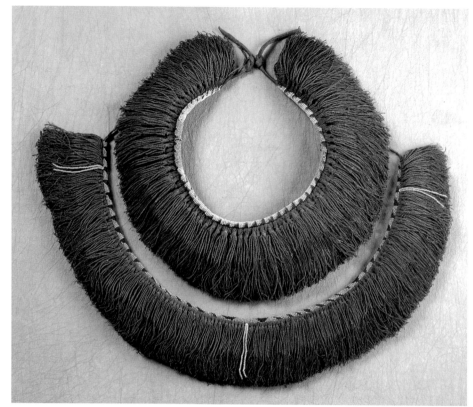

Figures 57a and 57b. **Basotho fringed skirts** (*thethane*), 19th century. Catalogue numbers 25 (top) and 18.

Basotho Fringed Skirts
Mary Axworthy

The *thethane*, a fringed skirt worn by newly initiated Basotho girls from the *bale* school in Lesotho, is made from the natural fibers of the indigenous gazania (*tsikitlane*) plant. The fibers are tightly twisted and attached to a leather band that is covered with beads.[1] Many hours are spent making these skirts that become a symbol of a Basotho girl's "feminine propriety." The skirt can be worn alone or under Western clothing.[2]

1   Caroline Crabtree and Pam Stallebrass, *Beadwork: A World Guide* (New York: Rizzoli, 2002), 60–61.
2   Barbara Tyrell, *Tribal Peoples of Southern Africa* (Cape Town: Gothic Printing, 1968), 97.

Basotho Initiation Veil (*lesira*)
Mary Axworthy

Distinctive to the Basotho people of Lesotho, Southeast Africa, is the *bale* (girls) school for the initiation of females into adulthood. This secret initiation school for girls is held during the summer months, and teaches the cultural values of the Basotho society to its young students. Customs of the *bale* school requires the initiates to cover their bodies in white clay, to signify their spiritual and physical separation from the community, until the end of the *bale* ceremony (lasting several months), and that they wear a traditional costume. Included in this costume is the hand-woven reed veil, called a *lesira*, that covers the face of the young female initiate.[1]

The reeds of the *lesira* are often decorated with glass beads and hand-rolled clay beads made by the older women of the village.[2] Along with the *lesira*, eight or more grass waist rings, sheepskin aprons and leather or cloth backskirts are worn. The waist rings, composed of a grass core, and bound with an endless plaited string of grass, has no beginning and no end, so that evil may not enter.[3]

During their schooling, the girls reside in a specially built house at the edge of the village, along with their teacher and accompanying large dogs. It is within this house that the girls receive their training for initiation to the rite of fertility and preparation for marriage. During daylight hours, *bale*

Figure 58. **Basotho initiation veil** (*lesira*). Catalogue number 601.

initiates venture into the countryside carrying medicinally treated forked sticks. Passersby are wise to present the girls with a small gift, or they run the risk of being battered by the forked-tipped sticks made specifically for this purpose.[4]

The *bale* initiation for young girls is still practiced in some remote villages of Lesotho, but has been discontinued in many areas due to Christian religious influence.[5]

1   Rhoda Levinsohn, *Art and Craft of Southern Africa: Treasures in Transition* (Craighall: Delta Books, 1984), 92.
2   Levinsohn, 92.
3   Barbara Tyrrell, *Tribal Peoples of Southern Africa* (Cape Town: Gothic Printing, 1968), 97.
4   Levinsohn, 92 and Tyrrell, 97 & 100.
5   Levinsohn, 92.

Zulu Earplugs
Mary Axworthy

The use of earplugs among the Zulu people of Southeast Africa is closely related to the long-standing custom of ear piercing. Ritual ear piercing was the first of a number of traditional ceremonies marking the transition from childhood to adulthood and was performed during the new moon or full moon cycles. The new moon (*ukwethwasa kwenyanga*) was associated with the time to begin making a new person, or adding a new unit to the family, while the full moon (*uma inyanga ihlangene*) was thought to be chosen when the children were being made "full" members of the family.[1] During the nineteenth century, pierced ears served as a distinguishing mark of the Zulu nation, and the large, decorative earplugs worn made it apparent to all, even from a distance, that the earlobes had been pierced.[2]

The practice of ear piercing was fairly common in many parts of eastern and southern South Africa, but the Zulu are unique in their characteristic enlargement of the earlobe. During the *Qhumbuza* ear piercing ceremony, a senior member, or healer, of the community would pierce the child's earlobe with a sharpened piece of iron. A small piece of corn stalk was placed in the newly created hole to stop the bleeding and ensure it would not close up. As the ear healed, larger and larger pieces of corn stalk were inserted into the hole, followed by reeds and progressively larger plugs, to gradually enlarge the hole until the desired shape was achieved (figure 53).[3]

The *Qhumbuza* ceremony seemed to lose its ritual and symbolic significance from about the 1950s onwards, and was thereafter practiced only on Zulu girls for aesthetic purposes.[4] With this new fash-

Figures 59a and 59b. **Zulu earplugs** (*amashaza*). Catalogue numbers 279 (top pair) and 281.

ionable use of earplugs, and the introduction of new materials, the earlier polished wood earplugs made from the hardwood of the red ivory tree, and painted lighter softwood discs were replaced by the popular "Marley Tile" vinyl asbestos earplugs. These new earplugs were made predominantly of softwoods, with finely worked plastic mosaic overlays, which were glued and/or pinned onto one or both sides of

the plug.[5] The new malleable materials available allowed more freedom of design, and many decorative patterns mimicked common everyday symbols such as road signs, letters of the alphabet and even logos of some well-known household products, such as the Sunbeam floor polish "sun" motif (figures 59a and 59b).[6] Another common motif found is the traditional slender crescent of the old,

Ritual ear piercing was the first of a number of traditional ceremonies marking the transition from childhood to adulthood...

Figure 60. **Zulu earplugs** (*amashaza*). Catalogue number 280.

Figure 61. **Zulu earplugs** (*amashaza*). Catalogue number 277.

Figure 62. **Zulu earplugs** (*amashaza*). Catalogue number 278.

or new moon, which could be a reference to the association of the moon with the original *Qhumbuza* ceremony (figure 60).[7]

With the new availability of colored plastics, Zulu artists also began incorporating the traditional color conventions of their regional beadwork, and the Msinga isishunka color sequence (white, red, black, dark green, yellow, light blue, and pink) is commonly found among earplugs from the mid-nineteenth century (figure 61). Another less common color convention found is the *uvalivali* pattern (figure 62). This older pattern, consisting of alternating bands of red and black or light blue and black, identified the wearer as a virgin (blue/black) or a married woman who was a virgin when she got married (red/black).[8]

In the 1960s and 1970s the thicker, more brittle Perspex material and other plastics largely replaced the vinyl asbestos "Marley Tiles." These materials were more difficult to work with, so earplug designs became simpler, but with larger, bolder

areas of color with a highly polished finish, frequently embellished with brass or chrome studs (figure 63). Despite the evolving changes in color, motif and materials, the underlying structural design of Zulu earplugs has remained consistent. In most cases, the circular disc of the earplug is divided into three segments: the equal sized lower and upper arcs, divided by a central parallel band.[9]

Since the 1980s, ear piercing has largely fallen out of favor with medium sized clip-on earplugs being produced for sale at the Mai-Mai market (the Zulu market place in Johannesburg). In many cases, people have actually had their previously pierced earlobes sewn up for fear of being labeled old fashioned.[10]

1   Frank Jolles, "Zulu Earplugs," in *Zulu Treasures: of Kings and Commoners* (KwaZulu Cultural Museum and Local History Museums: 1996), 171.

2   Jolles, "Zulu Earplugs," 171 & 175.

3   Alex Zaloumis and Ian Difford, *Zulu Tribal Art* (Cape Town: Amazulu Publishers, 2000), 213 and Frank Jolles, "Zulu Earplugs: A Study in Transformation," *African Arts* 30, no. 2 (1997): 46.

4   Jolles, "Zulu Earplugs," 171.

5   Jolles, "Zulu Earplugs," 172.

6   Zaloumis, 214.

7   Jolles, "Zulu Earplugs," 173.

8   Jolles, "Zulu Earplugs," 174.

9   Jolles, "Zulu Earplugs," 173.

10   Jolles, "Zulu Earplugs," 174.

Figure 63. **Zulu earplugs** (*iziqhaza*). Catalogue number 276.

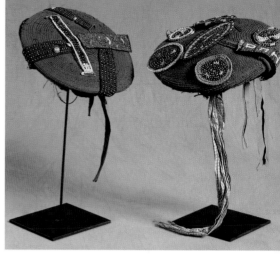

Figures 65a and 65b. **Zulu Valley of a Thousand Hills hats** (*inhloko/isicholo*). Catalogue numbers 328 (left) and 310.

Zulu Hats
Mary Axworthy

The interior of the elaborate hairdo was packed with dried herbs, and women were known to hide small personal treasures inside.

Among the Zulu, the head is considered sacred and a married woman, especially in rural areas, will never appear in public without some type of head covering, whether it be a scarf, a beret, a hat, or the traditional headdress.[1] Most contemporary headdresses are removable, but in the past many were made by weaving coarse knitting wool into the woman's hair to form a permanent fixture which was sealed on top. The interior of the elaborate hairdo was packed with dried herbs, and women were known to hide small personal treasures inside. This type of hair adornment was usually stained with red ochre pigment or a chemical dye and often smeared with fat or oil.[2]

The style of a Zulu woman's headdress, called an *inhloko* or *isicholo*, is usually determined to a degree by the culture to which she belongs.[3] Female members of the Shembe Church (*Ibandla*

Figure 66. **Zulu Msinga hat** (*inhloko/isicholo*). Catalogue number 309.

Figures 64a and 64b. **Zulu Shembe church hats** (*inhloko/isicholo*). Catalogue numbers 312 (left) and 311.

IamaNazaretha) wear a distinctive conical hat (figures 64a and 64b), and married women from the Valley of a Thousand Hills, wear a beret style headpiece, often ornately decorated with beaded panels or medallions (figures 65a and 65b). Women from the Msinga area don an assortment of headdresses in unique styles (figures 66 and 67), including a bifurcated horn-like headpiece, worn strictly by married women who can trace their ancestry to the Tukela Ferry region (figure 69).[4] One of the most unusual headdresses, also worn by Msinga women from the Tukela Ferry area, is comprised from a mixture of the woman's natural hair with coarse knitting wool that is shaped into a wide, disk-like form (figure 68).

1   Sue Derwent, *Zulu* (London: Struick, 1998), 99.
2   Aubrey Elliott, *The Zulu: Traditions and Culture* (Cape Town: Struik Publishers, 1995), 3.
3   Aubrey Elliott, *Zulu: Heritage of a Nation* (Cape Town: Struik Publishers, 1991), 18.
4   Peter Magubane, *Vanishing Cultures of South Africa* (New York: Rizzoli, 1998), 61.

Figure 67. **Zulu Msinga hat** (*inhloko/isicholo*). Catalogue number 314.

Figure 68. **Zulu Msinga hat** (*inhloko/isicholo*). Catalogue number 313.

Figure 69. **Double cone Zulu Msinga hat** (*inhloko/isicholo*). Catalogue number 323.

Zulu Warrior Dance Costume
Mary Axworthy

Under the leadership of the mighty King Shaka, the Zulu kingdom came to flourish during the early nineteenth century. Under Shaka's direction, the Zulu army increased from 500 odd warriors to a highly disciplined, well-trained regiment of up to 40,000 soldiers. Shaka's military genius and strategy also increased the Zulu region from 100 square miles to nearly 200,000 square miles during his twelve-year reign.[1] The Zulu male ceremonial dance costume (figure 70) is a visual celebration of this proud warrior heritage. Descendants of a nation founded on impressive military strength, many Zulu men still strongly identify with their glorious militant past. Through dance, Zulu men reenact military maneuvers and victorious battles that continue to live on in oral history.[2]

The prestigious leopard skin collar (*amambatha*) was once restricted by the king and bestowed upon worthy soldiers as a reward of valor. The warrior costume's front piece (*isinene*) consists of *izinjobo* (tails), which move on the thighs while walking, creating an important ceremonial stride.[3] Contemporary elements of ceremonial dress combine bicycle reflectors with the traditional leopard pelt.

Cowhide shields (*imibhumbuluzo*) also form an intricate part of military regalia. Small shields are used for ceremonies and stick-fighting and larger shields for dancing or war training. During battles, a large shield was used to conceal weapons, and when held horizontally while advancing across a hill, a military regiment could easily have been mistaken for a herd of cattle on the move.[4]

1   Sue Derwent, *Zulu* (London: Struik, 1998), 31.
2   Derwent, 14.
3   Derwent, 70.
4   Derwent, 91, 93.

Figure 70. **Zulu warrior dance costume**. Catalogue numbers 55 and 672 (shield).

Nursing Necklaces
Ruth Broudy

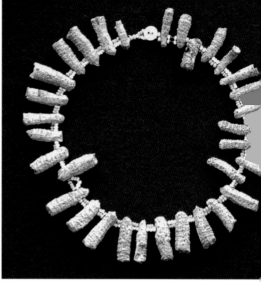

The Xhosa consider the milk of the mother as a wholesome food that nurtures the physical strength, good health and tranquility of the child. Xhosa infants are customarily nursed by their mothers for three years or more, by which time they are already walking and ready to digest an adult diet.[1]

Nursing necklaces, such as those seen in figures 71 and 72, are made for young women who are nursing babies and toddlers. The larger necklace (figure 71) is worn comfortably around the mother's neck and is positioned in such a manner that allows the child to touch the wooden rods, which have been treated with aromatic herbs and are soothing to the touch. When moved against each other, these rods produce a sound that is pleasant and calming to the child.[2]

In contrast, the rough texture of the dried roots or cobs on the smaller necklace feels uncomfortable against a mother's skin. Nevertheless, this coarse texture is pleasant to touch with the fingers. The Xhosa often thread pieces of the Cape honeysuckle, an indigenous healing plant, into the nursing necklace, believing it to encourage milk flow

Figure 72. **Xhosa Nursing Necklace** (*izinyango*)
The dried roots or cobs of smaller nursing necklaces are often threaded with pieces of Cape honeysuckle, an indigenous healing plant, believed to encourage milk flow and to make the baby strong. The cobs are kept moistened and the medicinal qualities are soothing to a teething baby and pleasing to the taste. Catalogue number 383.

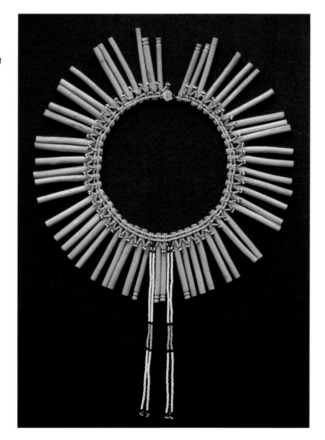

Figure 71. **Xhosa Nursing Necklace** (*izinyango*). The Xhosa peoples of Southeast Africa nurse their infants for three or more years until they are able to digest an adult diet. The wooden rods of this larger nursing necklace are treated with aromatic herbs that are soothing to the touch. When moved against each other, these rods produce a sound that is pleasant and calming to the child. Catalogue number 412.

and to make the baby strong and vigorous.[3] The cobs on the necklace are kept moistened and the medicinal qualities are soothing to a teething baby and pleasing to the taste.

To wean a child, a very bitter medicine mixed with a species of fly is tied around the neck of the child and smeared on the breast of the mother. The fly is said to make the child forget, while the medicine enables the child not to cry for the breast. The mother may not become pregnant again until the child has been weaned, at which time a goat is slaughtered for the purification of the mother and child, and sexual intercourse may again take place.[4]

1   Edward M. Smith Family Foundation, *Understanding Women in African Art*, African Art Exhibit (Mesa College, 2004).
2   Smith Family Foundation.
3   Margaret Roberts, *Indigenous Healing Plants* (Cape Town: Struik Publishers, Ltd., 1990), 12.
4   Eileen Jensen Krige, *The Social System of the Zulus* (Pietermaritzburg: Longmans Green and Co. Ltd., 1936), 73.

Selected Objects: Figurative

Mary Axworthy

Figure 73. **Northern Nguni puppets** (detail). Catalogue number 238.

Northern Nguni Puppets

For centuries, oral tradition has recognized the use of puppets, in religious and ritual context, throughout Africa. The earliest written account of African puppet shows dates back to the seventeenth century. Dramatic reenactments of heroes, and past historical events, preserve religious beliefs and moral values, encouraging social cohesion while entertaining African youth.[1]

According to Rayda Becker, this fine example of articulated puppets is probably Tsonga or Sotho in origin. Becker notes the wooden joints are similar in construction to those found in the northern province (Limpopo) of South Africa, but because of their small size, they could have easily traveled, being collected and decorated anywhere in the region.[2]

Becker recalls a puppeteer in Tzaneen who carved groups of small figures with articulated limbs, which he then attached to a circular metal structure that hung from his guitar. The puppets danced as the musician strummed and sang. Another puppeteer tied a group of puppets together in a line (similar to the puppets shown) and then strung them between his legs. He made the figures move by slapping his legs while singing or telling stories.[3] A third way these charming puppets could be manipulated is by stretching the strings between the puppeteer's toes, delighting children among the audience.[4]

Anitra Nettleton adds that these puppets are of a type distributed by Tsonga diviner/healers across a large region from Mozambique through the South African Lowveld, and into northern KwaZulu-Natal.[5] The headrings carved on the three male figures represent a type of headgear worn by many northern Nguni, including the Zulu, Swazi and Tsonga.[6]

1   E.A. Dagan, *Emotions in Motion: Theatrical Puppets and Masks from Black Africa* (Montreal: Galerie Amrad African Arts, 1990), 30.
2   Rayda Becker, <rbecker@parliament.gov.za> "Re: Puppet Photo," 23 July 2004, personal email.
3   Rayda Becker, <rbecker@parliament.gov.za> "Re: Forgot to Ask." 28 July 2004, personal email.
4   Dagan, 70.
5   Anitra Nettleton, <nettletona@artworks.wits.ac.za> "RE: Venda (?) Lady & Tsonga (?) Puppets," 15 July 2004, personal email.
6   Rayda Becker and Anitra Nettleton, "Tsonga-Shangana Beadwork and Figures," in *Catalogue: Ten Years of Collecting (1979–1989)*, eds. David Hammond-Tooke and Anitra Nettleton (Johannesburg: University of the Witwatersrand, 1989), 12.

Northern Nguni Male and Female Figures

Few figures exist from the Southeast Africa region and because of the movement and mingling of peoples, establishing a definite origin and use for these art objects is extremely difficult and speculative. The figures that do exist seem to have been made in pairs and come from the Northern Province of South Africa, where initiation was an important rite of passage. Figurative pairs were thought to be associated with initiation schools and used for didactic purposes— to instruct both male and female initiates in proper social and sexual behavior.[1]

Lack of original provenance and history regarding the production and use of figurative works from Southeast Africa has recently led scholars to believe that some sculptural pairs were probably not made for "traditional" indigenous use, but may have been produced for a trade market.[2] The figures here were carved by an unknown, but recognizable artist, who produced figures with exceptionally large, staring eyes. Other works by this artist can be found in the Natal Museum and the Brenthurst Collection in Southern Africa.[3]

1   Karel Nel, "Consonant with Cattle-culture: The Art of the Portable," in *The Art of Southeast Africa* (Milan: 5 Continents Editions, 2002), 20 & 35.

2   Sandra Klopper, "'Zulu' Headrests and Figurative Carvings: The Brenthurst Collection and the Art of South-east Africa," in *Art and Ambiguity: Perspective on the Brenthurst Collection of Southern African Art* (Johannesburg: Johannesburg Art Gallery/Johannesburg City Council, 1991), 89.

3   Klopper, 96.

Figure 74. **Northern Nguni male and female figures**. Catalogue number 301.

Northern Nguni Female Figure

This unique Southeast African sculpture is a stylized representation of a female figure with looped extremities. Lack of extensive research in the field of southern African sculpture and the early misconception that all southern African sculpture was "Zulu," continues to make it difficult for scholars to accurately determine the origin of exquisite figurative pieces, such as this one.[1] Anitra Nettleton speculates that this piece is probably of Tsonga or Zulu origin.[2]

How this figure was used in society also remains a mystery. Freestanding sculpture among the Northern Nguni cultures have been thought to be linked to divination or used as didactic tools in initiation schools.[3] A similar figure in the British Museum is labeled as a "rhythm pounder," and Sandra Klopper suggests they may have been used as a grain pounder.[4]

Another sculptural example from this same artist can be found in the Conru Collection. Both pieces have the identical poker-work cross burnt into the surface of the wood at its base. Of notable difference, however, is the treatment of the head. The Conru anthropomorphic object is rather unusual, as the head is formed as a stylized vessel.[5]

1   Anitra Nettleton, "History and the Myth of Zulu Sculpture," *African Arts* 21, no. 3 (1988): 48.
2   Anitra Nettleton, <nettletona@artworks.wits.ac.za> "RE: Venda Objects," 15 July 2004, personal email.
3   Nettleton, "History and the Myth of Zulu Sculpture," 48.
4   Kevin Conru, *The Art of Southeast Africa* (Milan: 5 Continents Editions, 2002), 20 & 214 and Sandra Klopper, personal handwritten note, May 2004.
5   Conru, 214.

Figure 75. **Northern Nguni female figure with looped extremities**. Catalogue number 282.

Figure 76. **Swazi baboon figure**.
Catalogue number 302.

Swazi Baboon Figure

According to the owner of the Colonial Gallery in Assangy, South Africa, a *sangoma* healer in Swaziland originally owned this unique sculpture. The healer kept this piece in front of his place of business for over fifty years. The baboon sculpture was said to symbolize good health and was consistently rubbed by patrons, creating a shiny patina on the baboon's snout.

The baboon has a long history in Swazi oral tradition. One legend traces the baboon back to a time when it carried the Swazi people across a river to their new homeland. There are also many myths that link baboons with sorcerers, witches and *tokoloshes* (a short, hairy, dwarf-like creature). At night, it is said that the evil creatures ride their baboon familiars (spirits embodied in the baboons and held to attend and serve their intimate associates) facing backwards, holding the baboon's tail like a rein. The Swazi warn that anyone encountering a baboon being ridden at night should not speak a word until dawn, or risk being dumb struck.[1]

1 Penny Miller, *Myths and Legends of Southern Africa* (Cape Town: T.V. Bulpin Publications, 1979), 232.

Southern Africa Figure

This serene wooden sculpture, whose provenance originates from Zambia or Zimbabwe, was acquired from the Leof Collection, Cuernavaca Mexico. Anitra Nettleton proposes this figure may be Tsonga, or even Makonde, and possibly Nyamwezi, however, distinctive features of this sculpture suggests a connection with the Venda of southern Africa.[1]

A Venda female figure from the Conru collection (KC 200), a Northern Transvaal male/female pair of figures from the Horstmann collection in the Johannesberg Art Gallery (accession numbers 1992.11.2a and 1992.11.2b), and a Venda female figure from the Sotheby's New York auction catalogue (November 24, 1992) all share several dynamic features also present in this piece. All of the mentioned objects are crafted from the same type of pokerwork wood, exhibiting a lighter patina face with a triangular nose, and display powerful legs, bent at the knees, and bent arms.

Continued debate surrounding the true origin of this type of sculpture can be attributed to the history of migration and intermingling among southern African cultures. David Hammond-Tooke connects the Venda people with Zimbabwe, whom later moved southward, extending their influence over Sotho groups in South Africa.[2] This type of figure among the Venda would probably have been one half of a pair of male/female figures used during the Domba female initiation procedures to prepare young women for marriage and their adult roles in society.[3] As with the Venda, Tsonga figures were also commonly used for initiation practice.

1   Anitra Nettleton, <nettletona@artworks.wits.ac.za> "RE: Venda (?) Lady & Tsonga (?) Puppets." 15 July 2004, personal email.
2   David Hammond-Tooke, *The Roots of Black South Africa* (Parklands: Jonathan Ball Publishers, 1993), 13, 33.
3   Anitra Nettleton, "The Venda Model Hut," *African Arts* 18, no.3 (1985): 87.

Figure 77. **Southern Africa figure**. Catalogue number 283.

67

Southern African Spoon

Spoons hold special significance in the traditional Zulu household and are associated with numerous rituals and customs relating to spiritual beliefs, hygiene, food type and social status. They are typically made of natural materials (wood, clay, or grass), despite the long availability of metal and western mediums.[1] Zulu spoons are usually very personal, decorated, and often kept in a special woven grass pouch (*impontshi*). A spoon is never left lying around the household, and if it is not stored in its *impontshi*, it is placed in the eves of the cooking hut when not in use. The mistake of leaving a spoon standing in food, or sticking out of a pot, is believed to cause indigestion.[2]

Early speculation surrounding this type of large, figurative spoon suggested that because of its size, it was probably used as a serving spoon or ladle (*isixwembe*) for stews or soup and was probably commissioned for a special occasion from a well-known sculptor, rather than being made for utilitarian purposes.[3] The scarification marks on the thighs and lower back are distinctive to Zulu society, however, ornamentation on Zulu spoons are usually limited to the handle and consist most often of geometric motifs. Rarely do we see figurative spoon designs among Zulu cultures.[4]

The scarification marks and the blackened rim of the spoon's bowl are the only definite clues that point towards Zulu origin. Therefore, new theories consider the attribution of this type of spoon to other regions within southern Africa. Previous research done in the field by Anita Nettleton has shown that many African sculptures previously thought to be Zulu may actually be the work of Tsonga artists.[5]

Another possibility not to be ignored is the interesting parallels with the Ngoni (another Nguni-speaking people) who migrated northward from Natal in the early nineteenth century. Many of the wooden dance staffs produced by the Ngoni are decorated with female breasts and have a spherical head, usually truncated on one section, with a carved, concave shape. This link could indicate that this elegant figurative spoon might have been used as a dance staff, which would explain its larger-than-average size.[6] Another very similar spoon can be found on display at the Musee du Louvre (on permanent loan from the Musee de I'Homme Collection), in Paris (accession number 977.52.14).

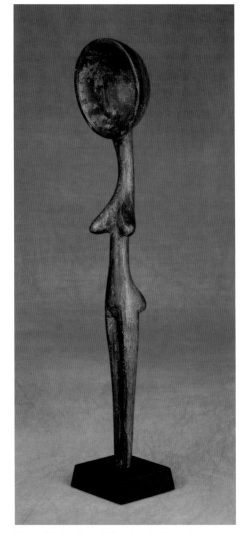

Figure 78. **Southern Africa female figured spoon.** Catalogue number 541.

1   Alex Zaloumis and Ian Difford, *Zulu Tribal Art* (Cape Town: Amazulu Publishers, 2000), 183.
2   Zaloumis and Difford, 183–184.
3   Marine Degli, "Zulu Sculpture," in *Sculptures: Africa Asia Oceania Americas*, ed. Jacques Kerchache (Paris: Reunion des Musees Nationaux, 2000), 38.
4   Manuel Valentin, "Zulu Sculpture," in *Sculptures: Africa Asia Oceania Americas*, ed. Jacques Kerchache (Paris: Reunion des Musees Nationaux, 2001), 208.
5   Valentin, 208.
6   Valentin, 208, 210.

Selected Objects: Staffs

Ruth Broudy

Northern Nguni Ceremonial Spear

This ceremonial spear is one of two known complete examples produced by the carver referred to as the Master of the Small Hands.[1] The majority of staffs and spears by this carver have been transformed into free-standing sculptures through the removal, probably by outside collectors, of the long shafts and blades still found on this surviving piece. Carvings of this kind were often acquired because of their prestige association with indigenous leaders, but also because they were relatively light and easy to carry.[2] All the examples by the Master of the Small Hands are carved from "red-ivory," a prized wood favored by artists in the region and one which was generally reserved for important leaders.[3] Common features noted on the finials of staffs identified by this carver are the treatment of such details as the hair, ear, facial features, arms, buttocks and legs and in the handling of the limbs, where there is a clear demarcation between the calves and thighs.[4] One feature, unique to this spear, is seen in the wooden handle which is inserted into the metal tip, rather than the metal tip being inserted into the wooden handle, that which is commonly observed in most spears.[5]

1 Annie Pérez, ed., *The Art of Southeast Africa from the Conru Collection* (Milan: 5 Continents Editions srl, 2002), 188. Besides this complete staff in the Smith Family Trust in California, another complete staff is located in the Cultural History Museum in Pretoria, South Africa.
2 Sandra Klopper, "Kings, Commoners and Foreigners: artistic production and the consumption of art in the Southeastern African region," in *The Art of Southeast Africa from the Conru Collection*, ed. Annie Pérez, 46 (Milan: 5 Continents Editions srl, 2002).
3 Bernard DeGrunne, *Mains de Maîtres* (Brussels, 2001), 247, 257.
4 Tom Phillips, ed., *Africa: The Art of a Continent* (Munich: Prestel Verlag, 1995), 225.
5 Ned Smith of the Edward M. Smith Family Art Foundation, personal communication.

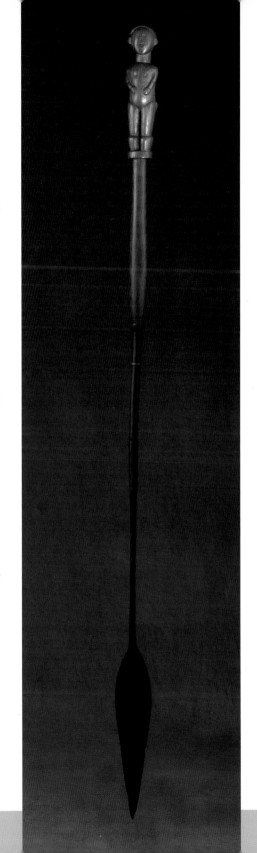

Figure 79. **Northern Nguni ceremonial spear with finial**. Catalogue number 572.

Figures 80a and 80b. **Lesotho etched walking staffs**. Catalogue numbers 597 (top) and 598.

San Walking Staff

This rare etched bamboo walking staff (figure 80a) with native fauna and flora motifs is one of only thirteen known to exist today.[1] Information relevant to this stick can conceivably be understood from a comparison with similar decorated sticks referenced in literature or known to exist in some museums, such as the stick in the Morija Museum in South Africa. The type of wood used for this staff, known as Southern Mountain, is an indigenous bamboo that grows uniquely in Lesotho and in the neighboring areas of Natal, the Orange Free State and the Eastern Cape Province in the Republic of South Africa.[2] The bamboo consists of eight panels, which are natural divisions formed by growth segments of the bamboo, each panel being decorated with a variety of engravings, including birds, antelopes, firearms, horses, a horse and rider, snakes, and a warthog. Such images date the stick to sometime after the late 1820s, as the horse, horse riding, and firearms were unknown in the area prior to that time.[3] Many of the engravings on the etched staff have been enhanced and decorated with pokerwork, a burning-in of the lines and dots which allows the designs to stand out against the light color of the bamboo. The subject matter depicted on this staff belongs to the group of so-called "conventional" or "traditional" designs, which is characterized by a smaller number of larger engravings of birds, animals, humans, firearms, snakes, and plants arranged in unrelated groups, often turned upside down or sideways. In contrast, sticks with "anecdotal" designs tend to illustrate scenes depicting activities or events rather than random groupings of images.[4] Little as yet is known about the significance of the images depicted on these sticks and efforts to compare their meanings to those illustrated in rock art have proved to be futile. This is because humans dominate the paintings in shelters while the birds, fish, reptiles, and plants, so common on many

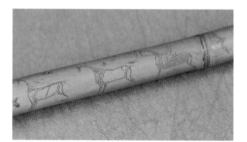

Figure 81. **Detail of figure 80a.**

70

of the sticks, are atypical for the painting sites.[5] The rounded knob on the end of this staff suggests that it probably served as a walking stick, although sticks of this type have also been referred to as messenger sticks, which served to legitimize messengers, with the sender being recognized by means of the decorations.[6]

1   Ned Smith of the Edward M. Smith Family Art Foundation, personal communication.
2   K.C. Palgrave, *The Trees of Southern Africa* (Cape Town: Struik, 1977), 63.
3   V. Ellenberger, "The First Horses to be Seen in Basutoland," *Basutoland Witness* 9, no.1 (1955): 6–7.
4   Johanna A.M. Giesen, ed., *Lesotho, Kingdom in the Sky* (The Netherlands: Afrika Museum, Berg en Dal, 1993), 211–12.
5   Giesen, 213.
6   Giesen, 213–14.

Figure 82. **Detail of figure 80a.**

San Staff

This very rare staff (figure 80b) is an example of an "anecdotal" stick with scenes that illustrate unfamiliar objects and activities, commonly associated with Europeans.[1] The event depicted is that of a battle scene at Prynnsberg during the Boer War in the Clocolan region of South Africa (see pages 4–5). The center panel illustrates the Boers on horseback fleeing the Prynnsberg Estate as the English take over (figure 4).[2] Because the Boers successfully resisted British encroachments during the First Boer War in 1880–1881, this staff probably references the Second Boer War of 1899–1902, where the Boer troops were defeated by British forces. Thus, the staff would correctly be dated to the early years of the twentieth century. In addition to the main battle scene, the stick depicts images that include cavalry, horses drawing a chariot, rifles, a building— all illustrating the remarkable marvels accompanying the arrival of a foreign culture. The carved designs are accentuated with pokerwork and hatching that has been made to stand out by rubbing them with dirt and body grease.[3] The elaborate separations between the panels, the many figures filled in with hatching (parallel engraved closely spaced lines), and the unusual geometric patterns which characterize this stick, have also been found on some of the few remaining examples, introducing the possibility that we are looking at the work of a single artist or only a few artists.[4] While the original function of this example is unknown, the shape of the ends and the rather short size of the stick do not suggest that it may have served as a walking stick. Rather, sticks of this type with anecdotal scenes most probably were meant to serve as a record of events, as a didactic tool to explain to others what had been encountered. They are regarded as a late development, fulfilling a very different purpose from sticks with conventional or traditional subject matter.[5]

1   Johanna A.M. Giesen, ed., *Lesotho, Kingdom in the Sky* (The Netherlands: Afrika Museum, Berg en Dal, 1993), 211.
2   Ned Smith of the Edward M. Smith Family Art Foundation, personal communication.
3   A.C. Hoffman and E. Bernard, *Bushman Engravings on Walking Sticks, Magic Sticks, a Calabash, and Ostrich Egg Shells* (Bloemfontein: Researches of the Nasionale Museum, 1969), 2.8: 238–242
4   Giesen, 212.
5   Giesen, 213–14.

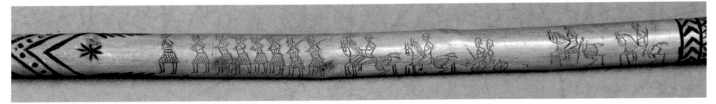

Figure 83. **Detail of figure 80b.**

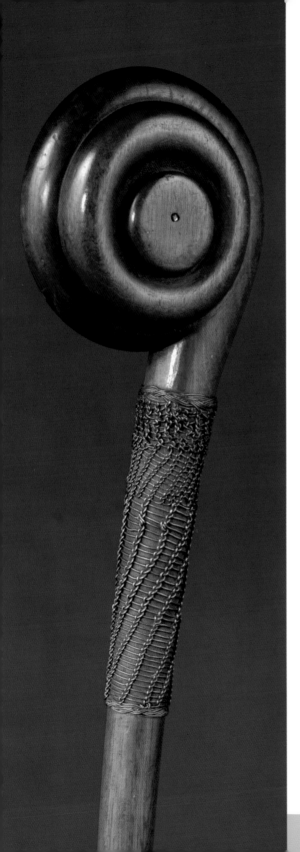

Swazi Staff

Like their Zulu neighbors, the art of the Swazi includes little free-standing figurative sculpture, but headrests and staffs in abundance.[1] The staff seen in this example is carved from ivory wood and has an offset head formed by five disc shape lozenges. Such a staff is noted as being typically Swazi and is associated with the regiments of the reign of King Sobhuza.[2] Staffs of this kind were commonly obtained as tribute or through trade and were often modified by their owners, primarily through the addition of brass and copper wire.[3] Indigenous communities regarded the imported brass and copper as two differently colored varieties of the same metal which was considered as the "gold" of the region.[4] As such, the wirework details frequently found on staffs and sticks from the Southeast African region serve both to individualize them and to affirm the fact that they are among a man's most valued personal possessions.

1   Sandra Klopper, "Zulu Art", in *Catalogue: The Standard Bank Foundation Collection of African Art* (1979–1986) (Johannesburg: University of the Witwatersrand Art Galleries, 1986). This catalogue is not paginated.

2   Karel Nel, "Consonant with Cattle-Culture: the Art of the Portable," in *The Art of Southeast Africa from the Conru Collection*, ed. Annie Pérez, 33–34 (Milan: 5 Continents Editions srl, 2002).

3   Sandra Klopper, "Kings, Commoners and Foreigners: artistic production and the consumption of art in the Southeastern African region," in *The Art of Southeast Africa from the Conru Collection*, ed. Annie Pérez, 46 (Milan: 5 Continents Editions srl, 2002).

4   A. T. Bryant, *The Zulu People: As They Were Before the White Man Came* (Pietermaritzburg: Shuter and Shooter, 1949), 159.

Figure 84. **Swazi staff** (spiral finial), detail.
Catalogue number 592.

Tsonga Staff with Finial

Among the principal artists working in the Colony of Natal was the Baboon Master, whose workshop produced figurative staffs of this kind. Works attributed to this carver are among the most distinctive carvings produced in late nineteenth century Southeast Africa. The Baboon Master worked in the region of Pietermaritzburg and Durban in the 1880s and 1890s, and carved sticks incorporating the form of a baboon into the handle, as well as staffs with single indigenous male and female figures. This maternity staff finial portrays a woman wearing the traditional topknot coiffure of married Zulu-speaking women of the Natal Chiefdoms.[1] In the nineteenth and twentieth centuries, figured staffs of this kind were carried by elderly women of high status who had produced children. During young men's initiation, these figures were used by instructors as a means of communicating with the spirits of influential ancestral women.[2] Common to staffs by the Baboon Master is the tall and slender compact treatment of form and delicately carved facial features that barely protrude beyond the ovoid mass of the head. Although the babies wrapped around the mothers' abdomens are given individual sculptural identity, points of contact and overlap between them and their mothers are used to strengthen the overall emphasis on gently pronounced swelling masses.[3]

1   Sandra Klopper, "'Zulu' Headrests and Figurative Carvings: the Brenthurst Collection of Southeast Africa", in *Art and Ambiguity: Perspectives on the Brenthurst Collection of Southern African Art*, exh. cat. (Johannesburg: Johannesburg Art Gallery, 1991), 89–96.
2   Edward M. Smith Family Foundation, *Understanding Women in African Art*, African Art Exhibit (San Diego: Mesa College, 2004).
3   Klopper, 93.

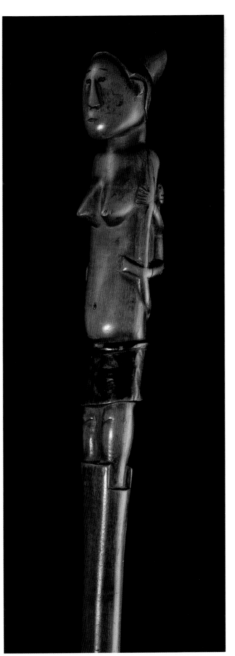

Figure 85. **Tsonga maternity staff** (front and back details). Catalogue number 574.

Figure 86. **Northern Nguni staff**. Catalogue number 589.

Northern Nguni Staff

    This staff, possibly of the kind carved by Tsonga and Venda artists for sale to tourists in the early part of the twentieth century,[1] suggests the fisted coiled staff that was looted from the Ondini *kraal* of the last independent Zulu king, Cetshwayo, during the Anglo-Zulu War of 1879. Since staffs with similar motifs had a ceremonial function,[2] the fisted hand is a possible indication of leadership, while the coiling around the shaft may be a stylized reference to snakes, and therefore to an integration of political and ancestral powers.[3] Among the peoples of southern Africa, including the Venda, Zulu, and Tsonga, snakes are treated with great respect and are regarded as a sign of the presence of the ancestors.[4] Thus a staff of this kind, which has little traditional significance in tourist trade, once represented the identity and authority of the people who owned them with the snakes signifying the power of the ancestors that spiraled out into the daily matters of those in physical existence.

1   This walking staff was thus identified by Anitra Nettleton, through correspondence on July 15, 2004, in which she states, "The staff is of a kind carved by Venda and Tsonga carvers for sale to tourists from early in the 20th Century—it has little traditional significance."

2   Gillian Berning, "Artefacts of the Zulu Kings", in *Zulu Treasures: of Kings and Commoners*, exh. cat. (KwaZulu: KwaZulu Cultural Museum and the Local History Museums, 1996), 62.

3   Sandra Klopper, "Zulu Art", in *Catalogue: The Standard Bank Foundation Collection of African Art* (1979–1986) (Johannesburg: University of the Witwatersrand Art Galleries, 1986). This catalogue is not paginated.

4   Karel Nel, "Consonant with Cattle-Culture: the Art of the Portable," in *The Art of Southeast Africa from the Conru Collection*, ed. Annie Pérez, 31–32 (Milan: 5 Continents Editions srl, 2002).

Zulu Dance Staff

Weddings and coming-of-age ceremonies are important events in the life of all communities. Zulu girls dedicate many hours preparing ornaments for family members and themselves in celebration of these special events. In Natal, young women join age-grade groups, organized by their communities. Each group has distinctive beaded dancing regalia which includes a thin staff or dancing stick, such as the one illustrated here. These staffs, decorated in specific colors and patterns, are used during special dancing performances.[1] The beadwork colors seen on this staff are typical of the Msinga region which follows a seven-color palette known as *isishunka* and includes the colors white, light blue, dark green, pale yellow, pink, red, and black. The white bands, in combination with light blue beads, indicate that this dancing stick is one that is used for marriage, as the color combination of white and light blue signifies fidelity or faithfulness.[2] When a girl is ready to marry, she appears in public with her dancing stick to dance amid her friends for what is symbolically the final dance before she leaves them in marriage.[3]

1   Jean Morris and Eleanor Preston-Whyte, *Speaking with Beads: Zulu Arts from Southern Africa* (London: Thames and Hudson, 1994), 38–39.
2   R.G. Twala, "Beads as Regulating the Social Life of the Zulu and Swazi," *African Studies* 10, no.3 (1958): 113–123.
3   Morris and Preston-Whyte, 39.

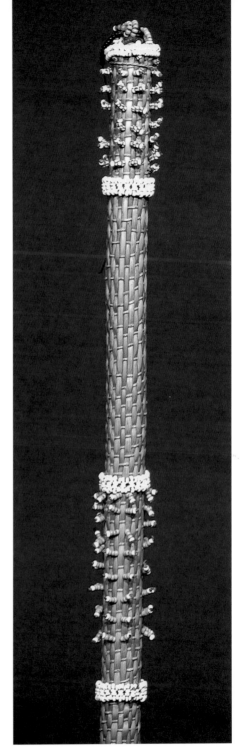

Figure 87. **Zulu dance staff** (detail).
Catalogue number 583.

75

Figure 88. **Zulu staff** (detail).
Catalogue number 573.

Zulu Staff

This staff is an example of those produced throughout Southeast Africa in the nineteenth and early twentieth centuries by carvers from Tsonga-speaking groups who supplied the Zulu kingdom with staffs as part of the tribute they were forced to pay Shaka and his successors.[1] The finial of this staff is presented as four, barrel-like flanges with an open ring in the upper chamber, a possible indication of status or the right to bear office.[2]

1   C. de B. Webb and J. Wright, eds., *The James Stuart Archive I* (Pietermaritzburg: University of Natal Press, 1976), 64.
2   Gillian Berning, "Artefacts of the Zulu Kings", in *Zulu Treasures: of Kings and Commoners*, exh. cat. (KwaZulu: KwaZulu Cultural Museum and the Local History Museums, 1996), 63.

Zulu Walking Staff

Long, walking sticks of this kind are known as *izimboko* and are traditionally carried by elderly men and women. Considerably longer than those used by men and boys, their purpose is to give support, rather than for defense and fighting.[1] Enormous symbolic power and value is often attached to Zulu walking sticks, such as the one seen in this example, where the bowl finial with crossbar below suggests a female figure, and hence references ancestral powers. Along with the capacity for sticks to contain an ancestral presence and to be intimately bound up with the identity of the man to whom it belongs, common stylistic elements found on sticks also represent the man's peer group or community.[2]

1   J.W. Grossert, *Zulu Crafts* (Pietermaritzburg: Shuter and Shooter, 1976), 48.
2   Karel Nel, "Consonant with Cattle-Culture: the Art of the Portable," in *The Art of Southeast Africa from the Conru Collection*, ed. Annie Pérez, 33 (Milan: 5 Continents Editions srl, 2002).

Figure 89. **Zulu walking stick with bowl-shaped finial** (detail). Catalogue number 595.

Selected Objects: Utilitarian

Mary Axworthy
and Ruth Broudy

Figure 91. **Basotho birds**. (Left to right) Catalogue numbers 290, 289, 286, 285 and 284.

Basotho Vessels
Mary Axworthy

Combining the spiritual elements of earth, fire and water, pottery remains one of the most fundamental arts of the Basotho people, and the crafting of this art has remained virtually unchanged for over nine thousand years. Women have traditionally assumed the role of pottery making among the Basotho, and clay vessels have filled the household functions of storing grain, water, beer making and cooking.[1]

The Basotho potter begins by setting a coil of clay on a piece of broken pottery or flat stone. The clay coils are layered one at a time and smoothed out as the pot is built upwards in the desired shape. Once the rim is completed, the vessel is turned over to complete the base. The pot is then set aside to dry in the sun, until it stiffens to a specific hardness, before it can be burnished with a small, smooth stone to create the characteristic sheen seen in many Basotho pieces.[2]

Firing of the pottery is accomplished by placing the clay objects in a hole dug into the ground and covered with dried cow dung mixed with straw. Loose rocks are dispersed among the pots to aid in heat retention and a final layer of pot shards, or a tin sheet, can also be placed over the pit to increase the firing temperature.[3]

Traditionally, very little surface design has been employed in Basotho pottery, but beautiful pieces, like the unique bird vessels shown here, have been created by using a different colored "slip," a thin mixture of clay and water, brushed onto the pottery before firing. The irregular black markings found on both the clay birds and the large pot are a result of reduction and smoke during the firing process.[4]

Figure 90. **Basotho pot**. Catalogue number 455.

1   Graham Taylor, "Basotho Pottery," *Sethala Magazine*, 10 May 1988, <http://www.lesoff.co.za/artline/Traditional/BasothoPottery.htm> (15 July 2004).
2   Taylor, 1988.
3   Taylor, 1988.
4   G. Clark and L. Wagner, *Potters of Southern Africa* (Cape Town: C. Struik, 1974), 147.

Zulu Milkpails
Ruth Broudy

In the cattle-based culture of southern Africa, milk plays a significant role in the daily lives of the people. It is not only an enduring staple, ensuring less dependence upon ground crops, but it is also a symbol of devotion to the ancestors, as well as the medium that binds two families through marriage. The consumption of milk, therefore, offers the daily ritualistic bond between past, present, and future.[1] When a milker approaches the cattle to be milked, he holds the milkpail above his head, an act meant to emphasize the honoring of cattle and their importance in maintaining good relations among the living and the dead.[2] The functional milkpail, whose place is in the cattle *kraal*, is important as a container not only for vital everyday food, but also as symbolic receptacle to represent the goodwill of the ancestral spirits who cause the cattle to prosper so that the continuity of the family is assured.[3]

Since the mid-nineteenth century, milkpails have been used throughout the region of present-day KwaZulu-Natal. Economically and emotionally, the Nguni depend more on their cattle than their inland neighbors who are more adept agriculturalists. This is illustrated by the attitude towards cow's milk: the men from most inland areas do not drink milk, which is regarded as food for women and children, but among the Nguni, milk is one of the staple foods, even though their cattle yield very little, two to three litres a day being considered the average.[4] Because milkpails are associated with cattle, and through cattle, with the man's ancestors, women are discouraged from touching their husband's milkpail. Women are also excluded from the process of milking and apportioning milk. A young bride may not share the milk and meat from her husband's home until the birth of her first child and until the gift of a goat has been exchanged between her husband's and father's families. The goat is known as the "goat of the spoon," for with it is given the spoon which the wife uses for eating sour milk and other food in her husband's household.[5]

The Zulu milkpail illustrated on the left in figure 92 is decorated with the *amasumpa* (wart) design. It consists of rows of small blocks, between which the width of separation varies, as well as the shape of the blocks, which taper slightly to the top in a pyramidal fashion. Many items decorated in this way suggest that the motif originated in the heartland of the Zulu kingdom and alludes to associated status and power. Situated below the neck of the vessel, small wooden motifs have been added, serving as grips to prevent the pail from slipping during the milking process (figures 92a and 92b). At times, breastlike motifs are carved near the neck of the vessel, suggesting female lactation and, thus, the idea of fertility.[6]

Milkpails of this kind are never used for storing milk, which is decanted in other vessels, usually clay pots, wooden containers in the form of wide-bellied, narrow-mouthed clay pots commonly produced in the region, or calabash vessels. Milk is rarely consumed fresh and in most instances it is left to form sour milk, known as *amasi*.[7] Once decanted, milkpails are placed upside down on a wooden pole, where they are allowed to drain and dry out until the next milking session.

Figures 92a and 92b. **Zulu Milkpails** (*ithunga*). The container on the left displays the wart-like *amasumpa* decoration, a pattern that affirms the importance of milk in the cattle-based culture of the Zulu. The milkpail serves, not only as a container for essential everyday food, but also as a symbolic receptacle to represent the goodwill of the ancestral spirits who cause the cattle to prosper so that the continuity of the family group is assured. The vessel on the right sits on a circular base, which is the smallest diameter of the object. The side lugs are situated well below the neck of the vessel and serve as grips, preventing the pail from slipping during the milking process. While milkpails of this type are used by the Zulu in the daily ritual of milking, they are never used for storing milk, which is decanted into other containers, usually clay pots, wooden or calabash vessels, and left to form sour milk, known as *amasi*. Catalogue numbers 354 (left) and 355.

1. Annie Pérez, ed., *The Art of Southeast Africa: from the Conru Collection* (Milan: 5 Continents Editions srl, 2002), 11.
2. C. de B. Webb and J. Wright, eds., *The James Stuart Archive 1* (Pietermaritzburg: University of Natal Press, 1976), 328.
3. Axel-Ivar Berglund, *Zulu Thought-Patterns and Symbolism* (London: C. Hurst and Company, 1976), 110.
4. Eileen Jensen Krige, *The Social Systems of the Zulus* (Pietermaritzburg: Longmans Green and Co. Ltd., 1936), 394.
5. Marion Mangon, ed., *Ubuntu: Arts et culture d'Afrique du Sud* (Paris: la Réunion des musées nationaux, 2002), 148.
6. Tom Phillips, ed., *Africa: The Art of a Continent* (New York: Prestel Verlag, 1999), 204, 226.
7. Krige, 207.

Figures 93a and 93b.
Northern Nguni incised vessels. Catalogue numbers 216 (left) and 217.

Northern Nguni Vessels
Mary Axworthy

These vessels exhibit a combed surface decoration unique to the Northern Nguni. The shorter vessel with exterior structures is deeply incised with broad bands of decoration, carved from a single piece of wood. Vessels of this type are so unique in style and execution, it is possible a single artist or workshop may have produced them.[1]

Although the use of these large vessels is unclear, early theories suggest they were used to store sour milk, beer or food. More recent thought proposes these vessels were used by royalty as court-sized tobacco or snuff containers. The taller vessel does closely resemble the form and surface decoration of some small, personal snuff containers made for individual use. The larger vessels could conceivably have been used in the courts of influential kings or chiefs, to offer tobacco or snuff (tobacco in its inhalable form) to dignitaries at gatherings, or feasts to honor the ancestors. Since tobacco and snuff were scarce and valuable commodities, sharing it would have been viewed as a sign of wealth and generosity.[2]

1   Tom Phillips, ed., *Africa: The Art of a Continent* (Munich; New York: Prestel, 1995), 223.
2   Karel Nel, "Consonat with Cattle-culture: The Art of the Portable," in *The Art of Southeast Africa* (Milan: 5 Continents Editions, 2002), 28.

Figure 94. **Xhosa figurative pipe**.
Catalogue number 499.

Figures 95a and 95b. **Zambia Ila Tonga pipes**.
Catalogue numbers 508 (left) and 509.

Pipes
Mary Axworthy

Tobacco (*Nicotiana*) and cannabis (*Cannabis sativa*) are not indigenous to Africa and there is no concrete evidence that establishes when or where they were introduced. The Portuguese most likely introduced tobacco to southern Africa in the fifteenth and sixteenth centuries, and cannabis was probably imported from Asia even earlier.[1]

The smoking of cannabis among Southeast African cultures appears to have been reserved for men. The "water-pipes" used for smoking cannabis were of a considerably different style from the tobacco pipes used today, and consisted of a container for water, a reed stem and a bowl of stone or clay for the leaves.[2]

The earliest tobacco pipes known for use in Southeast Africa were simple cylindrical forms made of bone and stone. From these original stone shapes, tobacco pipes evolved into more and more elaborate forms, and by the early twentieth century a wide variety of carved and decorated wooden pipes could be found throughout Southeast Africa, particularly among the Xhosa in the Eastern Cape (figures 94, 96a and 96b).[3] Some innovative and expressive pipes made from clay can also still be found in some regions (figures 95a and 95b).

As with snuff containers, pipes were used as markers of social status, and the size, shape and decoration varied according to sex, age and profession. Proper etiquette surrounding tobacco smoking included that a lit pipe had to be shared with all members of the community present, and each individual always carried their own removable mouthpiece.[4]

1   Ann Wanless, "Public Pleasures: Smoking and Snuff-taking in Southern Africa," in *Art and Ambiguity: Perspective on the Brenthurst Collection of Southern African Art* (Johannesburg: Johannesburg Art Gallery/ Johannesburg City Council 1991), 127.
2   Wanless, 127–128.
3   Wanless, 140.
4   Wanless, 140.

Figures 96a and 96b. **Xhosa (Thembu) pipes**. Catalogue numbers 507 (left) and 506.

Zulu Snuff Spoons
Mary Axworthy

The delicate ivory snuff spoon on the right also doubled as a comb. The long tines could be worn stuck through the hair as ornament, while the c-shaped spoon served to deliver snuff to both nostrils simultaneously. The bridge between the comb/handle and spoon is engraved with a fine pattern, on both examples, in which a black pigment has been rubbed in to enhance the design.[1]

Ivory snuff spoons were generally reserved for chiefs and those who could afford them. The ivory was delicately shaved with a knife and the long teeth carefully sawed with a rough piece of iron. The work took a great deal of patience and was no easy task.[2]

Snuff spoons were also often used as sweat scrapers, making them very personal to the owner. Once the spoon contained these elements of the user's body, it could then be used for making powerful medicine.[3]

1   Karel Nel, "Consonat with Cattle-culture: The Art of the Portable," in *The Art of Southeast Africa* (Milan: 5 Continents Editions, 2002), 29.
2   Patricia Davison, "Some Nguni Crafts Part 2: The Uses of Horn, Bone and Ivory," *Annals of the South African Museum* (Cape Town: The Rustica Press, 1997), 146.
3   Ann Wanless, "Public Pleasures: Smoking and Snuff-taking in Southern Africa," in *Art and Ambiguity: Perspective on the Brenthurst Collection of Southern African Art* (Johannesburg: Johannesburg Art Gallery/ Johannesburg City Council 1991), 140.

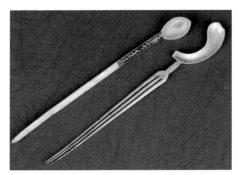

Figure 97. **Zulu snuff spoons** (*izitshengula*). Catalogue numbers 519 (left) and 500.

Figure 98. **Xhosa snuff containers**. (Left to right) Catalogue numbers 504, 503 and 505.

Snuff Containers
Mary Axworthy

Tobacco has been a highly enjoyed and valuable commodity among black southern African communities for centuries and holds a very important place in social ritual. Symbolically, it is closely associated with fertility, the complementary nature of the sexes, and ideas of growth and change.[1] Tobacco is also linked with the power of the ancestors, referred to as *shades*, and was a popular offering to the spirits along with beer and meat.[2] Many healers and diviners used tobacco to "clear their heads," enhancing their ability to receive the voices of the spirits.[3]

Inhaling tobacco, known as "the taking of snuff," was a formal part of major feasts, and was enjoyed by both the living and the spirits of the dead (figure 47). It was most often shared amongst community members and was rarely taken alone.[4] Elaborate rituals exist around the taking of snuff and strict rules of etiquette apply in regards to both the giving and taking of tobacco. Tobacco has long been viewed as a symbol of wealth and power, and among the Zulu, the most important person of the community was expected to supply the snuff at ceremonial gatherings.[5]

Although the use of tobacco has always been a public activity, the paraphernalia surrounding its use is very personal. Snuff containers belong strictly to an individual, both male and female, and serve as a symbol of status, as well as important objects of personal adornment. Snuff containers have been worn in the form of earplugs, beaded and suspended from necklaces, belts (figure 99) and bandoliers, worn as ornamentation in the hair, and incorporated as decoration into walking sticks.[6]

Snuff containers can be made of various materials including wood, ivory, horn, bone, seedpods, calabashes (gourds), reeds, cartridge cases and metal or glass containers.[7] Many of these containers are further embellished with beads, wirework or etching.

Figure 99. **Zulu woman**. This Zulu woman wears a beaded snuff container hanging from her waist. Photograph taken in approximately 1900. Appendix A-7.

83

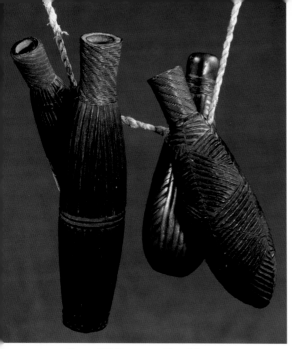

Figure 100. **Tsonga snuff containers**. Catalogue number 501.

Figure 101. **Sotho snuff containers**. (Left to right) Catalogue numbers 522, 523 and 524.

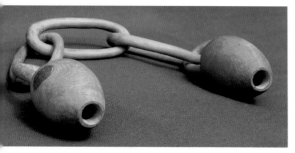

Figure 102. **Tsonga snuff containers**. Catalogue number 517.

Figure 103. **Zulu snuff containers** (*ishungu*). Catalogue numbers 531 (left) and 530.

Among the Sotho, traditional snuff containers were made of animal horn, making use of the natural hollow of the horn, which was plugged from underneath to seal the cavity. A mouth was made by drilling a small hole into the horn, which was then fitted with a stopper. Many of these horn snuff containers depict human or animal figures (figure 105).[8] With the introduction of Western materials, innovative new metal, mirror and glass designs developed (figure 101) and the feminine influence can be found in small beaded gourd containers, referencing the mythological link between calabashes and birth/gestation (figure 104).[9] Horn, metal and beaded gourd snuff containers are also commonly found among the Xhosa cultures (figure 98).

The Tsonga are known for their carved, drop-like wooden snuff containers, many of which are intricately etched with fine linear designs (figure 100). Bulbous snuff containers, joined by a carved wooden chain, are commonly seen among Tsonga groups and are frequently found attached to the end of headrests (figure 102).[10]

Delicate wire decorated gourds were made into snuff containers by various cultures throughout southern Africa (figure 103). The wirework designs probably varied from one region to another, but lack of provenance history often makes it difficult to ascribe a specific design to a definite geographic location or group.[11]

A very distinctive type of snuff container, found among the Xhosa, is made from the blood and hide scrapings of an animal that been sacrificed as an offering to the ancestors.[12] Blood and tissue scraped from the intestinal lining of the animal was mixed with small amounts of ochre pigment or powdered clay to create a stiff paste. The paste was then spread over a clay model and left to dry. After the form was dry, an opening was cut into the snuff container and the clay core removed.[13] These organic receptacles are most often found in the forms of

Figure 104. **Sotho snuff container**. Catalogue number 521.

elephants, antelopes, cattle (figure 106) and people.[14] A spiky texture is found on many of the animal snuff forms, which is created by lifting and stretching the surface membrane of the container with a sharp tool while still malleable.[15] The container can also be left smooth to create a natural, skin-like texture (figure 107).

1   Ann Wanless, "Public Pleasures: Smoking and Snuff-taking in Southern Africa," in *Art and Ambiguity: Perspective on the Brenthurst Collection of Southern African Art* (Johannesburg: Johannesburg Art Gallery/Johannesburg City Council 1991), 143.
2   Wanless, 130.
3   Wanless, 131.
4   Wanless, 128.
5   Wanless, 132.
6   Alex Zaloumis and Ian Difford, *Zulu Tribal Art* (Cape Town: Amazulu Publishers, 2000), 126 and Wanless, 133.
7   Zaloumis, 125.
8   Tom Phillips, ed., *Africa: The Art of a Continent* (Munich: New York: Prestel, 1995), 213.
9   Wanless, 137.
10 Kevin Conru, *The Art of Southeast Africa* (Milan: 5 Continents Editions, 2002), 209.

Figure 106. **Xhosa snuff container**. Catalogue number 510.

11 Conru, 202.
12 Phillips, 215.
13 Wanless, 169.
14 Conru, 196.
15 Phillips, 315.

Figure 107. **Nguni snuff container**. Catalogue number 516.

Figure 105 (below). **Sotho snuff container**. Catalogue number 502.

Zulu Meat Platters
Mary Axworthy

Zulu meat platters were used extensively during the late nineteenth and twentieth century to cut, carry and serve raw and cooked meat during ritual celebrations and to honor the ancestors. These platters are usually oval or rectangular in shape with rounded corners, a handle on each side and four short supports on the often decorated bottom. Both the handles and underside of the platters tended to develop a deep, rich patina from the constant saturation of oils from the roasted meat. The shallow, concave serving portion was scraped clean after each use, leaving it covered in scratches or cut-marks, evidence of years of use.[1]

The majority of Zulu meat platters have decorative panels on the blackened underside of the bowl. This decoration was probably executed as a means of identifying ownership and status, as well as providing an aesthetic aspect, as meat platters were often used to cover one another (to retain heat as well as keep flies away).[2] The large platter shown is decorated with the common *amasumpa* (warts) design, a grid-like design consisting of a series of shallow, raised pyramids. This design is repeatedly found on Zulu meat platters, milk pails, headrest and clay pots, and is associated as a symbol for herds of cattle.[3]

1   Alex Zaloumis and Ian Difford, *Zulu Tribal Art* (Cape Town: Amazulu Publishers, 2000), 271.
2   Tom Phillips, ed., *Africa: The Art of a Continent* (Munich; New York: Prestel, 1995), 224.
3   Karel Nel, "Consonat with Cattle-Culture: The Art of the Portable," in *The Art of Southeast Africa* (Milan: 5 Continents Editions, 2002), 26.

Figure 108. **Zulu meat platters** (*ugqoko*). (Left to right) Catalogue numbers 353, 348 and 351.

Figure 109. **Zulu bowl**. Catalogue number 219.

Zulu Bowls
Mary Axworthy

The Zulu, being a primarily cattle-culture in the nineteenth and early twentieth century, were migratory, moving fairly regularly as natural resources were depleted by the herds. As such, the art of the Zulu consisted of a few, highly prized possessions that could easily be transported as the need arose. Typical pastoralist objects include walking sticks, milking pails, headrests, grass mats, snuff containers, and wooden food platters and bowls.[1]

The importance of cattle to the survival of the people, and as a link to their ancestors, lent itself to a natural representation in Zulu art forms. The single bowl seen here creates the allusion of a bull, ox, or cow, as evident from the stylized head, legs and tail. The triple compartment bowl represents two animals, which is also often found in Zulu headrests, invoking the idea of a herd of cattle, the symbol of social harmony, wealth, pride and power.[2]

1   Karel Nel, "Consonat with Cattle-Culture: The Art of the Portable," in *The Art of Southeast Africa* (Milan: 5 Continents Editions, 2002), 17–18.
2   Nel, 22.

Figure 110. **Zulu bowl**. Catalogue number 218.

Zulu Baskets
Mary Axworthy

These bulb-shaped baskets are tightly woven containers commonly used for storing liquids. They share an unmistakable resemblance to Zulu coiled clay pots, which largely replaced baskets as a means of transporting beer and water, when migrating cultures settled.[1]

KwaZulu-Natal hosts a variety of grasses and palms suitable for basketmaking, but the most popular material for baskets is the foliage of the *ilala* palm (*Hyhaene natalensis*), found along the eastern coastal areas of South Africa. Only the young leaf shoots are harvested with the leaves split and put in the sun daily, for about a week, to dry out. After the leaves have dried, they are split into very thin threads for fine baskets, or wider threads for coarse baskets.[2]

The *isichumo* basket is commonly used to transport beer and is fitted with a lid. They are typically made using the coiling technique and are very tightly woven to hold liquids. The dried grasses swell when wet, making the basket watertight.[3] Although basketry is usually considered a woman's art among Southeast African cultures, adult Zulu men traditionally made these baskets.[4]

The ribbed design on the smaller basket is created using the grasshopper stitch that is worked in vertical parallel lines to the simple basic weave. Basket decoration does not serve any necessary function, and can therefore be viewed as a means of artistic expression.[5] This basket also features a small hide loop attached to one edge, functioning as a handle that could be used to stabilize the basket in transport and later used as a means of hanging it up for storage.[6]

1   Alex Zaloumis and Ian Difford, *Zulu Tribal Art* (Cape Town: Amazulu Publishers, 2000), 161.
2   Jannie Van Heerden, "Zulu Grassweaving," in *Zulu Treasures: of Kings and Commoners* (KwaZulu Cultural Museum and Local History Museums, 1996), 132.
3   Van Heerden, 133.
4   Carolee Kennedy, *The Art and Material Culture of the Zulu-Speaking Peoples* (Los Angeles: UCLA Museum of Cultural History, 1978), 3.
5   Rhoda Levinsohn, *Basketry: A Renaissance in Southern Africa* (Cleveland Heights: Protea Press, 1979), 53.
6   E. M. Shaw, "The Basketwork of Southern Africa Part 1: Technology," *Annals of the South African Museum* (Cape Town: The Rustica Press, 1992), 168.

Figure 111 (below). **Zulu coiled baskets** (*isichumo*). Catalogue numbers 155 (left) and 154.

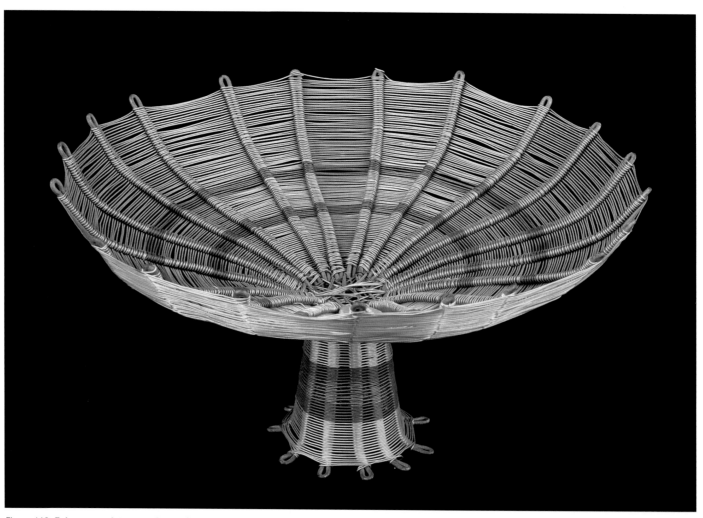

Figure 112. **Zulu woven plate on pedestal**. Catalogue number 181.

Selected Objects: Contemporary

Mary Axworthy,
Beth Baniadam and
Nancy El-Haddad

Figure 113. **Zulu wire basket by Elliot Mkhize**.
Catalogue number 161.

Zulu wire basketry
Mary Axworthy and *Beth Baniadam*

The beginnings of Zulu wire basketry were initiated long ago by the highly esteemed metalsmith profession. Village blacksmiths crafted ornamental metal wire that was incorporated into decorated dance staffs and gourds. This art form later evolved into elegant artistic wire forms and eventually developed into the colorful plastic-coated telephone wire basketry produced today.

In the nineteenth century, Zulu King Shaka kept tight control over the gathering of ore, the production of metal, and the creation of metal objects.[1] Brass could only be used under Shaka's direct supervision, which afforded great prestige to those who received it. When European traders began importing mass-produced metal items into southern Africa, King Shaka's political control over metal goods was broken and brass eventually lost its social importance.[2]

By the turn of the century, metal wire was readily available in the local marketplace. Brass and copper wire were used to embellish many personal items that were commonly used to hold snuff, medicine and cosmetics (figure 103), and carved staffs and spears were often adorned with wire, usually wrapped around the upper portion of the staff or finial (figure 84). Innovative new basketry forms were created out of the imported wire material as well. The Prynnsberg collection includes an impressive set of wire basketry in various shapes and sizes that include plates (figure 112), eggholders, cups, candleholders, bracelets, napkin rings, and spoons. These unique objects incorporate both copper and brass wire and were created using the same coiling technique employed by Zulu grass weavers.

Figure 114. **Zulu wire basket by Elliot Mkhize**.
Catalogue number 189.

With the introduction of inexpensive, plastic-coated telephone wire, basketry in the mid-twentieth century took another creative turn. Contemporary artist, Elliot Mkhize of Durban, South Africa, learned the art of grass basket making in the 1960s and quickly adapted the colorful new material into his basketry work. Mkhize began creating beer pot covers (*imbenge*) with telephone wire instead of grass (figure 113), utilizing the same coiling technique used for traditional grass *imbenge* (figure 56). One of these whimsical baskets incorporates the intricate design of a bird and numerous insects (figure 114). The writing above the bird, *ingududu*, translates to "ground hornbill."[3] After transitioning to a full time artist, Mkhize began sharing his innovative ideas with other artists, launching a new urban art form.[4]

1   Frans Roodt, "Zulu Metalworking," in *Zulu Treasures: of Kings and Commoners, A Celebration of the Material Culture of the Zulu People* (Durban: KwaZulu Cultural Museum and the Local History Museums, 1996), 95.

2   Roodt, 98.

3   Translation courtesy of Marianna Visser, Head of African Languages of the University of Stellenbosch, South Africa.

4   *Sunday Times*, "Wired for Beauty," 16 April 1995, p. 27, col. 1.

Josephine Ghesa Sculpture
Mary Axworthy and *Nancy El-Haddad*

Described as having "an original voice, who does not abide by the rules of classical sculpture,"[1] contemporary artist Josephine Ghesa works her magic in clay at the Ardmore Ceramic Art Studio in KwaZulu-Natal, South Africa. Josephine coils terracotta into tantalizing combinations of human and animal forms, in which she blends the legends of her Sotho childhood with a uniquely personal mythology. These sculptures are then fired to 1200 degrees and finished in a variety of mediums that can include anything from oil paint to boot polish.[2]

Josephine was born in 1958 at Thabazeka in Lesotho, South Africa. She was orphaned at an early age and lived

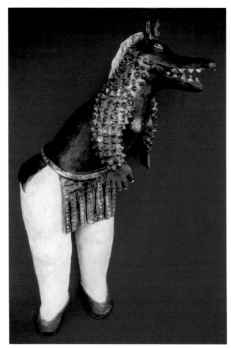

Figure 115. **Contemporary sculpture by Josephine Ghesa**. Catalogue number 287.

with her grandmother for five years, learning her trade as a potter for the local, rural community. Josephine earned a meager living continuing her grandmother's business after her death, making clay pots and drinking vessels for sale through a man in Ficksburg, South Africa. Eventually, Josephine married William Ghesa and with him had six children. An unfortunate turn of events left Josephine and her children homeless, when her husband kicked her out after taking another wife.[3]

After an unsuccessful search for work in Lesotho, Josephine found temporary work as a "mealie gleaner," gathering grain after the Indian corn harvest on a farm in Bergville. Hating this work, Josephine continued to search for better employment and in 1990, joined Fee Halsted-Berning's ceramic studio (Ardmore Ceramic Art Studio) in KwaZulu-Natal.[4] Fee instructed Josephine in the fundamentals of coiling and creating forms in clay, and Josephine soon found her calling. Fee recognized a unique talent in Josephine. Coming from a Sotho background, unlike the other resident Zulu artists at Ardmore, Josephine created large fired and painted earthenware sculptures that were quite different from the utilitarian and decorative pieces made by the other artists.[5]

Josephine was visited in her dreams by her grandfather, who had been a *sangoma* (diviner) in Lesotho. Her grandfather presented her with gifts of beads and cigarettes, an indication that her destiny was also to become a *sangoma* for her people.[6] But Josephine had finally found her voice in her clay creations, and instead of following the calling of her ancestors, she followed her heart. Her dreams and imagination took on new

Figure 116. **Contemporary sculpture by Josephine Ghesa.** Catalogue number 288.

life through her hands, and the earth she molded, and through them, a personal expression of her visions was realized.

Josephine's artistic inspiration draws from mythology and spiritualism, invoking her viewers to widen their perception of the world that exists outside their daily experience. Her sculptures possess a dreamlike, somewhat surreal quality that is unique, sometimes disturbing, and at other times amusing.[7]

Josephine Ghesa is developing a strong presence in the contemporary art world in South Africa. She won the National Regional Sculpture Prize in 1990, the Natal Biennial Merit Award in 1993 and the sculpture prize at the Brett Kebble Art Awards in 2003. She was a guest artist at the 1997 South Africa National Ceramic Exhibition and continues to exhibit her work widely.[8]

1   Margaret Von Klemperer, "Ardmore Ceramics Selected for Kebble Awards," *The Witness*, 4 September 2003. Quote from Richard Smith, Brett Kebble Art Awards curator.

2   Contemporary African Music & Arts Archive, "Josephine Ghesa," <http://www.cama.org.za/CAMA/countries/southafr/Makers/ghesa/HTML/> (24 May 2004).

3   Ardmore Ceramic Art Studio, "The Artists of Ardmore—Duma, Ghesa and Gumbi," <http://www.ardmoreceramics.co.za/ardmore-artists.html> (15 July 2004).

4   Ardmore, 15 July 2004.

5   Gloria Bates, "Sangoma Visions," (2001), 1–2.

6   Gillian Scott, *Ardmore: An African Discovery* (Cape Town: Fernwood Press, 1998), 21.

7   Bates, 2–3.

8   Contemporary African Music & Arts Archive, 24 May 2004.

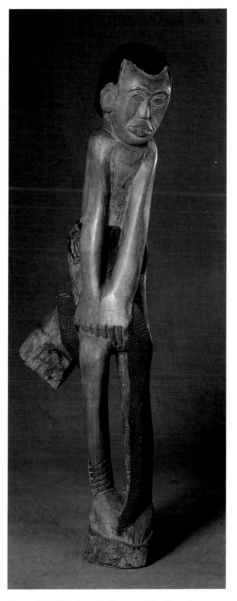

Figure 117. **Venda male figure with python by Owen Ndou**. Catalogue number 293.

Owen Ndou Sculpture
Mary Axworthy

Owen Ndou was born in 1964 in Gwamasenga, Venda, and currently resides in Hamutsha. Owen was drawn to sculpting at a very young age and started carving full time in 1984. He considers his responsibility as an artist to be a communicator to people's spiritual nature and explores themes dealing with religion, culture and mythology.[1]

This sculpture depicts an African man holding a large python. The python is associated with the Venda creation myth in which the python of the pool of creation, Lake Fundudzi, "vomited forth all animal and human creation from the pool."[2] The python is also considered to be a healer, and the bringer or withholder of rain, among the Venda.[3]

1   Mukondeni Fine Arts Gallery. "Owen Ndou Homepage," <http://www.mukondeni.com/html/Owen%20Ndou.htm> (29 June 2004).
2   Anitra Nettleton, "Venda Art," in *Catalogue: Ten Years of Collection (1979–1989)*, eds. David Hammond-Tooke and Anitra Nettleton (Johannesburg: University of the Witwatersrand, 1989), 5.
3   Nettleton, 7.

Catalogue
of the
Collection

The catalogue of the Southeast African Collection of the Edward M. Smith Family Art Foundation is organized according to types of objects. Dimensions are noted in inches; height precedes width precedes depth, unless specified otherwise.

*illustrated

APRONS, SKIRTS, LOINDRESSES

1. Zulu skirt (*itete*)
Cotton textile, glass beads, brass buttons; 3.5 x 25
Twentieth century; FSA-018-01

2. Zulu skirt (*itete*)
Cotton textile, glass beads, sisal fiber, brass buttons; 9.5 x 33
Twentieth century; FSA-018-02

3. Zulu skirt (*itete*)
Cotton textile, glass beads, sisal fiber; 21 x 20.5
Twentieth century; FSA-018-03

4. Zulu skirt (*itete*)
Cotton textile, glass beads, sisal fiber; 19.5 x 22
Twentieth century; FSA-018-04

5. Zulu skirt (*itete*)
Cotton textile, glass beads, sisal fiber; 11 x 34.5
Twentieth century; FSA-018-05

6. Zulu skirt (*itete*)
Cotton textile, glass beads, sisal fiber; 15 x 15
Twentieth century; FSA-018-06

7. Zulu skirt (*itete*)
Cotton textile, glass beads, sisal fiber; 12.5 x 26
Twentieth century; FSA-018-07

8. Zulu skirt (itete)
Cotton textile, glass beads, sisal fiber; 8 x 33.5
Twentieth century; FSA-018-08

9. Ndebele young girl's apron (*lighabi*)*
Glass beads, fiber; 4.5 x 7.5
Mid-twentieth century; PD-04, Figure 25b

10. Ndebele young girl's apron (*lighabi*)*
Glass beads, fiber; 8.5 x 11
Mid-twentieth century; PD-05, Figure 25a

11. Ndebele initiated girl's apron (*isiphephethu*)*
Glass beads, canvas, fiber; 12 x 15
Mid-twentieth century; PD-06, Figure 26

12. Ndebele married woman's apron (*liphotu*)*
Glass beads, hide, fiber; 22 x 24
Early twentieth century; PER-36, Figure 27
Purchased from the Gerald Block Collection, California

13. Ndebele married woman's apron (*ijogolo*)*
Glass beads, hide, fiber; 32 x 25.5
Early twentieth century; PER-38, Figure 44
Purchased from the African Heritage Trust Collection, Winchester, California

14. Xhosa girdle (*inkciyo*)*
Glass beads, fiber, metal; 20 x 30 x 2.5
Twentieth century; PER-39-01, Figure 41

15. Xhosa red ochre skirt*
Wool textile, glass beads, fur, buttons; 33 x 80.5
Twentieth century; PER-47, Figure 42b

16. Basotho fringed skirt (*thethane*)
Gazania fiber, hide, glass beads; 6 x 29 x 1
Circa mid-1850s; SA-041A-01
Purchased from the Prynnsberg Museum, Clocolan, South Africa, 1995

17. Basotho fringed skirt (*thethane*)
Gazania fiber, hide, glass beads; 5 x 29 x 2.5
Circa mid-1850s; SA-041A-02
Purchased from the Prynnsberg Museum, Clocolan, South Africa, 1995

18. Basotho fringed skirt (*thethane*)*
Gazania fiber, hide, glass beads; 4 x 33 x 1.25
Circa mid-1850s; SA-041A-03, Figure 57b
Purchased from the Prynnsberg Museum, Clocolan, South Africa, 1995

19. Nguni apron
Glass beads, fiber; 4.25 x 9
Nineteenth century; SA-054-17
Purchased from the Prynnsberg Museum, Clocolan, South Africa, 1995

20. Nguni apron with belt
Glass beads, fiber, button; 3.5 x 6.5
Nineteenth century; SA-054-18
Purchased from the Prynnsberg Museum, Clocolan, South Africa, 1995

21. Zulu black fiber skirt
Vegetable fiber, cowrie shells, glass beads; 12 x 16
Nineteenth century; SA-055-01
Purchased from the Prynnsberg Museum, Clocolan, South Africa, 1995

22. Zulu fishnet skirt
Hide, cowrie shells, glass beads; 10 x 42
Nineteenth century; SA-055-02
Purchased from the Prynnsberg Museum, Clocolan, South Africa, 1995

23. San red stained skirt
Hide, glass beads, red pigment; 7 x 12
Twentieth century; SA-055-03
Purchased from the Prynnsberg Museum, Clocolan, South Africa, 1995

24. Basotho fringed skirt (*thethane*)
Gazania fiber, hide, glass beads; 4.25 x 33
Nineteenth century; SA-066-01
Purchased from the Prynnsberg Museum, Clocolan, South Africa, 1995

25. Basotho fringed skirt (*thethane*)*
Gazania fiber, hide, glass beads; 5 x 35 x 2
Nineteenth century; SA-066-02, Figure 57a
Purchased from the Prynnsberg Museum, Clocolan, South Africa, 1995

26. Basotho fringed skirt (*thethane*)
Gazania fiber, hide, glass beads; 4.25 x 33
Nineteenth century; SA-066-03
Purchased from the Prynnsberg Museum, Clocolan, South Africa, 1995

27. Zulu man's rear apron (*ibeshu*)
Hide, glass beads; 21 x 27
Circa 1960s–1970; SA-092
Purchased from the African Art Center, Pietermaritzburg, South Africa

28. Zulu married woman's skirt (*isidwaba*)*
Hide, glass beads, metal; 29 x 26
Twentieth century; SA-093, Figure 35
Purchased from the African Art Center, Durban, South Africa;
collected by Nomusa Dube, 1995–1999

29. Zulu skirt mounted on wood
Hide, glass beads, shells, wood; 10 x 46
Nineteenth century; SA-118
Purchased from Craig Helms, Bonita, California

30. Xhosa married woman's ceremonial skirt (*umbhaco*)*
Wool textile, fur, glass beads, buttons; 33 x 68
Circa 1950s; SA-119A, Figure 42a
Purchased from the African Art Center, Pietermaritzburg, South Africa, 1997

31. Zulu loindress*
Glass beads, fiber; 6 x 9.5 x 32
Circa 1890-1910; SA-139, Figure 45
Purchased from the Dave DeRoche Gallery, San Francisco, California; Butterfield and Butterfield, 12/10/96, Lot 329

32. Lesotho skirt
Glass beads, fiber; 6 x 9.5
Early Twentieth century; SA-140
Purchased from Bud Lueck, El Cajon, California, from the Lapue Collection

33. Zulu Ceza-Nongoma pubic apron (*isigege*)
Glass beads, Job's tears seeds; 5.5 x 3.25
Circa 1940s; SA-205-01
Collected in South Africa, 1995

34. Zulu Ceza-Nongoma pubic apron (*isigege*)
Glass beads, Job's tears seeds; 6 x 7
Circa 1940s; SA-205-02
Collected in South Africa, 1995

35. Zulu Ceza-Nongoma pubic apron (*isigege*)*
Glass beads, Job's tears seeds; 6 x 6
Circa 1940s; SA-205-03, Figure 32b
Collected in South Africa, 1995

36. Zulu Ceza-Nongoma pubic apron (*isigege*)*
Glass beads, Job's tears seeds; 5 x 6
Circa 1940s; SA-205-04, Figure 32a
Collected in South Africa, 1995

37. Zulu Ceza-Nongoma pubic apron (*isigege*)
Glass beads, Job's tears seeds; 5 x 6 x 29.5
Circa 1950s; SA-206-01
Collected in Durban, South Africa

38. Zulu Maphumulo skirt or shawl (*itete*)
Glass beads, cotton textile; 8 x 13
Twentieth century; SA-210
Collected by Nomusa Dube in South Africa, 1995–1999

39. Zulu Msinga pregnancy apron (*umbodiya*)*
Goatskin and feet, fur, fiber, metal studs, beads; 28 x 20 x 1.25
Early/mid-twentieth century; SA-212, Figure 40
Collected by Nomusa Dube in South Africa, 1995–1999

40. Xhosa skirt
Hide, glass beads, sisal fiber; 9.5 x 17
Twentieth century; SA-214
Collected by Nomusa Dube in South Africa, 1995–1999

41. Zulu skirt (*itete*)
Cotton textile, cotton fiber, glass beads; 8 x 18
Twentieth century; SA-230-01
Collected by Nomusa Dube in South Africa, 1995–1999

42. Zulu skirt (*itete*)
Cotton textile, cotton fiber, glass beads; 30 x 17
Twentieth century; SA-230-02
Collected by Nomusa Dube in South Africa, 1995–1999

43. Zulu skirt (*itete*)
Cotton textile, cotton fiber, glass beads, brass buttons; 23 x 17
Twentieth century; SA-230-03
Collected by Nomusa Dube in South Africa, 1995–1999

44. Zulu loindress and belt*
Glass beads, sisal fiber, textile, brass; 4 x 8 x 24
Circa 1925; SA-241, Figure 31
Purchased from the African Art Center, Durban, South Africa, 1995

45. Ndebele married woman's apron (*ijogolo*)*
Glass beads, hide; 23 x 16
Late twentieth century; SA-249, Figure 28
Purchased from the African Art Center, Durban, South Africa, 1995

46. Lesotho apron
Glass beads, sisal fiber; 5.5 x 9.5
Circa 1890–1910; SA-250
Purchased from Bud Lueck, El Cajon, California, from the Lapue Collection

47. Zulu skirt
Glass beads, hide, fiber, brass button; 7 x 7.5
Twentieth century; SA-252
Purchased from Bud Lueck, El Cajon, California, from the Lapue Collection

48. Basotho girdle
Glass beads, fiber, brass button; 3 x 7 x 25
Nineteenth century; SA-266-01
Purchased from the Prynnsberg Museum, Clocolan, South Africa, 1995

49. Basotho girdle
Glass beads, fiber, brass button; 2.5 x 7 x 35
Nineteenth century; SA-266-02
Purchased from the Prynnsberg Museum, Clocolan, South Africa, 1995

50. Skirt (possibly Zulu)
Hide, fur, glass beads, fiber; length: 13.5
Nineteenth century; SA-267
Purchased from Craig Helms, Bonita, California

51. Zulu men's rear apron (*ibeshu*)*
Hide, metal studs, glass; 30 x 26.5
Twentieth century; SA-300, Figure 39
Purchased from the African Art Center, Durban, South Africa, 1995

52. Zulu pregnancy apron (*umbodiya*)
Hide, hooves, glass beads, brass buttons; 24.5 x 13
Circa 1950s; SA-301-01
Collected by Nomusa Dube in South Africa, 1995–1999

53. Zulu pregnancy apron (*umbodiya*)
Hide, hooves, fur, glass beads, brass buttons; 27 x 14
Circa 1950s; SA-301-02
Collected by Nomusa Dube in South Africa, 1995–1999

54. Zulu men's rear apron (*ibeshu*)
Hide, glass beads, textile; 26 x 27
Twentieth century; SA-312
Collected by Nomusa Dube in South Africa, 1995–1999

55. Zulu warrior dance costume*
Leopard skin, various other animal skin and hides,
animal claws, brass tacks, glass ornaments
Mid-twentieth century; SA-314, Figure 70
Collected by Nomusa Dube in South Africa, 1995–1999

56. Zulu Maphumulo skirt (*itete*)
Textile, glass beads, fiber; 14.5 x 35
Mid-twentieth century; SA-315
Collected by Nomusa Dube in South Africa, 1995–1999

57. Zulu Msinga skirt (*itete*)
Canvas, glass beads, brass studs, fiber; 13.5 x 15.5
Circa 1940s; SA-316-01
Collected by Nomusa Dube in South Africa, 1995–1999

58. Zulu Msinga skirt (*itete*)
Textile, glass beads, fiber; 13 x 17
Circa 1940s; SA-316-02
Collected by Nomusa Dube in South Africa, 1995–1999

59. Zulu Msinga skirt (*itete*)
Cotton textile, glass beads, fiber; 13.5 x 17
Circa 1950s; SA-317-01
Collected by Nomusa Dube in South Africa, 1995–1999

60. Zulu Msinga skirt (*itete*)
Cotton textile, glass beads, metal rivets, fiber; 27.5 x 20.5
Circa 1950s; SA-317-02
Collected by Nomusa Dube in South Africa, 1995–1999

61. Zulu Msinga skirt (*itete*)
Textile, glass beads, fiber; 16 x 21
Late twentieth century; SA-321-01
Purchased from the African Art Center, Durban, South Africa

62. Zulu Msinga skirt (*itete*)*
Textile, glass beads, fiber; 34 x 24
Late twentieth century; SA-321-02, Figure 38b
Purchased from the African Art Center, Durban, South Africa

63. Zulu Msinga skirt (*itete*)
Textile, glass beads, fiber; 17 x 13.5
Circa 1950s; SA-322-01
Collected by Nomusa Dube in South Africa, 1995–1999

64. Zulu Maphumulo skirt (*itete*)*
Textile, glass beads, fiber; 20.5 x 27.5
Circa 1950s; SA-322-02, Figure 38a
Collected by Nomusa Dube in South Africa, 1995–1999

65. Zulu skirt (*itete*)
Textile, glass beads, fiber; 25 x 16
Circa 1960s; SA-323-01
Collected by Nomusa Dube in South Africa, 1995–1999

66. Zulu skirt (*itete*)
Textile, glass beads, fiber; 17 x 18
Circa 1960s; SA-323-02
Collected by Nomusa Dube in South Africa, 1995–1999

67. Zulu skirt (*itete*)
Textile, glass beads, metal rivets, fiber; 10 x 20
Circa 1960s; SA-323-03
Collected by Nomusa Dube in South Africa, 1995–1999

68. Zulu Msinga skirt (*itete*)*
Textile, glass beads, fiber; 37 x 28
Late twentieth century; SA-325-01, Figure 36
Collected in Sundesia, Durban, South Africa, 1995

69. Zulu skirt (*itete*)
Textile, glass beads, fiber; 20 x 44
Late twentieth century; SA-325-02
Collected in Sundesia, Durban, South Africa, 1995

70. Zulu skirt (*itete*)
Textile, glass beads, metal, fiber; 16.5 x 18.5
Late twentieth century; SA-325-03
Collected in Sundesia, Durban, South Africa, 1995

ARM, LEG ORNAMENTS

71. Xhosa armbands (*isacholo*)
Brass; 5 x 5
Twentieth century; PER-39-04

72. Nguni anklets (group of 4)
Glass beads, fiber; 3.5 x 3.5 to 4 x 4
Nineteenth century; SA-054-20
Purchased from the Prynnsberg Museum, Clocolan, South Africa, 1995

73. Nguni anklet
Hide, glass beads, fiber; 4.5 x 4.5
Nineteenth century; SA-054-23
Purchased from the Prynnsberg Museum, Clocolan, South Africa, 1995

74. Nguni anklet
Glass beads, fiber; length: 7
Nineteenth century; SA-054-24
Purchased from the Prynnsberg Museum, Clocolan, South Africa, 1995

75. Nguni anklet
Glass beads; 3 x 3
Nineteenth century; SA-054-25
Purchased from the Prynnsberg Museum, Clocolan, South Africa, 1995

76. Zulu leg cover
Hide, glass beads; length: 22
Nineteenth century; SA-060-01
Purchased from the Prynnsberg Museum, Clocolan, South Africa, 1995

77. Zulu leg cover
Hide, glass beads; length: 22
Nineteenth century; SA-060-02
Purchased from the Prynnsberg Museum, Clocolan, South Africa, 1995

78. Zulu leg cover
Hide, glass beads; length: 16.5
Nineteenth century; SA-060-03
Purchased from the Prynnsberg Museum, Clocolan, South Africa, 1995

79. Zulu leg cover
Hide, glass beads; length: 19
Nineteenth century; SA-060-04
Purchased from the Prynnsberg Museum, Clocolan, South Africa, 1995

80. Arm band
Grass, colored pigment; 3 x 3
Nineteenth century; SA-063-23
Purchased from the Prynnsberg Museum, Clocolan, South Africa, 1995

81. Xhosa leg ornaments (*isitsaba*)
Hide, glass beads, sisal fiber, shell buttons; 4.5 x 8.5
Early/mid-twentieth century; SA-120
Purchased from the African Art Center, Pietermaritzburg, South Africa, 1997

82. Zulu arm wrap
Glass beads, cotton fiber; length: 12
Circa 1940s–1950s; SA-202-02
Purchased from the African Art Center, Durban, South Africa, 1996

83. Zulu arm wrap
Glass beads, cotton fiber; length: 13
Circa 1940s–1950s; SA-202-03
Purchased from the African Art Center, Durban, South Africa, 1996

84. Zulu arm wrap
Glass beads, cotton fiber; length: 12.5
Circa 1940s–1950s; SA-202-04
Purchased from the African Art Center, Durban, South Africa, 1996

85. Zulu arm wrap
Glass beads, cotton fiber; length: 12.5
Circa 1940s–1950s; SA-202-05
Purchased from the African Art Center, Durban, South Africa, 1996

86. Zulu ankle wrap
Glass beads, cotton fiber; length: 12.5
Circa 1940s–1950s; SA-202-06
Purchased from the African Art Center, Durban, South Africa, 1996

87. Zulu ankle wrap
Glass beads, cotton fiber; length: 12.5
Circa 1940s–1950s; SA-202-07
Purchased from the African Art Center, Durban, South Africa, 1996

88. Zulu Msinga arm/leg wrap
Glass beads, cotton fiber; length: 14
Twentieth century; SA-203-01
Purchased from the African Art Center, Durban, South Africa, 1996

89. Zulu Msinga arm/leg wrap
Glass beads, cotton fiber; length: 14.5
Twentieth century; SA-203-02
Purchased from the African Art Center, Durban, South Africa, 1995

90. Zulu Msinga arm/leg wrap
Glass beads, cotton fiber; length: 19
Twentieth century; SA-203-03
Purchased from the African Art Center, Durban, South Africa, 1995

91. Zulu Msinga arm/leg wrap
Glass beads, cotton fiber; length: 8
Twentieth century; SA-203-04
Purchased from the African Art Center, Durban, South Africa, 1995

92. Zulu Msinga arm/leg wrap
Glass beads, cotton fiber; length: 8.5
Twentieth century; SA-203-05
Purchased from the African Art Center, Durban, South Africa, 1995

93. Zulu Msinga arm/leg wrap
Glass beads, cotton fiber; length: 9
Twentieth century; SA-203-06
Purchased from the African Art Center, Durban, South Africa, 1995

94. Zulu Msinga arm/leg wrap
Glass beads, cotton fiber; length: 9
Twentieth century; SA-203-07
Purchased from the African Art Center, Durban, South Africa, 1995

95. Zulu Msinga arm/leg wrap
Glass beads, cotton fiber; length: 8.5
Twentieth century; SA-203-08
Purchased from the African Art Center, Durban, South Africa, 1995

96. Zulu Msinga arm/leg wrap
Glass beads, cotton fiber; length: 8
Twentieth century; SA-203-09
Purchased from the African Art Center, Durban, South Africa, 1995

97. Zulu Msinga arm/leg wrap
Glass beads, cotton fiber; length: 6.5
Twentieth century; SA-203-10
Purchased from the African Art Center, Durban, South Africa, 1995

98. Zulu Msinga arm/leg wrap
Glass beads, cotton fiber; length: 7.5
Twentieth century; SA-203-11
Purchased from the African Art Center, Durban, South Africa, 1995

99. Zulu Msinga arm/leg wrap
Glass beads, cotton fiber; length: 9
Twentieth century; SA-203-12
Purchased from the African Art Center, Durban, South Africa, 1995

100. Zulu Ceza-Nongoma leg ornaments
Glass beads, cotton fiber; 8 x 10.5
Circa 1950s; SA-206-02
Collected in Durban, South Africa

101. Zulu Ceza-Nongoma leg ornaments
Glass beads, cotton fiber; 4.5 x 9
Mid-twentieth century; SA-207
Collected in South Africa

102. Zulu Maphumulo leg ornament
Glass beads, cotton fiber; 6 x 9.5
Twentieth century; SA-208-01
Collected in Durban, South Africa, 1995

103. Zulu Maphumulo leg ornament
Glass beads, cotton fiber; 6 x 9.5
Twentieth century; SA-208-02
Collected in Durban, South Africa, 1995

104. Zulu anklet
Glass beads, fiber; length: 18.5
Early 1950s; SA-302-01
Collected by Nomusa Dube in South Africa, 1995–1999

105. Zulu anklet
Glass beads, fiber; length: 10
Early 1950s; SA-302-02
Collected by Nomusa Dube in South Africa, 1995–1999

106. Zulu anklet
Glass beads, fiber; length: 28
Early 1950s; SA-302-03
Collected by Nomusa Dube in South Africa, 1995-1999

107. Zulu Msinga armband
Glass beads, cotton fiber; length: 7
Circa 1950s; SA-304-01
Collected by Nomusa Dube in South Africa, 1995–1999

108. Zulu Msinga armband
Glass beads, cotton fiber; length: 9
Circa 1950s; SA-304-02
Collected by Nomusa Dube in South Africa, 1995–1999

109. Zulu Msinga anklet
Glass beads, cotton fiber; length: 9.5
Circa 1950s; SA-304-03
Collected by Nomusa Dube in South Africa, 1995–1999

110. Zulu Msinga anklet
Glass beads, cotton fiber; length: 9
Circa 1950s; SA-304-04
Collected by Nomusa Dube in South Africa, 1995–1999

111. Zulu Msinga anklet
Glass beads, cotton fiber; length: 8
Circa 1950s; SA-304-05
Collected by Nomusa Dube in South Africa, 1995–1999

112. Zulu Msinga anklet
Glass beads, cotton fiber; length: 9
Circa 1950s; SA-304-06
Collected by Nomusa Dube in South Africa, 1995–1999

113. Zulu Msinga anklet
Glass beads, cotton fiber; length: 9
Circa 1950s; SA-304-07
Collected by Nomusa Dube in South Africa, 1995–1999

114. Zulu Msinga anklet
Glass beads, cotton fiber; length: 9
Circa 1950s; SA-304-08
Collected by Nomusa Dube in South Africa, 1995–1999

115. Zulu armbands
Glass beads, cotton fiber; length: 7.5
Circa 1950s; SA-306-02
Collected by Nomusa Dube in South Africa, 1995–1999

116. Zulu anklet
Glass beads, cotton fiber; length: 13
Circa 1950s; SA-306-05
Collected by Nomusa Dube in South Africa, 1995–1999

117. Zulu anklet
Glass beads, cotton fiber; length: 12
Circa 1950s; SA-306-06
Collected by Nomusa Dube in South Africa, 1995–1999

118. Zulu armband/anklet
Glass beads, cotton fiber; length: 12
Twentieth century; SA-307-01
Collected by Nomusa Dube in South Africa, 1995–1999

119. Zulu armband/anklet
Glass beads, cotton fiber; length: 12.5
Twentieth century; SA-307-02
Collected by Nomusa Dube in South Africa, 1995–1999

120. Zulu armband/anklet
Glass beads, cotton fiber; length: 6.5
Twentieth century; SA-307-03
Collected by Nomusa Dube in South Africa, 1995–1999

121. Zulu armband/anklet
Glass beads, cotton fiber; length: 6.5
Twentieth century; SA-307-04
Collected by Nomusa Dube in South Africa, 1995–1999

122. Zulu anklets (pair)
Glass beads, cotton fiber; length: 14
Twentieth century; SA-307-05
Collected by Nomusa Dube in South Africa, 1995–1999

123. Zulu anklet
Glass beads, cotton fiber; length: 14
Twentieth century; SA-307-06
Collected by Nomusa Dube in South Africa, 1995–1999

124. Zulu anklets (pair)
Glass beads, cotton fiber; length: 11
Twentieth century; SA-307-07
Collected by Nomusa Dube in South Africa, 1995–1999

125. Zulu armband/anklet
Glass beads, cotton fiber; length: 12.5
Twentieth century; SA-307-08
Collected by Nomusa Dube in South Africa, 1995–1999

126. Zulu Shembe church anklet
Glass beads, cotton fiber; length: 6
Twentieth century; SA-308-01
Collected by Nomusa Dube in South Africa, 1995–1999

127. Zulu Maphumulo anklet
Glass beads, cotton fiber; length: 9.25
Twentieth century; SA-308-02
Collected by Nomusa Dube in South Africa, 1995–1999

128. Zulu anklets (pair)
Glass beads, cotton fiber; length: 9
Twentieth century; SA-308-05
Collected by Nomusa Dube in South Africa, 1995–1999

129. Zulu Ndwandwe anklets (pair)
Glass beads, cotton fiber; length: 7
Twentieth century; SA-308-06
Collected by Nomusa Dube in South Africa, 1995–1999

130. Zulu bracelet
Glass beads, cotton fiber; length: 10
Mid-twentieth century; SA-308A-01
Collected by Nomusa Dube in South Africa, 1995–1999

131. Zulu Maphumulo armband (pair)
Glass beads, cotton fiber; length: 7 to 8
Mid-twentieth century; SA-308A-02
Collected by Nomusa Dube in South Africa, 1995–1999

132. Zulu Shembe church armband
Glass beads, cotton fiber; length: 7
Mid-twentieth century; SA-308A-03
Collected by Nomusa Dube in South Africa, 1995–1999

133. Zulu Shembe church armband
Glass beads, cotton fiber; length: 7.75
Mid-twentieth century; SA-308A-04
Collected by Nomusa Dube in South Africa, 1995–1999

134. Zulu Msinga armband
Glass beads, cotton fiber; length: 11
Mid-twentieth century; SA-308A-07
Collected by Nomusa Dube in South Africa, 1995–1999

135. Zulu armband (pair)
Glass beads, cotton fiber; length: 6
Mid-twentieth century; SA-308A-08
Collected by Nomusa Dube in South Africa, 1995–1999

136. Zulu Maphumulo armband/anklet
Glass beads, fiber; 4 x 7.25
Twentieth century; SA-327-01
Purchased from the African Art Center, Durban, South Africa, 1995

137. Zulu Maphumulo armband/anklet
Glass beads, fiber; 4 x 7.25
Twentieth century; SA-327-02
Purchased from the African Art Center, Durban, South Africa, 1995

138. Zulu Maphumulo armband/anklet
Glass beads, fiber; 4.5 x 11
Twentieth century; SA-327-03
Purchased from the African Art Center, Durban, South Africa, 1995

BAGS, WALLETS, POUCHES

139. Xhosa purse (*isipaji*)*
Hide, glass, metal, brass; 32 x 5.5
Twentieth century; PER-49, Figure 42b

140. Zulu woven spoon pouch (*impontshi*)
Grass, glass beads; 7 x 4.5
Twentieth century; SA-017-01
Collected in South Africa

141. Zulu woven spoon pouch (*impontshi*)
Grass; 6 x 4.75
Twentieth century; SA-017-02
Collected in South Africa

142. Zulu woven spoon pouch (*impontshi*)
Grass; 6 x 4.75
Twentieth century; SA-017-03
Collected in South Africa

143. Nguni pouch
Glass beads, fiber, brass; 5.5 x 5.5
Nineteenth century; SA-054-12
Purchased from the Prynnsberg Museum, Clocolan, South Africa, 1995

144. Nguni pouch
Glass beads, textile, fiber; 3.75 x 3.25
Nineteenth century; SA-054-13
Purchased from the Prynnsberg Museum, Clocolan, South Africa, 1995

145. Nguni pouch
Glass beads, cotton textile, sisal fiber; 4.75 x 4
Nineteenth century; SA-054-14
Purchased from the Prynnsberg Museum, Clocolan, South Africa, 1995

146. Nguni pouch
Glass beads, fiber; 4.5 x 5
Nineteenth century; SA-054-15
Purchased from the Prynnsberg Museum, Clocolan, South Africa, 1995

147. Plaited purse
Reeds, fiber cordage; 6.25 x 5.5
Nineteenth century; SA-063-21
Purchased from the Prynnsberg Museum, Clocolan, South Africa, 1995

148. European purse
Ivory, silver, glass beads; 8 x 6.75
Nineteenth century; SA-070
Purchased from the Prynnsberg Museum, Clocolan, South Africa, 1995

149. Zulu woven spoon pouch (*impontshi*)
Grass, glass beads; 8.5 x 4
Twentieth century; SA-211-01
Collected by Nomusa Dube in South Africa, 1995–1999

150. Zulu woven spoon pouch (*impontshi*)
Grass, glass beads; 8 x 4.5
Twentieth century; SA-211-02
Collected by Nomusa Dube in South Africa, 1995–1999

151. Zulu woven spoon pouch (*impontshi*)
Grass; 8 x 4.5
Twentieth century; SA-211-03
Collected by Nomusa Dube in South Africa, 1995–1999

152. Zulu woven spoon pouch (*impontshi*)
Grass, glass beads; 8.5 x 5
Twentieth century; SA-211-04
Collected by Nomusa Dube in South Africa, 1995–1999

BASKETRY

153. Zulu wire basket (*imbenge*) by Elliot Mkhize
Colored telephone wire; 2 x 11.5 x 11.5
Twentieth century; FSA-009
Purchased from the African Art Center, Durban, South Africa

154. Zulu coiled basket with grasshopper stitching (*isichumo*)*
Ilala palm leaf; 6 x 8 x 8
Twentieth century; PER-04, Figure 111
Purchased from private collection, Australia

155. Zulu coiled beer basket (*isichumo*)*
Ilala palm leaf; 8 x 11.75 x 11.75
Nineteenth century; PER-10, Figure 111
Purchased from the Prynnsberg Museum, Clocolan, South Africa, 1995

156. Zulu Urkhamba contemporary coiled basket (*isichumo*)
Grass; 22 x 21 x 21
Twentieth century; SA-019
Collected in Sundesia, South Africa, 1995

157. Zulu contemporary coiled basket by Doris Zulu
Grass; 17 x 16
Twentieth century; SA-021
Collected in Sundesia, South Africa, 1995

158. Zulu contemporary coiled basket by Bongiwe Maphanga
Grass; 23 x 13
Twentieth century; SA-022
Collected in Sundesia, South Africa, 1995

159. Zulu contemporary coiled basket
Grass; 19.5 x 21 x 21
Twentieth century; SA-023
Collected in Sundesia, South Africa, 1995

160. Zulu coiled beer basket (*isichumo*)
Grass, hide; 9 x 9 x 9
Twentieth century; SA-024
Collected in South Africa, 1995

161. Zulu wire basket (*imbenge*) by Elliot Mkhize*
Colored telephone wire; 2 x 11.5 x 11.5
Twentieth century; SA-025, Figure 113
Purchased from the African Art Center, Durban, South Africa

162. Nguni beer sifter (*ivovo/ihluzo*)
Grass, horse hair; 20.5 x 5.5
Nineteenth century; SA-063-07
Purchased from the Prynnsberg Museum, Clocolan, South Africa, 1995

163. Nguni beer sifter (*ivovo/ihluzo*)
Grass; 28 x 6 3/4
Nineteenth century; SA-063-08
Purchased from the Prynnsberg Museum, Clocolan, South Africa, 1995

164. Nguni coiled basket
Grass; 6 x 15.5 x 15.5
Nineteenth century; SA-063-13
Purchased from the Prynnsberg Museum, Clocolan, South Africa, 1995

165. Nguni coiled basket
Grass; 6 x 15.5 x 15.5
Nineteenth century; SA-063-14
Purchased from the Prynnsberg Museum, Clocolan, South Africa, 1995

166. Nguni coiled basket
Grass; 8 x 21 x 21
Nineteenth century; SA-063-15
Purchased from the Prynnsberg Museum, Clocolan, South Africa, 1995

167. Nguni coiled basket
Grass, red and black pigment; 10.75 x 20.5 x 20.5
Nineteenth century; SA-063-16
Purchased from the Prynnsberg Museum, Clocolan, South Africa, 1995

168. Nguni coiled basket
Grass, horse hair; 8 x 20.5 x 20.5
Nineteenth century; SA-063-17
Purchased from the Prynnsberg Museum, Clocolan, South Africa, 1995

169. Nguni coiled basket
Grass; 7.75 x 19.25 x 19.25
Nineteenth century; SA-063-18
Purchased from the Prynnsberg Museum, Clocolan, South Africa, 1995

170. Coiled basket with lid
Grass, red, black and yellow pigment; 3.25 x 8.25
Nineteenth century; SA-063-19
Purchased from the Prynnsberg Museum, Clocolan, South Africa, 1995

171. Coiled basket with lid
Grass, red, black and yellow pigment; 3.5 x 9
Nineteenth century; SA-063-20
Purchased from the Prynnsberg Museum, Clocolan, South Africa, 1995

172. Coiled tray
Grass, colored pigment; 3.25 x 17.75 x 17.75
Nineteenth century; SA-063-24
Purchased from the Prynnsberg Museum, Clocolan, South Africa, 1995

173. Coiled tray
Grass; 18 x 18
Nineteenth century; SA-063-25
Purchased from the Prynnsberg Museum, Clocolan, South Africa, 1995

174. Zulu woven egg holders (group of 10)
Silver wire, copper wire; 2 x 1.5 x 1.5
Nineteenth century; SA-064-01
Purchased from the Prynnsberg Museum, Clocolan, South Africa, 1995

175. Zulu woven cup on pedestal
Silver wire, copper wire; 3.5 x 3 x 3
Nineteenth century; SA-064-02
Purchased from the Prynnsberg Museum, Clocolan, South Africa, 1995

176. Zulu woven cup on pedestal
Silver wire, copper wire; 3 x 2.75 x 2.75
Nineteenth century; SA-064-03
Purchased from the Prynnsberg Museum, Clocolan, South Africa, 1995

177. Zulu woven candleholder
Silver wire, copper wire; 3.5 x 6.5 x 6.5
Nineteenth century; SA-064-04
Purchased from the Prynnsberg Museum, Clocolan, South Africa, 1995

178. Zulu woven candleholder
Silver wire, copper wire; 3 x 4 x 4
Nineteenth century; SA-064-05
Purchased from the Prynnsberg Museum, Clocolan, South Africa, 1995

179. Zulu woven candleholder
Silver wire, copper wire; 3 x 7 x 7
Nineteenth century; SA-064-06
Purchased from the Prynnsberg Museum, Clocolan, South Africa, 1995

180. Zulu woven plate on pedestal
Silver wire, copper wire; 4.25 x 8 x 8
Nineteenth century; SA-064-07
Purchased from the Prynnsberg Museum, Clocolan, South Africa, 1995

181. Zulu woven plate on pedestal*
Silver wire, copper wire; 4.5 x 8.5 x 8.5
Nineteenth century; SA-064-08, Figure 112
Purchased from the Prynnsberg Museum, Clocolan, South Africa, 1995

182. Zulu woven spoons (group of 3)
Silver wire, copper wire; 6 x 2 x 2
Nineteenth century; SA-064-09
Purchased from the Prynnsberg Museum, Clocolan, South Africa, 1995

183. Zulu spoon/beer strainer (*isikhetho*)*
Ilala palm fibers, wire; 9.5 x 3.5 x 3.5
Nineteenth century
SA-064-10, Figure 50
Purchased from the Prynnsberg Museum, Clocolan, South Africa, 1995

184. Zulu woven napkin holders (group of 9)
Silver wire, copper wire; 2 x 2
Nineteenth century; SA-064-11
Purchased from the Prynnsberg Museum, Clocolan, South Africa, 1995

185. Zulu woven bracelets (group of 6)
Silver wire, copper wire; 2 x 2
Nineteenth century; SA-064-12
Purchased from the Prynnsberg Museum, Clocolan, South Africa, 1995

186. Zulu woven bracelets (group of 5)
Silver wire, copper wire; 2 x 2
Nineteenth century; SA-064-13
Purchased from the Prynnsberg Museum, Clocolan, South Africa, 1995

187. Zulu woven bracelets (set of 2)
Silver wire, copper wire; 2.5 x 2.5
Nineteenth century; SA-064-14
Purchased from the Prynnsberg Museum, Clocolan, South Africa, 1995

188. Zulu woven bracelets (set of 2)
Silver wire, copper wire; 2.5 x 2.5
Nineteenth century; SA-064-15
Purchased from the Prynnsberg Museum, Clocolan, South Africa, 1995

189. Zulu wire basket (*imbenge*) by Elliot Mkhize*
Colored telephone wire; 2.5 x 15 x 15
Twentieth century; SA-075, Figure 114
Purchased from the African Art Center, Durban, South Africa

190. Sotho coiled basket
Grass; 9 x 8 x 8
Early Twentieth century; SA-081
Collected by Nomusa Dube in South Africa, 1995–1999

191. Sotho coiled basket
Grass; 6.75 x 8 x 8
Early Twentieth century; SA-082
Collected by Nomusa Dube in South Africa, 1995–1999

192. Sotho coiled tray
Grass; 2.25 x 8.25 x 8.25
Early Twentieth century; SA-083
Collected by Nomusa Dube in South Africa, 1995–1999

193. Zulu Urkhamba contemporary coiled basket
Fiber; 12.5 x 14 x 14
Twentieth century; SA-091
Collected in Sundesia, South Africa, 1995

194. Zulu wire basket (*imbenge*) by Elliot Mkhize
Colored telephone wire; 7 x 8.5 x 8.5
Twentieth century; SA-115
Purchased in Durban, South Africa, 1996

195. Zulu contemporary coiled basket
Grass; 9 x 8 x 8
Twentieth century; SA-128
Purchased in South Africa

196. Zulu coiled basket
Grass; height: 19.5
Twentieth century; SA-339
Purchased in South Africa

BEADWORK PANELS AND STRIPS

197. Ndebele wedding train (*nyoga*)*
Glass beads, fiber; 80 x 13
Twentieth century; PD-02, Figure 29

198. Ndebele wedding train (*nyoga*)*
Glass beads, fiber; 89.5 x 11
Early twentieth century; PER-35, Figure 30
Purchased from the Gerald Block Collection, Winchester, California

199. Nguni panel
Glass beads, fiber; 5 x 7
Nineteenth century; SA-054-11
Purchased from the Prynnsberg Museum, Clocolan, South Africa, 1995

200. Ndebele blanket fringe
Glass beads, cotton fiber; length: 60
Twentieth century; SA-213-01
Collected in South Africa

201. Ndebele *linga koba* (long tears) one half of pair
Glass beads, cotton fiber; length: 50
Twentieth century; SA-213-02
Collected in South Africa

202. Shembe church panel
Glass beads, cotton fiber; length: 9
Twentieth century; SA-308-07
Collected by Nomusa Dube in South Africa, 1995–1999

203. Shembe church panel
Glass beads, cotton fiber; length: 9
Twentieth century; SA-308-08
Collected by Nomusa Dube in South Africa, 1995–1999

BEER POT COVERS

204. Zulu beer pot cover (*imbenge*)
Grass, glass beads; 2 x 7 x 7
Twentieth century; FSA-020-01

205. Zulu beer pot cover (*imbenge*)
Grass, glass beads; 2.5 x 8 x 8
Twentieth century; FSA-020-02

206. Zulu beer pot cover (*imbenge*)
Grass, glass beads; 2 x 7.5 x 7.5
Twentieth century; FSA-020-03

207. Zulu beer pot cover (imbenge)*
Grass, glass beads; 2.5 x 7.25 x 7.25
Twentieth century; PER-22, Figure 52, 55a
Collected by Nomusa Dube in South Africa, 1995–1999

208. Zulu beer pot cover (*imbenge*)
Reeds, fiber cordage, colored pigment; 8.5 x 9.5 x 9.5
Nineteenth century; SA-063-22
Purchased from the Prynnsberg Museum, Clocolan, South Africa, 1995

209. Zulu beer pot cover (*imbenge*)
Grass, glass beads; 2.5 x 9.5 x 9.5
Twentieth century; SA-086-01
Purchased from the African Art Center, Durban, South Africa

210. Zulu beer pot cover (*imbenge*)
Grass, glass beads; 2 x 8.5 x 8.5
Twentieth century; SA-086-02
Purchased from the African Art Center, Durban, South Africa

211. Zulu beer pot cover (*imbenge*)
Grass, glass beads; 2 x 8 x 8
Twentieth century; SA-086-03, Figure 51b, Figure 56
Purchased from the African Art Center, Durban, South Africa

212. Zulu beer pot cover (*imbenge*)*
Grass, glass beads; 2 x 8 x 8
Twentieth century; SA-086-04, Figure 56
Purchased from the African Art Center, Durban, South Africa

213. Zulu beer pot cover (*imbenge*)*
Grass, glass beads; 2 x 7 x 7
Mid-twentieth century; SA-201-01, Figure 56
Collected in South Africa, 1995

214. Zulu beer pot cover (*imbenge*)*
Grass, glass beads; 4 x 8 x 8
Mid-twentieth century; SA-201-02, Figure 56
Collected in South Africa, 1995

215. Zulu beer pot cover (*imbenge*)*
Grass, glass beads; 3 x 7 x 7
Mid-twentieth century; SA-201-03, Figure 52, 55b
Collected in South Africa, 1995

BOWLS

216. Northern Nguni incised vessel*
Wood; 13.5 x 16 x 14.25
Nineteenth century; PER-05, Figure 93a
Purchased from Sotheby's from the Carlos Monzino and Jacob Epstein collection

217. Northern Nguni incised vessel*
Wood; 18.5 x 10 x 10
Nineteenth century; PER-06, Figure 93b
Purchased from Calmel-Cohens, Paris, France

218. Zulu bowl*
Wood; 4 x 18.5 x 7.75
Nineteenth century; PER-07, Figure 110
Purchased from Alfonso Patino, Pinecrest, Florida

219. Zulu bowl*
Wood; 4.25 x 20.75 x 5.5
Early Twentieth century; PER-08, Figure 109
Purchased from Shelenge Dube, Natal, Durban

220. Barotse blackened bowl
Wood; 4.75 x 10
Nineteenth century; SA-045-01
Purchased from the Prynnsberg Museum, Clocolan, South Africa, 1995

221. Barotse blackened bowl
Wood; 4.25 x 8.5
Nineteenth century; SA-045-02
Purchased from the Prynnsberg Museum, Clocolan, South Africa, 1995

222. Barotse blackened bowl with carved aardvark lid
Wood; 3.5 x 7
Nineteenth century; SA-045-03
Purchased from the Prynnsberg Museum, Clocolan, South Africa, 1995

223. Barotse blackened dual bowl with handles
Wood; 2.5 x 18
Nineteenth century; SA-045-04
Purchased from the Prynnsberg Museum, Clocolan, South Africa, 1995

224. Barotse elongated oval blackened bowl
Wood; 2.5 x 30
Nineteenth century; SA-045-05
Purchased from the Prynnsberg Museum, Clocolan, South Africa, 1995

225. Barotse elongated oval blackened bowl
Wood; 2.75 x 22.5
Nineteenth century; SA-045-06
Purchased from the Prynnsberg Museum, Clocolan, South Africa, 1995

226. Zulu bowl
Wood; length: 19
Circa 1940s; SA-226
Collected by Nomusa Dube in South Africa, 1995–1999

CAPES, BLANKETS

227. Xhosa ceremonial cape (*isitofu*)*
Wool textile, braiding, buttons; 50 x 52
Twentieth century; SA-119, Figure 42a
Purchased from the African Art Center, Pietermaritzburg, South Africa, 1997

228. Zulu shoulder wrap
Cotton textile, glass beads; 46 x 28
Twentieth century; SA-231-01
Purchased from the African Art Center, Pietermaritzburg, South Africa, 1995

229. Zulu shoulder wrap
Cotton textile, glass beads; 46.5 x 22
Twentieth century; SA-231-02
Purchased from the African Art Center, Pietermaritzburg, South Africa, 1995

230. Zulu wedding cape (*isikoti* or *isibheklane*)
Glass beads, textile; length: 32
Twentieth century; SA-251
Collected by Nomusa Dube in South Africa, 1995–1999

231. Zulu wedding cape (*isikoti* or *isibheklane*)*
Cotton textile, glass beads, fiber; 32 x 36
Twentieth century; SA-309, Figure 34
Collected by Nomusa Dube in South Africa, 1995–1999

232. Zulu wedding cape (*isikoti* or *isibheklane*)
Cotton textile, glass beads, fiber; 28 x 35
Twentieth century; SA-310
Collected by Nomusa Dube in South Africa, 1995–1999

233. Xhosa Mfengu cape*
Textile, glass beads, buttons; 49.25 x 101.5
Twentieth century; SA-337, Figure 42b
Purchased from the African Art Center, Pietermaritzburg, South Africa

DOLLS/PUPPETS

234. Zulu trade doll by Mamethlo Mzila
Cotton textile, yarn, metal, wire, glass beads, hair; 14.25 x 7 x 4.5
Twentieth century; FSA-013-01

235. Zulu trade doll by Mamethlo Mzila
Cotton textile, metal, wire, glass beads, hair; 15.25 x 6.25 x 4
Twentieth century; FSA-013-02

236. Ndebele child figure (*umtwana wa madlozi*)*
Glass beads, textile, grass; 11 x 8 x 5
Twentieth century; PD-07, Figure 15a

237. Ndebele trade doll*
Glass beads, textile, metal; 39 x 7 x 7
Twentieth century; PD-08, Figure 20b

238. Northern Nguni puppets*
Wood, hide, glass beads, sisal fiber, metal; 9.5 x 15.5 x 2.5
Late nineteenth/early twentieth centuries; PER-01, Figure 73, cover
Purchased from the Prynnsberg Museum, Clocolan, South Africa, 1995

239. Lesotho child figure*
Glass beads, wood, textile; 10.5 x 3.25 x 3.25
Twentieth century; PER-37, Figure 18
Purchased from a private collection, France

240. Kamba doll
Wood, paint, metal tack; height: 7.25
Twentieth century; SA-004
Purchased from an antique store, San Diego, California

241. Zulu trade doll*
Textile, glass beads; 9 x 3 x 3
Twentieth century; SA-030-01, Figure 22a
Purchased from the African Art Center, Durban, South Africa

242. Zulu trade doll*
Textile, glass beads; 9 x 3 x 3
Twentieth century; SA-030-02, Figure 22b
Purchased from the African Art Center, Durban, South Africa

243. Pedi child figure
Wood, textile, glass beads, metal; height: 11.75
Late nineteenth/early twentieth centuries; SA-034
Purchased from the Antique Mall, Ocean Beach, California, 1995

244. Zulu doll on necklace
Wood, glass beads, button, sisal fiber; 8.5 x 1.5
Nineteenth century; SA-047
Purchased from the Prynnsberg Museum, Clocolan, South Africa, 1995

245. Ndebele trade doll*
Glass beads, textile, hide, metal, wood; 34 x 8 x 9
Twentieth century; SA-088, Figure 20a
Purchased from the Craft Center, Johannesburg, South Africa

246. Ndebele child figure (*umtwana wa madlozi*)
Glass beads, textile, grass; 7.75 x 4 x 4
Twentieth century; SA-096
Purchased from Bob Wilhelmson, Maui, Hawaii

247. Zulu Sangoma trade doll*
Glass beads, fiber, textile; 11.5 x 4 x 5
Circa 1960s; SA-104, Figure 21
Collected in Durban, South Africa, 1995

248. Ntwane child figure (*gimwane*)*
Plaited grass, wood, wool, glass beads, plastic beads, buttons, metal; 15 x 5 x 5
Circa 1950s–1960s; SA-105, Figure 16b
Purchased from an estate sale, San Diego, California

249. Xhosa trade doll
Ceramic, textile, thread, beads, buttons; height: 10
Twentieth century; SA-142
Purchased in South Africa, 1989

250. Herero Doll
Wood, red hide, seed beads, textile, metal; height: 2
Twentieth century; SA-200-01
Purchased from the Gerald Block Collection, Winchester, California

251. Herero Doll
Wood, red hide, seed beads, textile, metal; height: 2.5
Twentieth century; SA-200-02
Purchased from the Gerald Block Collection, Winchester, California

252. Herero Doll
Wood, red hide, seed beads, textile, metal; height: 25
Twentieth century; SA-200-03
Purchased from the Gerald Block Collection, Winchester, California

253. Herero Doll
Wood, red hide, seed beads, textile, metal; height: 32
Twentieth century; SA-200-04
Purchased from the Gerald Block Collection, Winchester, California

254. Herero Doll
Wood, red hide, seed beads, textile, metal; height: 36
Twentieth century; SA-200-05
Purchased from the Gerald Block Collection, Winchester, California

255. Ndebele child figure (*umtwana wa madlozi*)
Glass beads, textile, grass; height: 9
Circa 1960s; SA-217-01
Purchased from the Gerald Block Collection, Winchester, California

256. Ndebele child figure (*umtwana wa madlozi*)
Glass beads, textile, grass; height: 9
Circa 1960s; SA-217-02
Purchased from the Gerald Block Collection, Winchester, California

257. Tsonga child figure*
Glass beads, plastic beads, textile, buttons, tin core; 5 x 8 x 8
Mid-twentieth century; SA-218, Figure 19
Purchased from the Gerald Block Collection, Winchester, California

258. Nguni puppet
Myrtle wood, cotton cording; height: 19.5
Mid-twentieth century; SA-221
Collected in South Africa

259. Ndebele trade doll
Ceramic, hide, textile, glass beads, wire; height: 11.5
Twentieth century; SA-222
Collected in South Africa

260. Ntwane child figure (*gimwane*)*
Plaited grass, wood, wool, glass beads, plastic beads, buttons; 17 x 5 x 5
Twentieth century; SA-242, Figure 16a
Purchased from the Gerald Block Collection, Winchester, California

261. Ntwane trade doll*
Wood, glass beads, textile, metal, fiber; 20.5 x 5 x 5
Circa 1950s; SA-243, Figure 17
Purchased from the Gerald Block Collection, Winchester, California

262. Ndebele child figure (*umtwana wa madlozi*)
Glass beads, textile, grass; height: 8
Twentieth century; SA-244-01
Purchased from the Gerald Block Collection, Winchester, California

263. Ndebele child figure (*umtwana wa madlozi*)
Glass beads, textile, grass; height: 6
Twentieth century; SA-244-02
Purchased from the Gerald Block Collection, Winchester, California

264. Ndebele child figure (*umtwana wa madlozi*)
Glass beads, textile, grass; height: 9
Mid-twentieth century; SA-245-01
Purchased from the Gerald Block Collection, Winchester, California

265. Ndebele child figure (*umtwana wa madlozi*)
Glass beads, textile, grass, wire; height: 8
Mid-twentieth century; SA-245-02
Purchased from the Gerald Block Collection, Winchester, California

266. Ndebele child figure (*umtwana wa madlozi*)
Glass beads, textile, grass; height: 8.5
Mid-twentieth century; SA-245-03
Purchased from the Gerald Block Collection, Winchester, California

267. Ndebele child figure (*umtwana wa madlozi*)
Glass beads, textile, grass; height: 8
Mid-twentieth century; SA-245-04
Purchased from the Gerald Block Collection, Winchester, California

268. Ndebele child figure (umtwana wa madlozi)
Glass beads, textile, grass; height: 7.75
Twentieth century; SA-246-01
Purchased from the Gerald Block Collection, Winchester, California

269. Ndebele child figure (*umtwana wa madlozi*)*
Glass beads, textile, grass; 10 x 8 x 5
Twentieth century; SA-246-02, Figure 15b
Purchased from the Gerald Block Collection, Winchester, California

270. Ndebele trade doll
Wood, hide, glass beads, wire; height: 21
Twentieth century; SA-247-01
Purchased from the Gerald Block Collection, Winchester, California

271. Ndebele trade doll
Wood, hide, glass beads, wire; height: 20.5
Twentieth century; SA-247-02
Purchased from the Gerald Block Collection, Winchester, California

272. Ndebele trade doll
Wood, textile, glass beads, metal; height: 16
Twentieth century; SA-247-03
Purchased from the Gerald Block Collection, Winchester, California

273. Ndebele trade doll
Grass, glass beads, fiber; height: 12
Twentieth century; SA-247-04
Purchased from the Gerald Block Collection, Winchester, California

274. Zulu trade doll
Wood, textile, glass beads, fiber; height: 8
Twentieth century; SA-248-01
Purchased from the Gerald Block Collection, Winchester, California

275. Ndebele trade doll
Wood,hide, textile,fur, glass beads; height: 21
Twentieth century; SA-248-02
Purchased from the Gerald Block Collection, Winchester, California

EARPLUGS, EARRINGS

276. Zulu earplugs (*iziqhaza*)*
Wood, Perspex, metal; 2.5 x 2.5 x 1
Circa 1960s–1980s; FSA-008, Figure 63
Purchased from the African Art Center, Durban, South Africa

277. Zulu earplugs (*amashaza*)*
Wood, vinyl asbestos, metal; 2.5 x 2.5 x 1
Circa 1940s–1950s; PD-01, Figure 61

278. Zulu earplugs (*amashaza*)*
Wood, vinyl asbestos, metal; 1.5 x 1.5
Circa 1940s–1950s; PD-03, Figure 62
Collected by Nomusa Dube in Natal, South Africa, 1995–1999

279. Zulu earplugs (*amashaza*)*
Wood, vinyl asbestos, metal; 2.5 x 2.5 x 1
Circa 1940s–1950s; SA-095, Figure 59a
Purchased from the African Art Center, Durban, South Africa

280. Zulu earplugs (*amashaza*)*
Wood, vinyl asbestos, metal; 2.5 x 2.5 x 0.5
Circa 1940s–1950s; SA-220, Figure 60
Purchased from the African Art Center, Durban, South Africa

281. Zulu earplugs (*amashaza*)*
Wood, vinyl asbestos, metal; 2.75 x 2.75 x 0.5
Circa 1940s–1950s; SA-257, Figure 59b
Purchased from the Gerald Block Collection, Winchester, California

FIGURES

282. Northern Nguni female figure with looped extremities*
Wood; 25.25 x 11 x 5
Nineteenth century; PER-02, Figure 75
Purchased from Merton Simpson, Christie's London, 04/04/89

283. Southern Africa figure*
Wood; 19.75 x 5.5 x 4
Nineteenth century; PER-03, Figure 77
Purchased from Tad Dale, Santa Fe, New Mexico, from the Arnot Leof Collection, Cuernavaca, Mexico

284. Basotho bird*
Clay; 6.25 x 5.5 x 3.5
Late nineteenth/early twentieth centuries; PER-11, Figure 91
Purchased from the Prynnsberg Museum, Clocolan, South Africa, 1995

285. Basotho bird*
Clay; 6.25 x 6 x 4
Late nineteenth/early twentieth centuries; PER-12, Figure 91
Purchased from the Prynnsberg Museum, Clocolan, South Africa, 1995

286. Basotho bird*
Clay; 12 x 11 x 5.5
Late nineteenth/early twentieth centuries; PER-13, Figure 91
Purchased from the Prynnsberg Museum, Clocolan, South Africa, 1995

287. Contemporary sculpture by Josephine Ghesa*
Ceramic, paint; 32 x 14 x 13
Circa 1990s; PER-16, Figure 115
Purchased from the Ardmore Studio, KwaZulu-Natal, South Africa

288. Contemporary sculpture by Josephine Ghesa*
Ceramic, paint; 15.75 x 30.5 x 16.25
Circa 1990s; PER-17, Figure 116
Purchased from the Ardmore Studio, KwaZulu-Natal, South Africa

289. Basotho bird*
Clay; 5.25 x 6.25 x 3
Nineteenth century; PER-44, Figure 91
Purchased from the Prynnsberg Museum, Clocolan, South Africa, 1995

290. Basotho bird*
Clay; 6 x 5.5 x 3.5
Nineteenth century; PER-45, Figure 91
Purchased from the Prynnsberg Museum, Clocolan, South Africa, 1995

291. Nguni seated figure
Wood, seeds; height: 6
Early twentieth century; SA-002
Purchased from the Africa and Beyond Gallery, La Jolla, California

292. North Nguni/Tsonga Figure
Wood; 9.5 x 3.75 x 3.5
Early twentieth century; SA-027
Purchased from an antique store in the USA, 1996

293. Venda male figure with python by Owen Ndou*
Wood; 36 x 8 x 10
Twentieth century; SA-029, Figure 117
Collected in the field, Venda, South Africa, 1993

294. Nguni standing male figure
Wood; height: 10.75
Nineteenth/twentieth centuries; SA-037
Purchased from Michael Wyman, Chicago, Illinois

295. Nguni alligator poker work figure
Wood; length: 23.25
Nineteenth century; SA-061-01
Purchased from the Prynnsberg Museum, Clocolan, South Africa, 1995

296. Nguni bird poker work figure
Wood; 8 x 2.5
Nineteenth century; SA-061-02
Purchased from the Prynnsberg Museum, Clocolan, South Africa, 1995

297. Nguni water buffalo poker work figure
Wood; 4 x 8
Nineteenth century; SA-061-03
Purchased from the Prynnsberg Museum, Clocolan, South Africa, 1995

298. Nguni wild boar poker work figure
Wood; 4.25 x 7
Nineteenth century; SA-061-04
Purchased from the Prynnsberg Museum, Clocolan, South Africa, 1995

299. Nguni horned animal poker work figure
Wood, seeds; 3 x 9.5
Nineteenth century; SA-061-05
Purchased from the Prynnsberg Museum, Clocolan, South Africa, 1995

300. South African maternity figure by Raphael Magwala
Wood; 37 x 8.5
1995; SA-089
Purchased from the African Art Center, Durban, South Africa

301. Northern Nguni male and female figures*
Wood; 13 x 2.25 x 2
Late nineteenth early/twentieth centuries; SA-103, Figure 74
Purchased from Christie's London 06/24/96, Lot #169

302. Swazi baboon figure*
Wood, hide, fur, beads, fiber, shells; 31 x 9 x 9
Twentieth century; SA-109, Figure 76
Purchased from the Old Colonial Gallery, Assagai, South Africa

FLYWHISKS

303. Nguni flywhisk
Wood, wire, blond horse hair; length: 28
Nineteenth century; SA-056-01
Purchased from the Prynnsberg Museum, Clocolan, South Africa, 1995

304. Nguni flywhisk
Wood, wire, brown horse hair; length: 42
Nineteenth century; SA-056-02
Purchased from the Prynnsberg Museum, Clocolan, South Africa, 1995

305. Xhosa flywhisk
Glass beads, cowrie shells, wood, palm leaves; length: 33
Nineteenth century; SA-056-03
Purchased from the Prynnsberg Museum, Clocolan, South Africa, 1995

306. Xhosa flywhisk
Glass beads, cowrie shells, wood, palm leaves; length: 30
Nineteenth century; SA-056-04
Purchased from the Prynnsberg Museum, Clocolan, South Africa, 1995

307. Colonial flywhisk
Ivory, wood, wire, blonde horse hair; length: 21.5
Nineteenth century; SA-056-05
Purchased from the Prynnsberg Museum, Clocolan, South Africa, 1995

308. Nguni flywhisk
Ivory, wood, horn, wire, black horse hair; length: 32
Nineteenth century; SA-056-06
Purchased from the Prynnsberg Museum, Clocolan, South Africa, 1995

HEADDRESSES, HATS, HEADBANDS

309. Zulu Msinga hat (*inhloko/isicholo*)*
Natural fiber, textile; 5 x 17 x 17
Twentieth century; FSA-011, Figure 66
Purchased from the African Art Center, Durban, South Africa

310. Zulu Valley of a Thousand Hills hat (*inhloko/isicholo*)*
Natural fiber, glass beads, textile; 3 x 12 x 12
Twentieth century; FSA-012, Figure 65b
Purchased from the African Art Center, Durban, South Africa

311. Zulu Shembe Church hat (*inhloko/isicholo*)*
Natural fiber, human hair, textile; 6 x 8 x 8
Twentieth century; PER-18, Figure 64b
Collected by Nomusa Dube in South Africa, 1995–1999

312. Zulu Shembe Church hat (*inhloko/isicholo*)*
Natural fiber, human hair; 8 x 8 x 8
Twentieth century; PER-19, Figure 64a
Collected by Nomusa Dube in South Africa, 1995–1999

313. Zulu Msinga hat (*inhloko/isicholo*)*
Human hair, oil, red clay, red ochre pigment; 3.5 x 20 x 20
Twentieth century; PER-20, Figure 68
Purchased in Sundesia, Durban, South Africa

314. Zulu Msinga Hat (*inhloko/isicholo*)*
Cotton textile, glass beads; 4 x 17 x 17
Twentieth century; SA-007, Figure 67
Purchased from the African Art Center, Durban, South Africa

315. Lesotho twinned conical hat
Grass; 10 x 16.5 x 16.5
Nineteenth century; SA-035
Purchased from Craig Helms, Bonita, California

316. Lesotho woven hat
Grass; 6 x 13 x 13
Nineteenth century; SA-063-01
Purchased from the Prynnsberg Museum, Clocolan, South Africa, 1995

317. Lesotho woven hat
Grass; 8 x 13.5 x 13.5
Nineteenth century; SA-063-02
Purchased from the Prynnsberg Museum, Clocolan, South Africa, 1995

318. Lesotho woven hat
Grass; 12 x 12.25 x 12.25
Nineteenth century; SA-063-03
Purchased from the Prynnsberg Museum, Clocolan, South Africa, 1995

319. Lesotho woven hat
Grass; 6 x 14 x 14
Nineteenth century; SA-063-04
Purchased from the Prynnsberg Museum, Clocolan, South Africa, 1995

320. Lesotho woven hat
Grass; 11 x 13.5 x 13.5
Nineteenth century; SA-063-05
Purchased from the Prynnsberg Museum, Clocolan, South Africa, 1995

321. Lesotho woven hat
Grass; 9 x 11.5 x 11.5
Nineteenth century; SA-063-06
Purchased from the Prynnsberg Museum, Clocolan, South Africa, 1995

322. Double cone Zulu Msinga hat (*inhloko/isicholo*)
Hair; 9 x 18 x 8
Twentieth century; SA-100, Figure
Collected in the field by Shlenge Dube in South Africa

323. Double cone Zulu Msinga hat (*inhloko/isicholo*)*
Hair; 8 x 14 x 8
Twentieth century; SA-101, Figure 69
Collected in the field by Shlenge Dube in South Africa

324. Zulu Headring
Textile, glass beads; 10 x 5.75
Early twentieth century; SA-137
Purchased from an antique store in Springfield, Arkansas, 1996

325. Zulu Shembe Church hatband (*umnqwazi*)
Glass beads, cotton fiber; length: 20
Twentieth century; SA-209
Collected in Durban, South Africa, 1995

326. Xhosa headband (*amadiliza entloko*)
Glass beads, sisal fiber; length: 21
Twentieth century; SA-233-02
Purchased from the African Art Center, Pietermaritzburg, South Africa, 1995

327. Xhosa headband (*amadiliza entloko*)
Glass beads, sisal fiber; length: 20
Twentieth century; SA-233-03
Purchased from the African Art Center, Pietermaritzburg, South Africa, 1995

328. Zulu Valley of a Thousand Hills hat (*inhloko/isicholo*)*
Cotton fiber, glass beads, safety pins; 2 x 13 x 13
Twentieth century; SA-261, Figure 65a
Collected by Nomusa Dube in South Africa, 1995–1999

329. Zulu Msinga hat
Cotton fiber, glass beads; 4.25 x 17 x 17
Twentieth century; SA-262
Collected by Nomusa Dube in South Africa, 1995–1999

330. Zulu hat band
Glass beads, cotton fiber; length: 17
Circa 1950s; SA-306-03
Collected by Nomusa Dube in South Africa, 1995–1999

331. Zulu hat band
Glass beads, cotton fiber; length: 20
Circa 1950s; SA-306-04
Collected by Nomusa Dube in South Africa, 1995–1999

332. Xhosa headband (*amadiliza entloko*)
Glass beads, buttons; length: 10
Twentieth century; SA-336-02
Purchased from the African Art Center, Durban, South Africa, 1996

HEADRESTS

333. Zulu headrest (*izigqiki*)
Wood railroad tie; 6.5 x 21.25 x 3.5
Twentieth century; FSA-004

334. Tsonga/Shona headrest (*xiqamelo, mutsago*)*
Wood; 5.5 x 7 x 3.5
Nineteenth century; PER-33, Figure 8a
Purchased from Sotheby's, South Africa

335. Tsonga double headrest (*xiqamelo*)*
Wood; 6 x 20 x 7
Nineteenth century; PER-34, Figure 10
Purchased from Sotheby's, South Africa

336. Tsonga headrest (*xiqamelo*)*
Wood; 5 1/2 x 7 x 2 1/2
Nineteenth century; SA-003, Figure 8b
Purchased from the Prynnsberg Museum, Clocolan, South Africa, 1995

337. Zulu headrest (*izigqiki*)*
Wood; 5 x 13.25 x 3
Early Twentieth century; SA-011, Figure 14
Purchased from the African Art Center, Durban, South Africa

338. Zulu headrest (*izigqiki*)*
Wood; 5.5 x 12.75 x 2.5
Nineteenth century; SA-036, Figure 12
Purchased from the African Art Center, Durban, South Africa

339. Zulu headrest (*izigqiki*)
Wood; 7 x 11.5
Nineteenth century; SA-038
Purchased from Bud Lueck, El Cajon, California, from the Lapue Collection

340. Tsonga Headrest (*xiqamelo*)*
Wood; 5 x 7
Nineteenth century; SA-043-01, Figure 8c
Purchased from the Prynnsberg Museum, Clocolan, South Africa, 1995

341. Zulu Headrest (*izigqiki*)
Wood; 6 x 10
Nineteenth century; SA-043-02
Purchased from the Prynnsberg Museum, Clocolan, South Africa, 1995

342. Zulu headrest (*izigqiki*)
Wood railroad ties; 5 x 14
Twentieth century; SA-084
Collected by Nomusa Dube in South Africa, 1995–1999

343. Zulu double headrest (*izigqiki*)
Wood; 6.5 x 14
Twentieth century; SA-085A
Collected by Nomusa Dube in South Africa, 1995–1999

344. Zulu headrest (*izigqiki*)*
Wood; 6.5 x 19 x 3.5
Early twentieth century; SA-125, Figure 11
Collected by Nomusa Dube in South Africa, 1995–1999

345. Zulu double headrest (*izigqiki*)*
Wood; 6.75 x 25.5 x 2.25
Early twentieth century; SA-127, Figure 13
Purchased from Butterfield and Butterfield, 12/10/96; previously owned by the UCLA Fowler Museum of Cultural History, Los Angeles, California

MATS

346. Zulu mealie (corn) mat
Grass; 9 x 8
Twentieth century; SA-111
Purchased in Durban, South Africa, 1996

MEAT PLATTERS

347. Zulu meat platter (*ugqoko*)
Wood; 3.5 x 15
Circa 1930s; SA-067A
Collected by Nomusa Dube in South Africa, 1995

348. Zulu meat platter (*ugqoko*)*
Wood; 2.25 x 13.75 x 6.75
Twentieth century; SA-090, Figure 108
Purchased from the African Art Center, Durban, South Africa; collected by Nomusa Dube, 1995

349. Zulu meat platter (*ugqoko*)
Wood; length: 15
Circa 1920s; SA-224
Collected by Nomusa Dube in South Africa, 1995

350. Zulu meat platter (*ugqoko*)
Wood; length: 15
Circa 1930s; SA-225
Collected by Nomusa Dube in South Africa, 1995

351. Zulu meat platter (ugqoko)
Wood; 2.75 x 20.25 x 10.5
Early twentieth century; SA-258, Figure 108
Collected in the field by Nomusa Dube in Natal, South Africa, 1995–1999

352. Zulu meat platter (*ugqoko*)
Wood; length: 15
Late nineteenth/early twentieth centuries; SA-268
Collected by Nomusa Dube in South Africa, 1995

353. Zulu meat platter (ugqoko)*
Wood; 4 x 15.5 x 9
Late nineteenth/early twentieth centuries; SA-340, Figure 108

MILK PAILS

354. Zulu milk pail (*ithunga*)*
Wood; 15.5 x 6 x 5.5
Early twentieth century; FSA-005, Figure 92a
Purchased from the African Art Center, Durban, South Africa

355. Zulu milk pail (*ithunga*)*
Wood; 17.25 x 7.5 x 6
Circa 1920–1940; SA-009, Figure 92b
Purchased from the African Art Center, Durban, South Africa

MISCELLANEOUS

356. Gourd with long wood shaft
Gourd; 27.25 x 5 x 5
Late nineteenth/early twentieth centuries; SA-041-05
Purchased from the Prynnsberg Museum, Clocolan, South Africa, 1995

357. Gourd
Gourd; 4.5 x 5.5 x 5.5
Late nineteenth/early twentieth centuries; SA-041-06
Purchased from the Prynnsberg Museum, Clocolan, South Africa, 1995

358. Zulu powder-horn/medicine-horn (*uphondo lomsizi*)
Horn; 5.5 x 2 x 2
Nineteenth century; SA-051-18
Purchased from the Prynnsberg Museum, Clocolan, South Africa, 1995

359. Zulu powder-horn/medicine-horn (*uphondo lomsizi*)
Horn; 2.5 x 2.5 x 2
Nineteenth century; SA-051-19
Purchased from the Prynnsberg Museum, Clocolan, South Africa, 1995

360. Zulu powder-horn/medicine-horn (*uphondo lomsizi*)
Horn; 6.5 x 3 x 1
Nineteenth century; SA-051-20
Purchased from the Prynnsberg Museum, Clocolan, South Africa, 1995

361. Python skins (group of 6)
Snake skin; length: 58 (longest)
Nineteenth century; SA-058-04
Purchased from the Prynnsberg Museum, Clocolan, South Africa, 1995

362. Scoop shaped container
Gourd, wire; 5 x 3
Nineteenth century; SA-067-03
Purchased from the Prynnsberg Museum, Clocolan, South Africa, 1995

MUSICAL INSTRUMENTS

363. Lesotho girls initiation drum
Clay, hide; 9.75 x 9 x 9
Nineteenth century; SA-062-01
Purchased from the Prynnsberg Museum, Clocolan, South Africa, 1995

364. Nguni finger drum
Gourd, hide, fiber; 4 x 2
Nineteenth century; SA-062-02
Purchased from the Prynnsberg Museum, Clocolan, South Africa, 1995

365. Nguni waiststrap rattle
Hide, stone, seeds; length: 58
Nineteenth century; SA-062-03
Purchased from the Prynnsberg Museum, Clocolan, South Africa, 1995

366. Nguni leg rattle
Hide, stone, seeds; length: 19
Nineteenth century; SA-062-04
Purchased from the Prynnsberg Museum, Clocolan, South Africa, 1995

367. Sanza-Bushman instrument
Wood, metal, tortoise shell, fiber; 9 x 7.25
Nineteenth century; SA-062-05
Purchased from the Prynnsberg Museum, Clocolan, South Africa, 1995

368. Hollowed gourd
Gourd; 11 x 5.5
Nineteenth century; SA-062-06
Purchased from the Prynnsberg Museum, Clocolan, South Africa, 1995

369. Lyre (*kissar*)
Wood, hide, sinew fiber, reptile skin; 21 x 16
Nineteenth century; SA-068
Purchased from the Prynnsberg Museum, Clocolan, South Africa, 1995

370. Nguni xylophone
Gourds, wood, hide; 24 x 36
Nineteenth century; SA-069
Purchased from the Prynnsberg Museum, Clocolan, South Africa, 1995

NECK, SHOULDER, CHEST ORNAMENTS

371. Zulu necklace
Glass beads, metal, cotton fiber; length: 116
Twentieth century; FSA-017-01

372. Zulu necklace
Stone beads, glass beads, cotton fiber; 3.5 x 10.5
Twentieth century; FSA-017-02

373. Zulu necklace
Glass beads, cotton fiber; 2.25 x 22
Twentieth century; FSA-017-03

374. Zulu necklace
Glass beads, cotton fiber; 2.25 x 7
Twentieth century; FSA-017-04

375. Zulu necklace
Glass beads, cotton fiber; 1.25 x 15
Twentieth century; FSA-017-05

376. Zulu necklace
Glass beads, cotton fiber; 1 x 14.5
Twentieth century; FSA-017-06

377. Zulu necklace
Glass beads, cotton fiber; 1.25 x 11.5
Twentieth century; FSA-017-07

378. Zulu necklace
Glass beads, cotton fiber; 1 x 13
Twentieth century; FSA-017-08

379. Zulu necklace
Glass beads, brass buttons, cotton fiber; length: 16
Twentieth century; FSA-017-09

380. Zulu necklace
Glass beads, brass buttons, cotton fiber; length: 8
Twentieth century; FSA-017-10

381. Zulu necklace
Glass beads, cotton fiber; 80 x 1.25
Twentieth century; FSA-017-11

382. Xhosa necklace
Brass; length: 21
Twentieth century; PER-39-03

383. Xhosa nursing necklace (*izinyango*)*
Wood, herbal materials, fiber, glass beads, button; 7.5 x 7.5 x 0.5
Twentieth century; PER-41, Figure 72
Purchased from the African Art Center, Pietermaritzburg, South Africa

384. Xhosa neck ornament (*amaqhina*)*
Glass beads, fiber; 19.25 x 8.25
Twentieth century; PER-42, Figure 42b
Purchased from the African Art Center, Pietermaritzburg, South Africa

385. Xhosa neck ornament (*intshinga*)*
Glass beads, animal hair, fiber; 15 x 1.5
Twentieth century; PER-43, Figure 42b
Purchased from the African Art Center, Pietermaritzburg, South Africa

386. Xhosa necklace*
Brass, glass beads, buttons; 8 x 8
Twentieth century; PER-46, Figure 42a

387. Xhosa necklace (*isidanga*)*
Glass beads, fiber; length: 31
Twentieth century; PER-48, Figure 42b

388. Nguni necklace
Glass beads, seed beads, fiber; 3.5 x 3.5
Nineteenth century; SA-054-19
Purchased from the Prynnsberg Museum, Clocolan, South Africa, 1995

389. Nguni necklace with pendant
Hide, glass beads, seeds; 11.5 x 2.5
Nineteenth century; SA-054-27
Purchased from the Prynnsberg Museum, Clocolan, South Africa, 1995

390. Nguni pendant
Hide, glass beads, seeds; 2.5 x 2.5
Nineteenth century; SA-054-28
Purchased from the Prynnsberg Museum, Clocolan, South Africa, 1995

391. Nguni necklace
Glass beads, fiber; length: 8.25
Nineteenth century; SA-054-29
Purchased from the Prynnsberg Museum, Clocolan, South Africa, 1995

392. Nguni necklace
Glass beads, brass button, sisal fiber; length: 14.75
Nineteenth century; SA-054-30
Purchased from the Prynnsberg Museum, Clocolan, South Africa, 1995

393. Nguni necklace
Glass beads, fiber; length: 14
Nineteenth century; SA-054-31
Purchased from the Prynnsberg Museum, Clocolan, South Africa, 1995

394. Nguni necklace
Glass beads, fiber; length: 37
Nineteenth century; SA-054-32
Purchased from the Prynnsberg Museum, Clocolan, South Africa, 1995

395. Nguni necklace
Glass beads, button, fiber; length: 9
Nineteenth century; SA-054-33
Purchased from the Prynnsberg Museum, Clocolan, South Africa, 1995

396. Nguni necklace
Glass beads, fiber; length: 14
Nineteenth century; SA-054-34
Purchased from the Prynnsberg Museum, Clocolan, South Africa, 1995

397. Nguni necklace
Hide, glass beads, fiber; 4 x 4
Nineteenth century; SA-054-35
Purchased from the Prynnsberg Museum, Clocolan, South Africa, 1995

398. Nguni necklace
Wood beads, glass beads, sisal fiber; 6.5 x 6.5
Nineteenth century; SA-054-36
Purchased from the Prynnsberg Museum, Clocolan, South Africa, 1995

399. Rosary
Wood beads, metal; length: 18.5
Nineteenth century; SA-054-37
Purchased from the Prynnsberg Museum, Clocolan, South Africa, 1995

400. Rosary
Beads, metal; length: 16
Nineteenth century; SA-054-38
Purchased from the Prynnsberg Museum, Clocolan, South Africa, 1995

401. Nguni necklace
Glass beads, fiber, brass buttons; length: 8.5
Nineteenth century; SA-054-39
Purchased from the Prynnsberg Museum, Clocolan, South Africa, 1995

402. Nguni necklace
Glass beads, seed beads, sisal fiber; length: 9
Nineteenth century; SA-054-40
Purchased from the Prynnsberg Museum, Clocolan, South Africa, 1995

403. Nguni necklace
Glass beads, fiber; length: 4
Nineteenth century; SA-054-41
Purchased from the Prynnsberg Museum, Clocolan, South Africa, 1995

404. Nguni necklace
Glass beads, seed beads, fiber; length: 22
Nineteenth century; SA-054-44
Purchased from the Prynnsberg Museum, Clocolan, South Africa, 1995

405. Zulu necklace (*umgexo*)
Cotton fiber, glass beads, hide; length: 12
Late nineteenth century; SA-087
Purchased from the African Art Center, Pietermaritzburg, South Africa

406. Zulu Msinga necklace
Cotton and sisal fiber, grass, brass buttons; length: 18
Mid- to late twentieth century; SA-204-01
Collected in Durban area, South Africa, 1995

407. Xhosa collar with necklace (*imiphalaza*)*
Glass beads, buttons, fiber; 99.5 x 9.75
Circa 1920s; SA-215, Figure 42b

408. Xhosa collar (*amathumbu*)*
Glass beads, sisal fiber, button; 9.25 x 13.75
Circa 1920s; SA-216-01, Figure 42b
Collected by Nomusa Dube in South Africa, 1992

409. Xhosa collar (*amathumbu*)*
Glass beads, sisal fiber, button; 14 x 21
Circa 1920s; SA-216-02, Figure 42a
Collected by Nomusa Dube in South Africa, 1992

410. Xhosa collar (*amathumbu*)
Glass beads, sisal fiber, button; length: 21
Circa 1920s; SA-216-03
Collected by Nomusa Dube in South Africa, 1992

411. Xhosa collar (*amathumbu*)*
Glass beads, sisal fiber, button; length: 20.5
Circa 1920s; SA-216-04, Figure 42a
Collected by Nomusa Dube in South Africa, 1992

412. Xhosa nursing necklace (*izinyango*)*
Wood, herbal materials, fiber, glass beads, button; 16 x 11 x 0.5
Circa 1940s; SA-219, Figure 71
Purchased from the African Art Center, Pietermaritzburg, South Africa, 1995

413. Xhosa necklace
Glass beads, sisal fiber; 10.5 x 10.5
Twentieth century; SA-233-01
Purchased from the African Art Center, Pietermaritzburg, South Africa, 1995

414. Xhosa necklace
Glass beads, sisal fiber; 11 x 12
Twentieth century; SA-233-04
Purchased from the African Art Center, Pietermaritzburg, South Africa, 1995

415. Xhosa collar (*amathumbu*)
Glass beads, sisal fiber; 12.5 x 13
Twentieth century; SA-234-01
Collected by Nomusa Dube in South Africa, 1995–1999

416. Xhosa collar (*amathumbu*)*
Glass beads, sisal fiber; 9.5 x 12
Twentieth century; SA-234-02, Figure 42a
Collected by Nomusa Dube in South Africa, 1995–1999

417. Xhosa collar (*amathumbu*)
Glass beads, sisal fiber; 13 x 18
Twentieth century; SA-234-03
Collected by Nomusa Dube in South Africa, 1995–1999

418. Xhosa collar (*amathumbu*)
Glass and shell beads, sisal fiber; 9 x 9
Late nineteenth/early twentieth centuries; SA-235-01
Collected by Nomusa Dube in South Africa, 1995–1999

419. Xhosa collar (*amathumbu*)*
Glass and shell beads, sisal fiber; 9 x 12.5
Late nineteenth/early twentieth centuries; SA-235-02, Figure 42b
Collected by Nomusa Dube in South Africa, 1995–1999

420. Xhosa collar (*amathumbu*)
Glass and shell beads, sisal fiber; 10 x 10
Late nineteenth/early twentieth centuries; SA-235-03
Collected by Nomusa Dube in South Africa, 1995–1999

421. Xhosa necklace and collar (*imiphalaza*)
Glass beads, sisal fiber, buttons; 64 x 9.75
Early twentieth century; SA-236
Collected by Nomusa Dube in South Africa, 1995–1999

422. Xhosa necklace*
Glass beads, sisal fiber, button; 9 x 8 1/2
Twentieth century; SA-237-01, Figure 23c
Collected by Nomusa Dube in South Africa, 1995-1999

423. Xhosa necklace*
Glass beads, sisal fiber, buttons; 12 x 12
Twentieth century; SA-237-02, Figure 23b
Collected by Nomusa Dube in South Africa, 1995–1999

424. Xhosa necklace*
Glass beads, sisal fiber, buttons; 9.5 x 9
Twentieth century; SA-237-03, Figure 23a
Collected by Nomusa Dube in South Africa, 1995–1999

425. Zulu necklace
Glass beads, cotton fiber; length: 23
Twentieth century; SA-238-01
Collected by Nomusa Dube in South Africa, 1995–1999

426. Zulu necklace
Glass beads, cotton fiber; length: 16
Twentieth century; SA-238-02
Collected by Nomusa Dube in South Africa, 1995–1999

427. Zulu necklace
Glass beads, cotton fiber; length: 18
Twentieth century; SA-238-03
Collected by Nomusa Dube in South Africa, 1995–1999

428. Zulu necklace
Glass beads, cotton fiber; length: 17
Twentieth century; SA-238-04
Collected by Nomusa Dube in South Africa, 1995–1999

429. Zulu necklace
Glass beads, cotton textile, sisal fiber; length: 19.25
Circa 1930s; SA-256
Purchased from Sotheby's, 05/08/96, Lot 326

430. Zulu necklace
Glass beads, fiber; 8.5 x 8.5
Mid-twentieth century; SA-265
Collected by Nomusa Dube in South Africa, 1995–1999

431. Zulu Msinga necklace
Glass beads, fiber, brass buttons; length: 14
Circa 1950s; SA-305-01
Collected by Nomusa Dube in South Africa, 1995–1999

432. Zulu Msinga necklace
Glass beads, fiber, brass buttons; length: 15
Circa 1950s; SA-305-02
Collected by Nomusa Dube in South Africa, 1995–1999

433. Zulu Msinga necklace
Glass beads, fiber, brass buttons; length: 11
Circa 1950s; SA-305-03
Collected by Nomusa Dube in South Africa, 1995–1999

434. Zulu Msinga necklace
Glass beads, fiber, brass buttons; length: 12
Circa 1950s; SA-305-04
Collected by Nomusa Dube in South Africa, 1995–1999

435. Zulu Msinga necklace
Glass beads, fiber, brass buttons; length: 17
Circa 1950s; SA-305-05
Collected by Nomusa Dube in South Africa, 1995–1999

436. Zulu necklace
Glass beads, cotton fiber; length: 17
Circa 1950s; SA-306-01
Collected by Nomusa Dube in South Africa, 1995–1999

437. Zulu Nongoma tab necklace
Glass beads, cotton fiber; 28 x 5
Twentieth century; SA-308-03
Collected by Nomusa Dube in South Africa, 1995–1999

438. Zulu tab necklace
Glass beads, cotton fiber; 28 x 5
Twentieth century; SA-308-04
Collected by Nomusa Dube in South Africa, 1995–1999

439. Zulu Msinga necklace
Glass beads, cotton fiber; length: 18
Mid-twentieth century; SA-308A-05
Collected by Nomusa Dube in South Africa, 1995–1999

440. Zulu necklace
Glass beads, cotton fiber; length: 14
Mid-twentieth century; SA-308A-06
Collected by Nomusa Dube in South Africa, 1995–1999

441. Zulu collar
Glass beads, sisal fiber; length: 27.5
Circa 1910s; SA-313-01
Collected by Nomusa Dube in South Africa, 1995–1999

442. Zulu collar
Glass beads, sisal fiber; length: 26
Circa 1910s; SA-313-04
Collected by Nomusa Dube in South Africa, 1995–1999

443. Zulu Nongoma bandolier
Glass beads, fiber; length: 20
Twentieth century; SA-320-01
Collected by Nomusa Dube in South Africa, 1995–1999

444. Zulu Nongoma bandolier
Glass beads, fiber; length: 22
Twentieth century; SA-320-02
Collected by Nomusa Dube in South Africa, 1995–1999

445. Zulu Nongoma bandolier
Glass beads, fiber; length: 24
Twentieth century; SA-320-03
Collected by Nomusa Dube in South Africa, 1995–1999

446. Zulu Nongoma bandolier
Glass beads, fiber; length: 22
Twentieth century; SA-320-04
Collected by Nomusa Dube in South Africa, 1995–1999

447. Zulu Msinga necklace
Glass beads, fiber; length: 27
Twentieth century; SA-320-05
Collected by Nomusa Dube in South Africa, 1995–1999

448. Xhosa necklace (*amaqhina*)*
Glass beads, buttons, fiber; 3 x 4
Twentieth century; SA-335-01, Figure 42a
Purchased from the African Art Center, Durban, South Africa, 1996

449. Xhosa necklace (*amaqhina*)*
Glass beads, button, fiber; length: 8
Twentieth century; SA-335-02, Figure 42a
Purchased from the African Art Center, Durban, South Africa, 1996

450. Xhosa necklace (*amaqhina*)
Glass beads, buttons, fiber; length: 7.75
Twentieth century; SA-335-03
Purchased from the African Art Center, Durban, South Africa, 1996

451. Xhosa necklace (*isidanga*)
Glass beads, button; length: 41
Twentieth century; SA-336-01
Purchased from the African Art Center, Durban, South Africa, 1996

452. Xhosa necklace (*isidanga*)
Glass beads, fiber; length: 24
Twentieth century; SA-343-01
Purchased from the African Art Center, Durban, South Africa, 1995

453. Xhosa necklace (*isidanga*)
Glass beads, sisal fiber; length: 64
Twentieth century; SA-343-02
Purchased from the African Art Center, Durban, South Africa, 1995

454. Xhosa necklace (*isidanga*)
Glass beads, fiber; length: 30.5
Twentieth century; SA-343-03
Purchased from the African Art Center, Durban, South Africa, 1995

POTTERY

455. Lesotho pot*
Clay; 16 x 19 x 19
Late nineteenth/early twentieth centuries; PER-14, Figure 90
Purchased from the Prynnsberg Museum, Clocolan, South Africa, 1995

456. Lesotho beer pot*
Clay; 11.25 x 13 x 13
Twentieth century; PER-21, Figure 54
Purchased from the Prynnsberg Museum, Clocolan, South Africa, 1995

457. Zulu beer pot (*uphiso*)*
Clay; 16 x 13 x 13
Early twentieth century; SA-014, Figure 52
Collected in South Africa, 1995

458. Zulu beer pot (*ukhamba*)
Clay; 11.5 x 14 x 14
Twentieth century; SA-015
Purchased from the African Art Center, Durban, South Africa

459. Lesotho redware bowl
Clay; 4 x 8 x 8
Nineteenth century; SA-048-01
Purchased from the Prynnsberg Museum, Clocolan, South Africa, 1995

460. Lesotho redware bowl
Clay; 5.5 x 7.5 x 7.5
Nineteenth century; SA-048-02
Purchased from the Prynnsberg Museum, Clocolan, South Africa, 1995

461. Lesotho redware bowl
Clay; 5 x 8 x 8
Nineteenth century; SA-048-03
Purchased from the Prynnsberg Museum, Clocolan, South Africa, 1995

462. Lesotho redware bowl
Clay; 5.5 x 6.75 x 6.75
Nineteenth century; SA-048-04
Purchased from the Prynnsberg Museum, Clocolan, South Africa, 1995

463. Lesotho redware bowl
Clay; 5 x 7.5 x 7.5
Nineteenth century; SA-048-05
Purchased from the Prynnsberg Museum, Clocolan, South Africa, 1995

464. Lesotho redware bowl
Clay; 4.5 x 8.25 x 8.25
Nineteenth century; SA-048-06
Purchased from the Prynnsberg Museum, Clocolan, South Africa, 1995

465. Lesotho redware bowl
Clay; 4 x 7.75 x 7.75
Nineteenth century; SA-048-07
Purchased from the Prynnsberg Museum, Clocolan, South Africa, 1995

466. Lesotho redware bowl
Clay; 4 x 8 x 8
Nineteenth century; SA-048-08
Purchased from the Prynnsberg Museum, Clocolan, South Africa, 1995

467. Lesotho black cylinder pot
Clay; 9.75 x 6.25 x 6.25
Nineteenth century; SA-048-09
Purchased from the Prynnsberg Museum, Clocolan, South Africa, 1995

468. Lesotho redware bowl with lid
Clay; 6.25 x 6 x 6
Nineteenth century; SA-048-10
Purchased from the Prynnsberg Museum, Clocolan, South Africa, 1995

469. Lesotho redware pot
Clay; 9.25 x 9.25 x 9.25
Nineteenth century; SA-048-11
Purchased from the Prynnsberg Museum, Clocolan, South Africa, 1995

470. Lesotho black plate
Clay; 3 x 9.25 x 9.25
Nineteenth century; SA-048-12
Purchased from the Prynnsberg Museum, Clocolan, South Africa, 1995

471. Lesotho plate
Clay; 1.25 x 11.5 x 11.5
Nineteenth century; SA-052-01
Purchased from the Prynnsberg Museum, Clocolan, South Africa, 1995

472. Lesotho plate
Clay; 4 x 12 x 12
Nineteenth century; SA-052-02
Purchased from the Prynnsberg Museum, Clocolan, South Africa, 1995

473. Lesotho plate
Clay; 1.75 x 11.25 x 11.25
Nineteenth century; SA-052-03
Purchased from the Prynnsberg Museum, Clocolan, South Africa, 1995

474. Lesotho pedestal
Clay; 5 x 7 x 7
Nineteenth century; SA-052-04
Purchased from the Prynnsberg Museum, Clocolan, South Africa, 1995

475. Lesotho oval serving bowl
Clay; 6 x 7.75 x 5.25
Nineteenth century; SA-052-05
Purchased from the Prynnsberg Museum, Clocolan, South Africa, 1995

476. Lesotho painted bowl
Clay, black paint; 4.25 x 12 x 12
Nineteenth century; SA-052-06
Purchased from the Prynnsberg Museum, Clocolan, South Africa, 1995

477. Lesotho painted bowl
Clay, black and white paint; 4.5 x 8.25 x 8.25
Nineteenth century; SA-052-07
Purchased from the Prynnsberg Museum, Clocolan, South Africa, 1995

478. Lesotho mug
Clay; 6 x 4.5 x 4.5
Nineteenth century; SA-052-08
Purchased from the Prynnsberg Museum, Clocolan, South Africa, 1995

479. Lesotho bowl with pedestal base
Clay; 5.5 x 6 x 6
Nineteenth century; SA-052-09
Purchased from the Prynnsberg Museum, Clocolan, South Africa, 1995

480. Lesotho container lids (group of 4)
Clay; 1.5 x 2 x 2 to 2 x 4 x 4
Nineteenth century; SA-052-10
Purchased from the Prynnsberg Museum, Clocolan, South Africa, 1995

481. Lesotho bowl
Clay; 1.75 x 5 x 5
Nineteenth century; SA-052-11
Purchased from the Prynnsberg Museum, Clocolan, South Africa, 1995

482. Zulu beer pot (*ukhamba*)*
Clay; 10 x 13 x 13
Circa 1950s; SA-066A, Figure 51a
Collected by Nomusa Dube in South Africa, 1995

483. Zulu beer pot (*ukhamba*)
Clay; 12 x 14 x 14
Circa 1950s; SA-068A
Collected by Nomusa Dube in South Africa, 1995

484. Zulu storage vessel/marriage pot (*uphiso*)
Clay; 10 x 10.25 x 10.25
Circa 1910; SA-069A
Collected by Nomusa Dube in South Africa, 1995;
previously owned by Mungubane Ntshaba

485. Zulu beer pot (*ukhamba*)
Clay; 9 .5 x 12 x 12
Circa 1950s; SA-070A
Collected by Nomusa Dube in South Africa, 1995

486. Lesotho red ware pot
Clay; 12 x 12 x 12
Circa 1850s; SA-270
Purchased from the Prynnsberg Museum, Clocolan, South Africa, 1995

487. Lesotho red ware pot
Clay; 13 x 13.5 x 13.5
Circa 1850s; SA-271
Purchased from the Prynnsberg Museum, Clocolan, South Africa, 1995

488. Lesotho red ware pot
Clay; 12.5 x 12.5 x 12.5
Circa 1850s; SA-272
Purchased from the Prynnsberg Museum, Clocolan, South Africa, 1995

489. Lesotho red ware pot
Clay; 14 x 14.5 x 14.5
Circa 1850s; SA-273
Purchased from the Prynnsberg Museum, Clocolan, South Africa, 1995

490. Lesotho red ware pot
Clay; 14 x 13 x 13
Circa 1850s; SA-274
Purchased from the Prynnsberg Museum, Clocolan, South Africa, 1995

491. Lesotho red ware pot
Clay; 13.5 x 13 x 13
Circa 1850s; SA-275
Purchased from the Prynnsberg Museum, Clocolan, South Africa, 1995

492. Lesotho red ware pot
Clay; 12 x 14 x 14
Circa 1850s; SA-276
Purchased from the Prynnsberg Museum, Clocolan, South Africa, 1995

493. Lesotho red ware pot
Clay; 13.5 x 15 x 15
Circa 1850s; A-277
Purchased from the Prynnsberg Museum, Clocolan, South Africa, 1995

494. Lesotho red ware pot
Clay; 13 x 12 x 12
Circa 1850s; SA-278
Purchased from the Prynnsberg Museum, Clocolan, South Africa, 1995

495. Lesotho flaring red ware bowl
Clay; 5.5 x 7 x 7
1600–1800 AD; SA-279
Purchased from the Prynnsberg Museum, Clocolan, South Africa, 1995

496. Lesotho flaring red ware bowl
Clay; 5.5 x 6 x 6
1600–1800 AD; SA-280
Purchased from the Prynnsberg Museum, Clocolan, South Africa, 1995

497. Lesotho flaring red ware bowl
Clay; 4 x 7 x 7
1600–1800 AD; SA-282
Purchased from the Prynnsberg Museum, Clocolan, South Africa, 1995

498. Lesotho red ware vessel/ashtray
Clay; 4.5 x 6 x 6
1600–1800 AD; SA-283
Purchased from the Prynnsberg Museum, Clocolan, South Africa, 1995

SMOKING IMPLEMENTS

499. Xhosa figurative pipe*
Wood, glass beads, hide, seeds; 6 x 1.5 x 7
Nineteenth century; F01-SA-330, Figure 94
Purchased from Christie's Amsterdam, 12/2000

500. Zulu snuff spoon (*izitshengula*)/hair ornament*
Ivory; 8 x 1 x 0.25
Late nineteenth/early twentieth centuries; PER-09, Figure 97
Purchased from Sotheby's, South Africa

501. Tsonga snuff containers*
Wood; 9.5 x 5.5 x 1.25
Nineteenth century; PER-23, Figure 100
Purchased from Sotheby's, South Africa

502. Sotho snuff container*
Horn; 5.5 x 2.5 x 2.5
Late nineteenth/early twentieth centuries; PER-24, Figure 105
Purchased from Christie's, Amsterdam

503. Xhosa snuff container*
Horn, wood; 2 x 2 x 2
Nineteenth century; PER-25, Figure 98
Purchased from Sotheby's, South Africa

504. Xhosa snuff container*
Horn, wood; 3 x 1.75 x 1.75
Nineteenth century; PER-26, Figure 98
Purchased from Sotheby's, South Africa

505. Xhosa snuff container*
Horn, wood; 3 x 1.5 x 1.5
Nineteenth century; PER-27, Figure 98
Purchased from Sotheby's, South Africa

506. Xhosa (*Thembu*) pipe*
Wood, horn, metal; 5.25 x 1.75 x 4.5
Late nineteenth/early twentieth centuries; PER-28, Figure 96b

507. Xhosa (Thembu) pipe*
Wood, horn, metal; 6.25 x 1.75 x 5.5
Late nineteenth/early twentieth centuries; PER-29, Figure 96a

508. Zambia Ila Tonga pipe*
Clay; 5.5 x 3.25 x 3.5
Late nineteenth/early twentieth centuries; PER-30, Figure 95a

509. Zambia Ila Tonga pipe*
Clay; 3 x 2.5 x 3
Late nineteenth/early twentieth centuries; PER-31, Figure 95b

510. Xhosa snuff container*
Animal intestine, blood, clay; 3.25 x 3 x 5.25
Nineteenth century; PER-32, Figure 106

511. Xhosa snuff container
Gourd, glass beads, sinew fiber; 5 x 4 x 4
Nineteenth century; SA-041-01
Purchased from the Prynnsberg Museum, Clocolan, South Africa, 1995

512. Xhosa snuff container
Gourd, glass beads, sinew fiber; 5 x 3.5 x 3.5
Nineteenth century; SA-041-02
Purchased from the Prynnsberg Museum, Clocolan, South Africa, 1995

513. Xhosa snuff container
Gourd, glass beads, sinew fiber; 3.25 x 4 x 4
Nineteenth century; SA-041-03
Purchased from the Prynnsberg Museum, Clocolan, South Africa, 1995

514. Xhosa snuff container
Gourd, glass beads, sinew fiber; 2.75 x 4 x 4
Nineteenth century; SA-041-04
Purchased from the Prynnsberg Museum, Clocolan, South Africa, 1995

515. Gourd cup
Gourd; 3.25 x 4.25 x 4.25
Late nineteenth/early twentieth centuries; SA-041-07
Purchased from the Prynnsberg Museum, Clocolan, South Africa, 1995

516. Nguni snuff container*
Animal intestine, blood, clay; 3 x 2.5 x 2.5
Nineteenth century; SA-042, Figure 107
Purchased from the Prynnsberg Museum, Clocolan, South Africa, 1995

517. Tsonga snuff containers*
Wood; 14 x 1.5 x 1.5
Nineteenth century; SA-045-07, Figure 102
Purchased from the Prynnsberg Museum, Clocolan, South Africa, 1995

518. Xhosa pipe (*inqawe*)*
Wood, glass beads, fiber; 7.5 x 3 x 2.5
Late nineteenth century; SA-046, Figure 43
Purchased from the Prynnsberg Museum, Clocolan, South Africa, 1995

519. Zulu snuff spoon (*izitshengula*)*
Ivory; 8 x 1
Late nineteenth century; SA-051-06, Figure 97
Purchased from the Prynnsberg Museum, Clocolan, South Africa, 1995

520. Xhosa snuff container
Metal, fiber, glass beads; 2 x 2 x 2
Late nineteenth century; SA-054-01
Purchased from the Prynnsberg Museum, Clocolan, South Africa, 1995

521. Sotho snuff container*
Gourd, fiber, glass beads; 2.5 x 2 x 2
Late nineteenth century; SA-054-02, Figure 104
Purchased from the Prynnsberg Museum, Clocolan, South Africa, 1995

522. Sotho snuff container*
Metal, mirror, glass beads, fiber; 12 x 2.75 x 1.25
Late nineteenth century; SA-054-03, Figure 101
Purchased from the Prynnsberg Museum, Clocolan, South Africa, 1995

523. Sotho snuff container*
Metal, mirror, glass beads, fiber; 12 x 2 x 1
Late nineteenth century; SA-054-04, Figure 101
Purchased from the Prynnsberg Museum, Clocolan, South Africa, 1995

524. Sotho snuff container*
Metal, mirror, glass beads, fiber; 7 x 1.75 x 0.75
Late nineteenth century; SA-054-05, Figure 101
Purchased from the Prynnsberg Museum, Clocolan, South Africa, 1995

525. Sotho snuff container
Metal, mirror, glass beads, fiber; 6.5 x 1.75
Late nineteenth century; SA-054-06
Purchased from the Prynnsberg Museum, Clocolan, South Africa, 1995

526. Nguni pipe cleaner
Metal, glass beads, fiber; length: 9.5
Nineteenth century; SA-054-07
Purchased from the Prynnsberg Museum, Clocolan, South Africa, 1995

527. Nguni pipe cleaner
Metal, glass beads, fiber; length: 13.5
Nineteenth century; SA-054-08
Purchased from the Prynnsberg Museum, Clocolan, South Africa, 1995

528. Nguni pipe cleaner
Metal, glass beads, fiber; length: 7.75
Nineteenth century; SA-054-09
Purchased from the Prynnsberg Museum, Clocolan, South Africa, 1995

529. Nguni pipe cleaner
Metal, glass beads, fiber; length: 14.5
Nineteenth century; SA-054-10
Purchased from the Prynnsberg Museum, Clocolan, South Africa, 1995

530. Zulu Snuff container (*ishungu***)***
Gourd, wire; 3 x 4 x 4
Nineteenth century; SA-067-01, Figure 103
Purchased from the Prynnsberg Museum, Clocolan, South Africa, 1995

531. Zulu snuff container (*ishungu***)***
Gourd, wire; 3 x 3 x 3
Nineteenth century; SA-067-02, Figure 103
Purchased from the Prynnsberg Museum, Clocolan, South Africa, 1995

532. South Africa gourd pipe
Gourd, clay; length: 24
Twentieth century; SA-121
Purchased from the Old Colonial Gallery, Durban, South Africa

533. Xhosa tobacco pouch (*iingxowa***)***
Cotton textile, glass beads; 15 x 10.5
Twentieth century; SA-232, Figure 42a
Purchased from the African Art Center, Pietermaritzburg, South Africa, 1995

534. Zulu snuff container (*ishungu***)**
Horn; height: 5
Nineteenth century; SA-264
Purchased from the Prynnsberg Museum, Clocolan, South Africa, 1995

SPOONS

535. Zulu spoon
Wood; length: 15
Twentieth century; FSA-006-01

536. Zulu spoon
Wood; length: 15.75
Twentieth century; FSA-006-02

537. Zulu spoon
Wood; length: 14.25
Twentieth century; FSA-006-03

538. Zulu spoon
Wood; length: 15
Twentieth century; FSA-006-04

539. Zulu spoon
Wood; length: 15.5
Twentieth century; FSA-006-05

540. Zulu spoon
Wood; length: 15
Twentieth century; FSA-006-06

541. Southern Africa female figured spoon (*isixwembe***)***
Wood; 19 x 4 x 2.25
Late nineteenth/early twentieth centuries; PER-15, Figure 48, 78
Purchased from the Countess Victoria Romieri Collection

542. Zulu spoon*
Wood; 13.5 x 2.5 x 1.5
Twentieth century; PER-50, Figure 49a

543. Zulu spoon*
Wood; 13.25 x 2.5 x 1.5
Twentieth century; PER-51, Figure 49b

544. Zulu ceremonial spoon
Wood; length: 21
Early twentieth century; SA-016-01
Purchased from the African Art Center, Durban, South Africa

545. Zulu ceremonial spoon
Wood; length: 21
Early twentieth century; SA-016-02

546. Zulu ceremonial spoon
Wood; length: 21
Early twentieth century; SA-016-03

547. Zulu spoon
Horn; length: 15
Nineteenth century; SA-051-01
Purchased from the Prynnsberg Museum, Clocolan, South Africa, 1995

548. Zulu spoon
Horn; length: 11.75
Nineteenth century; SA-051-02
Purchased from the Prynnsberg Museum, Clocolan, South Africa, 1995

549. Zulu spoon
Horn; length: 12.5
Nineteenth century; SA-051-03
Purchased from the Prynnsberg Museum, Clocolan, South Africa, 1995

550. Zulu spoon
Horn; length: 11
Nineteenth century; SA-051-04
Purchased from the Prynnsberg Museum, Clocolan, South Africa, 1995

551. Zulu spoon
Horn; length: 5.25
Nineteenth century; SA-051-05
Purchased from the Prynnsberg Museum, Clocolan, South Africa, 1995

552. Zulu blackened poker work spoon (*ukhezo***)**
Wood; length: 18.5
Nineteenth century; SA-051-07
Purchased from the Prynnsberg Museum, Clocolan, South Africa, 1995

553. Zulu blackened poker work spoon (*ukhezo***)**
Wood; length: 16
Nineteenth century; SA-051-08
Purchased from the Prynnsberg Museum, Clocolan, South Africa, 1995

554. Zulu blackened poker work spoon (*ukhezo***)**
Wood; length: 13.5
Nineteenth century; SA-051-09
Purchased from the Prynnsberg Museum, Clocolan, South Africa, 1995

555. Zulu blackened poker work spoon (*ukhezo***)**
Wood; length: 15.25
Nineteenth century; SA-051-10
Purchased from the Prynnsberg Museum, Clocolan, South Africa, 1995

556. Zulu blackened poker work spoon (*ukhezo***)**
Wood; length: 17.5
Nineteenth century; SA-051-11
Purchased from the Prynnsberg Museum, Clocolan, South Africa, 1995

557. Zulu blackened poker work spoon (*ukhezo***)**
Wood; length: 10
Nineteenth century; SA-051-12
Purchased from the Prynnsberg Museum, Clocolan, South Africa, 1995

558. Zulu blackened poker work spoon (*ukhezo***)**
Wood; length: 19.75
Nineteenth century; SA-051-13
Purchased from the Prynnsberg Museum, Clocolan, South Africa, 1995

559. Zulu blackened poker work spoon (*ukhezo***)**
Wood; length: 12.5
Nineteenth century; SA-051-15
Purchased from the Prynnsberg Museum, Clocolan, South Africa, 1995

560. Zulu blackened poker work spoon (*ukhezo***)**
Wood; length: 10.75
Nineteenth century; SA-051-16
Purchased from the Prynnsberg Museum, Clocolan, South Africa, 1995

561. Zulu blackened poker work spoon (*ukhezo***)**
Wood; length: 14.5
Nineteenth century; SA-051-17
Purchased from the Prynnsberg Museum, Clocolan, South Africa, 1995

562. Zulu blackened poker work spoon (*ukhezo***)**
Wood; length: 13.25
Nineteenth century; SA-051-21
Purchased from the Prynnsberg Museum, Clocolan, South Africa, 1995

563. Zulu ceremonial ladle with rifle-shaped handle (*izixembe***)**
Wood; 12 x 4.5 x 3.5
Nineteenth century; SA-074
Purchased from James Willis, San Francisco, California

564. Zulu oval-shaped spoon
Wood; length: 16
Early twentieth century; SA-079-01
Purchased from the African Art Center, Durban, South Africa

565. Zulu pear-shaped spoon
Wood; length: 16
Early twentieth century; SA-079-02
Purchased from the African Art Center, Durban, South Africa

566. Zulu pear-shaped spoon
Wood; length: 16
Early twentieth century; SA-079-03
Purchased from the African Art Center, Durban, South Africa

567. Zulu spoon*
Wood; 14.5 x 2.5 x 1.25
Late nineteenth/early twentieth centuries; SA-129-01, Figure 49c
Collected by Nomusa Dube in South Africa, 1995–1999

568. Zulu spoon*
Wood; 15 x 2.5 x 0.75
Late nineteenth/early twentieth centuries; SA-129-02, Figure 49d
Collected by Nomusa Dube in South Africa, 1995–1999

569. Zulu spoon
Wood; length: 12.5
Late nineteenth/early twentieth centuries; SA-129-03
Collected by Nomusa Dube in South Africa, 1995–1999

STAFFS, WALKING STICKS, DANCE WANDS

570. Zulu Knobkerrie
Wood; length: 29
Twentieth century; FSA-002-01
Collected in South Africa, 1995

571. South Africa walking stick with human head finial
Wood; length: 34.5
Twentieth century; FSA-010

572. Northern Nguni ceremonial spear*
Wood, metal; 59 x 3 x 2.5
Nineteenth century; NSA-001, Figure 79
Purchased from Alfonso Patino, Pinecrest, Florida

573. Zulu staff*
Wood; 51.25 x 2.5 x 1
Nineteenth century; PER-40, Figure 88
Purchased from Richard Ulevitch, Del Mar, California

574. Tsonga Maternity Staff*
Wood; 42 x 2 x 2 inches
Nineteenth century; PER-52, Figure 85
Purchased from Wally Zolman, Indianapolis, Indiana

575. Zulu dance wand
Wood, glass beads, sisal; length: 34
Nineteenth century; SA-001
Purchased from David DeRoche, San Francisco, California

576. Zulu spiral staff with knob finial
Wood; length: 51
Nineteenth century; SA-033-01
Purchased from Craig Helms, Bonita, California

577. Zulu sangoma stick
Wood; 28.5 x 2 x 1
Circa 1950s; SA-033-02
Belonged to sangoma Phumizile Mazula Kwanaze from Melmoth, South Africa

578. Zulu knobkerrie
Wood; 17 x 3.5
Nineteenth century; SA-049-01
Purchased from the Prynnsberg Museum, Clocolan, South Africa, 1995

579. Zulu knobkerrie
Wood; 22 x 4
Nineteenth century; SA-049-02
Purchased from the Prynnsberg Museum, Clocolan, South Africa, 1995

580. San root stock club
Root stock wood; length: 22.5
Nineteenth century; SA-058-01
Purchased from the Prynnsberg Museum, Clocolan, South Africa, 1995

581. San root stock club
Root stock wood; length: 25.5
Nineteenth century; SA-058-02
Purchased from the Prynnsberg Museum, Clocolan, South Africa, 1995

582. San root stock club
Root stock wood; length: 26.5
Nineteenth century; SA-058-03
Purchased from the Prynnsberg Museum, Clocolan, South Africa, 1995

583. Zulu dance staff*
Wood, reed fiber, glass beads; 30.5 x 1 x 1
Nineteenth century; SA-059-01, Figure 87
Purchased from the Prynnsberg Museum, Clocolan, South Africa, 1995

584. Nguni staff/walking stick
Wood, reed fiber, glass beads; length: 33.25
Nineteenth century; SA-059-02
Purchased from the Prynnsberg Museum, Clocolan, South Africa, 1995

585. Nguni staff/walking stick
Wood, wire; length: 38.5
Nineteenth century; SA-059-03
Purchased from the Prynnsberg Museum, Clocolan, South Africa, 1995

586. Nguni staff/walking stick
Wood, wire; length: 40.75
Nineteenth century; SA-059-04
Purchased from the Prynnsberg Museum, Clocolan, South Africa, 1995

587. Nguni staff/walking stick
Wood; length: 36.25
Nineteenth century; SA-059-05
Purchased from the Prynnsberg Museum, Clocolan, South Africa, 1995

588. Nguni staff/walking stick
Wood, cork, wire; length: 19.5
Nineteenth century; SA-059-06
Purchased from the Prynnsberg Museum, Clocolan, South Africa, 1995

589. Northern Nguni spiral staff*
Wood; 58.5 x 2 x 1.5
Twentieth century; SA-071, Figure 86
Purchased from Alfonso Patino, Pinecrest, Florida,
from the Marvin Chasen Collection

590. South African male figure walking stick
Wood; length: 53
Early twentieth century; SA-073
Purchased from Alfonso Patino, Pinecrest, Florida,
from the Marvin Chasen Collection

591. Tsonga maternity staff
Wood; 35 x 1.75 x 2
Age unknown; SA-110
Purchased from Alfonso Patino, Pinecrest, Florida

592. Swazi staff (spiral finial)*
Wood, metal; 24 x 3.5 x 2
Twentieth century; SA-126, Figure 84
Purchased from Butterfield and Butterfield, 12/10/96, Lot 326

593. Zulu cane/walking stick
Wood, metal rivets; length: 37.5
Twentieth century; SA-132

594. Zulu walking stick
Wood; 56 x 3 x 3
Nineteenth century; SA-133
Purchased from Alfonso Patino, Pinecrest, Florida

595. Zulu walking stick with bowl-shaped finial*
Wood; 50.5 x 7.5 x 4
Nineteenth century; SA-134, Figure 89
Purchased from Alfonso Patino, Pinecrest, Florida

596. San walking stick with bird finial
Wood; length: 51
Early twentieth century; SA-135
Purchased from Alfonso Patino, Pinecrest, Florida

597. Lesotho etched walking staff*
Wood; 41.75 x 1.5 x 1.5
Circa mid-1800s; SA-254, Figure 80a, 81, 82
Purchased from the Prynnsberg Museum, Clocolan, South Africa, 1995

598. Lesotho etched walking staff*
Wood; 37.25 x 1 x 1
Circa mid-1800s; SA-255, Figure 4, 80b, 83
Purchased from the Prynnsberg Museum, Clocolan, South Africa, 1995

STOOLS

599. Barotse stool
Wood; 7 x 17.5
Nineteenth century; SA-044
Purchased from the Prynnsberg Museum, Clocolan, South Africa, 1995

600. Mangbetu stool
Wood; 16.5 x 10 x 10
Twentieth century; SA-085
Purchased from the African Art Center, Durban, South Africa;
collected by Nomusa Dube, 1995–1999

VEILS

601. Basotho initiation veil (*lesira*)*
Reeds, glass beads, buttons; 11 x 8 x 8
Nineteenth/twentieth centuries; SA-190, Figure 58
Purchased from the Prynnsberg Museum, Clocolan, South Africa, 1995

WAISTBANDS, BELTS

602. Zulu belt
Grass, glass beads, sisal fiber, metal tacks; length: 28
Twentieth century; FSA-016-01

603. Zulu belt
Grass, glass beads, sisal fiber, metal tacks; length: 32
Twentieth century; FSA-016-02

604. Zulu belt
Grass, glass beads, sisal fiber, metal tacks; length: 30.5
Twentieth century; FSA-016-03

605. Zulu belt
Glass beads, grass, sisal fiber; length: 25.5
Twentieth century; FSA-016-04

606. Zulu belt
Glass beads, grass, sisal fiber; length: 38
Twentieth century; FSA-016-05

607. Zulu belt
Glass beads, sisal fiber; length: 34
Twentieth century; FSA-016-06

608. Zulu belt
Glass beads, grass, sisal fiber, metal; length: 31.5
Twentieth century; FSA-016-07

609. Xhosa belt (*umjajo*)
Brass; length: 14.5 feet
Twentieth century; PER-39-02

610. Nguni belt
Glass beads, sisal fiber; length: 30
Nineteenth century; SA-054-26
Purchased from the Prynnsberg Museum, Clocolan, South Africa, 1995

611. Nguni Western belt adapted with local beadwork
Hide, metal, glass beads; length: 35
Nineteenth century; SA-065-01
Purchased from the Prynnsberg Museum, Clocolan, South Africa, 1995

612. Nguni Western belt adapted with local beadwork
Hide, metal, glass beads; length: 35
Nineteenth century; SA-065-02
Purchased from the Prynnsberg Museum, Clocolan, South Africa, 1995

613. Zulu belt
Glass beads, cotton fiber; length: 36
Circa 1940–1950s; SA-202-01
Purchased from the African Art Center, Durban, South Africa, 1996

614. Zulu Msinga belt
Cotton and sisal fiber, grass, brass buttons; length: 27
Mid- to late twentieth century; SA-204-02
Collected in Durban area, South Africa, 1995

615. Zulu Msinga belt
Cotton and sisal fiber, grass, brass buttons; length: 31
Mid- to late twentieth century; SA-204-03
Collected in Durban area, South Africa, 1995

616. Zulu Msinga belt
Cotton and sisal fiber, grass, brass buttons; length: 37
Mid- to late twentieth century; SA-204-04
Collected in Durban area, South Africa, 1995

617. Zulu Msinga belt
Cotton and sisal fiber, grass, brass buttons; length: 34
Mid- to late twentieth century; SA-204-05
Collected in Durban area, South Africa, 1995

618. Zulu Msinga belt
Cotton and sisal fiber, grass, brass buttons; length: 27.5
Mid- to late twentieth century; SA-204-06
Collected in Durban area, South Africa, 1995

619. Xhosa belt (*isaziso sesinqe*)
Glass beads, sisal fiber; length: 30
Twentieth century; SA-233-05
Purchased from the African Art Center, Pietermaritzburg, South Africa, 1995

620. Xhosa belt (*isaziso sesinqe*)
Glass beads, sisal fiber; length: 28.5
Twentieth century; SA-233-06
Purchased from the African Art Center, Pietermaritzburg, South Africa, 1995

621. Zulu belt
Glass beads, sisal fiber, brass; length: 31
Circa 1890–1910; SA-240
Purchased from the African Art Center, Durban, South Africa

622. Zulu belt
Glass beads, fiber; length: 37.5
Late nineteenth/early twentieth centuries; SA-260
Collected by Nomusa Dube in South Africa, 1995–1999

623. Zulu belt
Glass beads, sisal fiber; length: 68
Late nineteenth/early twentieth centuries; SA-263
Purchased from the Prynnsberg Museum, Clocolan, South Africa, 1995

624. Zulu belt
Glass beads, fiber; length: 36
Early 1950s; SA-302-04
Collected by Nomusa Dube in South Africa, 1995–1999

625. Zulu belt
Glass beads, fiber; length: 36
Early 1950s; SA-302-05
Collected by Nomusa Dube in South Africa, 1995–1999

626. Zulu Msinga belt (*isifociya/ixhama*)
Grass, glass beads, cotton fiber, brass and tin tacks; length: 29
Circa 1940s; SA-311-01
Collected by Nomusa Dube in South Africa, 1995–1999

627. Zulu Msinga belt (*isifociya/ixhama*)
Grass, glass beads, cotton fiber, brass and tin tacks; length: 28
Circa 1940s; SA-311-02
Collected by Nomusa Dube in South Africa, 1995–1999

628. Zulu Msinga belt (*isifociya/ixhama*)
Grass, glass beads, cotton fiber, brass and tin tacks; length: 29.5
Circa 1940s; SA-311-03
Collected by Nomusa Dube in South Africa, 1995–1999

629. Zulu Msinga belt (*isifociya/ixhama*)
Grass, glass beads, cotton fiber, brass and tin tacks; length: 29.5
Circa 1940s; SA-311-04
Collected by Nomusa Dube in South Africa, 1995–1999

630. Zulu Msinga belt (*isifociya/ixhama*)
Grass, glass beads, cotton fiber, brass and tin tacks; length: 29.5
Circa 1940s; SA-311-05
Collected by Nomusa Dube in South Africa, 1995–1999

631. Zulu belt
Glass beads, sisal fiber; length: 27.5
Circa 1910s; SA-313-02
Collected by Nomusa Dube in South Africa, 1995–1999

632. Zulu belt
Glass beads, sisal fiber; length: 19
Circa 1910s; SA-313-03
Collected by Nomusa Dube in South Africa, 1995–1999

633. Zulu Msinga belt
Glass beads, fiber; length: 30
Twentieth century; SA-318-01
Collected by Nomusa Dube in South Africa, 1995–1999

634. Zulu Msinga belt
Glass beads, fiber; length: 38
Twentieth century; SA-318-02
Collected by Nomusa Dube in South Africa, 1995–1999

635. Zulu Msinga belt
Glass beads, fiber; length: 32
Twentieth century; SA-318-03
Collected by Nomusa Dube in South Africa, 1995–1999

636. Zulu belt
Glass beads, fiber; length: 24
Twentieth century; SA-318-04
Collected by Nomusa Dube in South Africa, 1995–1999

637. Zulu Msinga belt
Glass beads, grass; 1.25 x 29
Late twentieth century; SA-326-01
Purchased from the African Art Center, Durban, South Africa, 1995

638. Zulu Msinga belt
Glass beads, grass; 1.5 x 27.5
Late twentieth century; SA-326-02
Purchased from the African Art Center, Durban, South Africa, 1995

639. Zulu belt
Glass beads, fiber; length: 32
Late twentieth century; SA-328-01
Purchased from the African Art Center, Durban, South Africa, 1995

640. Zulu belt
Glass beads, fiber; length: 29.5
Late twentieth century; SA-328-02
Collected in Sundesia, Durban, South Africa, 1995

641. Zulu belt
Glass beads, fiber; length: 22
Late twentieth century; SA-328-03
Collected in Sundesia, Durban, South Africa, 1995

642. Zulu belt
Glass beads, brass tacks, fiber; length: 33.75
Late twentieth century; SA-328-04
Collected in Sundesia, Durban, South Africa, 1995

643. Xhosa belt (*isaziso sesinqe*)
Glass beads, buttons; length: 29.5
Twentieth century; SA-336-03
Purchased from the African Art Center, Durban, South Africa, 1996

WAISTCOATS, VESTS

644. Xhosa body harness/waistcoat (*umwayo*)
Glass beads, shell beads, buttons, fiber; 19.25 x 6.25
Twentieth century; SA-259
Collected by Nomusa Dube in South Africa, 1995–1999

645. Zulu men's vest
Textile, glass beads, buttons; 27 x 13
Twentieth century; SA-324-01
Purchased from the African Art Center, Pietermaritzburg, South Africa

646. Zulu men's vest
Textile, glass beads, buttons, metal; 27 x 14
Twentieth century; SA-324-02
Purchased from the African Art Center, Pietermaritzburg, South Africa

WEAPONS, TOOLS

647. Zulu Ax (*isizenze*)
Wood, metal; 18.5 x 9 x 1.5
Twentieth century; SA-039-01
Purchased from Gerard Becker, Temecula, California

648. Zulu Ax (*isizenze*)
Wood, metal; 23 x 6.25 x 1.5
Twentieth century; SA-039-02
Purchased from Gerard Becker, Temecula, California

649. San bow
Wood, reeds; length: 58.5
Nineteenth century; SA-050-01
Purchased from the Prynnsberg Museum, Clocolan, South Africa, 1995

650. San bow
Wood, reeds; length: 55
Nineteenth century; SA-050-02
Purchased from the Prynnsberg Museum, Clocolan, South Africa, 1995

651. San arrows (group of 7)
Wood, metal; length: Approximately 28.5
Nineteenth century; SA-050-03
Purchased from the Prynnsberg Museum, Clocolan, South Africa, 1995

652. San arrows (set of 2)
Wood, metal; length: 42.75
Nineteenth century; SA-050-04
Purchased from the Prynnsberg Museum, Clocolan, South Africa, 1995

653. San quiver
Hide; length: 29
Nineteenth century; SA-050-05
Purchased from the Prynnsberg Museum, Clocolan, South Africa, 1995

654. Zulu spearhead
Metal; length: 18.25
Nineteenth century; SA-050-06
Purchased from the Prynnsberg Museum, Clocolan, South Africa, 1995

655. Zulu spearhead
Wood, metal; length: 9.5
Nineteenth century; SA-050-07
Purchased from the Prynnsberg Museum, Clocolan, South Africa, 1995

656. Zulu spearhead
Wood, metal; length: 11.5
Nineteenth century; SA-050-08
Purchased from the Prynnsberg Museum, Clocolan, South Africa, 1995

657. Zulu spearhead
Wood, metal; length: 17
Nineteenth century; SA-050-09
Purchased from the Prynnsberg Museum, Clocolan, South Africa, 1995

658. Zulu spear (*umkhonto*)
Wood, metal; length: 51
Nineteenth century; SA-050-10
Purchased from the Prynnsberg Museum, Clocolan, South Africa, 1995

659. Zulu spear (*umkhonto*)
Wood, metal; length: 43.75
Nineteenth century; SA-050-11
Purchased from the Prynnsberg Museum, Clocolan, South Africa, 1995

660. Zulu spear (umkhonto)
Wood, metal; length: 55
Nineteenth century; SA-050-12
Purchased from the Prynnsberg Museum, Clocolan, South Africa, 1995

661. Zulu spear (*umkhonto*)
Wood, metal; length: 61.5
Nineteenth century; SA-050-13
Purchased from the Prynnsberg Museum, Clocolan, South Africa, 1995

662. Zulu spear (*umkhonto*)
Wood, metal; length: 68.25
Nineteenth century; SA-050-14
Purchased from the Prynnsberg Museum, Clocolan, South Africa, 1995

663. Zulu spear (*umkhonto*)
Wood, metal; length: 17.25
Nineteenth century; SA-050-15
Purchased from the Prynnsberg Museum, Clocolan, South Africa, 1995

664. Zulu spear (*umkhonto*)
Wood, metal; length: 56.75
Nineteenth century; SA-050-16
Purchased from the Prynnsberg Museum, Clocolan, South Africa, 1995

665. Zulu spear (*umkhonto*)
Wood, metal; length: 52.25
Nineteenth century; SA-050-17
Purchased from the Prynnsberg Museum, Clocolan, South Africa, 1995

666. Zulu spear (*umkhonto*)
Wood, metal; length: 48.5
Nineteenth century; SA-050-18
Purchased from the Prynnsberg Museum, Clocolan, South Africa, 1995

667. Zulu spear (*umkhonto*)
Wood, metal; length: 42.5
Nineteenth century; SA-050-19
Purchased from the Prynnsberg Museum, Clocolan, South Africa, 1995

668. Zulu machete
Wood, steel; length: 32
Nineteenth century
SA-050-20
Purchased from the Prynnsberg Museum, Clocolan, South Africa, 1995

669. Zulu axe with bulb top (*isizenze*)
Wood, steel, wire; 26.25 x 6.75 x 2
Nineteenth century; SA-053-01
Purchased from the Prynnsberg Museum, Clocolan, South Africa, 1995

670. Zulu axe with painted blade (*isizenze*)
Wood, steel, wire; 34.25 x 7 x 1.25
Nineteenth century; SA-053-02
Purchased from the Prynnsberg Museum, Clocolan, South Africa, 1995

671. Nguni whip
Hide, metal; length: 32
Nineteenth century; SA-054-43
Purchased from the Prynnsberg Museum, Clocolan, South Africa, 1995

672. Zulu shield (*umbhumbuluzo*)*
Hide; 34.5 x 18.5 x 1.5
Nineteenth century; SA-057-01, Figure 70
Purchased from the Prynnsberg Museum, Clocolan, South Africa, 1995

673. Zulu shield (*umbhumbuluzo*)
Hide; 23.5 x 15 x 4
Nineteenth century; SA-057-02
Purchased from the Prynnsberg Museum, Clocolan, South Africa, 1995

674. Zulu shield (*umbhumbuluzo*)
Hide; 15.25 x 11 x 1.75
Nineteenth century; SA-057-03
Purchased from the Prynnsberg Museum, Clocolan, South Africa, 1995

675. Nguni broom
Grass, glass beads, fiber; length: 28.5
Nineteenth century; SA-063-09
Purchased from the Prynnsberg Museum, Clocolan, South Africa, 1995

676. Nguni broom
Grass, wire, fiber; length: 28.5
Nineteenth century; SA-063-10
Purchased from the Prynnsberg Museum, Clocolan, South Africa, 1995

677. Nguni broom
Grass, textile; lemgth: 24
Nineteenth century; SA-063-11
Purchased from the Prynnsberg Museum, Clocolan, South Africa, 1995

678. Nguni broom
Grass, glass beads, fiber; length: 28.5
Nineteenth century; SA-063-12
Purchased from the Prynnsberg Museum, Clocolan, South Africa, 1995

Appendix

Historical Photography

To help illustrate cultural context, photography from the late nineteenth and early twentieth centuries have been included to suggest how a variety of Southeast African art objects may have been worn, used and seen. Many of the photographic images were produced during the 1880s–1890s for use on postcards marketed to white tourists and colonials. While these early images serve as a contextual resource, the subject matter was recorded through the filters of a colonial perspective that included cultural, social and gender prejudice. Photographers working in studio and field situations routinely manipulated settings, props, costumes and poses to accentuate the exoticness of their subjects. While the original captions identifying the subject matter of these photographs is often vague or incorrect, and sometimes offensive, it is provided below for documentary purposes. Keeping all of these potential problems in mind, this careful selection of early photographs should enhance the viewer's ability to recreate some measure of art historical understanding and cultural appreciation for the art presented.

All historical photos/postcards
courtesy of Sally A. Fall.

A-1 "A Zulu Youth"
The photographer is thought to be George T. Ferneyhough.
The publisher is unknown; the card is printed in England.

A-2 "Native Maidens"
Copyright E.323
Photographer / publisher unknown.

A-3 "A Typical Zulu Woman"
Copyright E.995
Photographer / publisher unknown.

A-4 "Zulu girls dressing hair"
Published by Sallo Epstein & Co., Durban.
Postally used December 5, 1904
Photographer unknown.

A-5 "Zulus snuffing"
No. 2265 Published by A. Rittenberg, Durban.
Postally used August 15, 1909
Photographer unknown.

A-6 "Native Reserve"
Photo. S.A.R. / N. V. / 8
TOKIM Production; Printed in England.
Photographer unknown.

A-7 "A Chief's Betrothed"
Copyright E.319
Photographer / publisher unknown.

Bibliography

Ardmore Ceramic Art Studio, "The Artists of Ardmore—Duma, Ghesa and Gumbi," Ardmore Ceramic Art Studio, http://www.ardmoreceramics.co.za/ardmore-artists.html

Argyle, John and Eleanor Preston-Whyte, eds. *Social System and Traditional in Southern Africa: Essays in Honour of Eileen Krige*. Cape Town: Oxford UP, 1978.

Baasch, Peter. Telephone interview with Mary Axworthy, 29 July 2004.

Bates, Gloria. "Sangoma Visions." Unpublished essay, 2001.

Battis, Walter. *The Art of Africa*. Pietermaritzburg: Shuter and Shooter, 1958.

Becker, Peter. *Inland Tribes of Southern Africa*. London: Granada, 1979.

Becker, Rayda. "Headrests: Tsonga Types and Variations." In *Art and Ambiguity: Perspectives on the Brenthurst Collection of Southern African Art*, exh. cat. Johannesburg: Johannesburg Art Gallery, 1991.

———. "Ku Veleka Vukosi…To Bear Children is Wealth…: Tsonga Figures." In *Evocations of the Child: Fertility Figures of the Southern African Region*. Cape Town: Human & Rousseau, 1998.

———. "Re: Puppet Photo." Personal email to Mary Axworthy, 23 July 2004.

———. "Re: Forgot to Ask." Personal email to Mary Axworthy, 28 July 2004.

Becker, Rayda and Anitra Nettleton. "Tsonga-Shangana Beadwork and Figures." In *Catalogue: Ten Years of Collecting (1979–1989)*, edited by David Hammond-Tooke and Anitra Nettleton. Johannesburg: University of the Witwatersrand, 1989.

Bedford, Emma. "Exploring Meanings and Identities: Beadwork from the Eastern Cape in the South African National Gallery." In *Ezakwantu: Beadwork from the Eastern Cape*. South African National Gallery, 1993.

Berglund, Axel-Ivar. *Zulu Thought-Patterns and Symbolism*. London: Hurst, 1976.

Berliner, Paul F. *The Soul of Mbira*. Berkeley: University of California Press, 1978.

Berning, Gillian. "Artifacts of Zulu Kings." In *Zulu Treasures: of Kings and Commoners*, exh. cat. Kwazulu: Kwazulu Cultural Museum and Local History Museums, 1966.

Bourdillon, Michael F.C. "Social and Religious Life in Traditional Zimbabwe." In *Legacies of Stone: Zimbabwe Past and Present*, vol. 1, edited by William Dewey. Tervuren: Royal Museum for Central Africa, 1997.

Bristowe, Anthea. "Going Cuckoo at Clocolan." *Sunday Times* [Johannesburg] 31 March 1996 sec. 2:17.

Broster, Joan A. *Red Blanket Valley*. Johannesburg: H. Keartland, 1967.

———. The Tembu: Their Beadwork, Songs and Dances. Cape Town: Purnell, 1976.

Bryant, A.T. *The Zulu People: As They Were Before the White Man Came*. New York: Negro Universities Press, (multiple editions) 1948, 1949, 1967, 1970.

Calana, Zolile and Patrick Holo. *Xhosa Proverbs and Metaphors*. Cape Town: Kwela, 2002.

Cameron, Elisabeth L. *Isn't S/he a Doll?: Play and Ritual in African Sculpture*. Los Angeles: UCLA Fowler Museum of Cultural History, 1996.

———. "In Search of Children: Dolls and Agency in Africa." *African Arts* 30.2 (Spring 1997): 18–34.

Carey, Margaret. *Beads and Beadwork of East and South Africa*. Princes Risborough: Shire, 1986.

———. "Gender in African Beadwork: An Overview." In *Beads and Bead Makers: Gender, Material Culture and Meaning*, edited by Lidia D. Sciama and Joanne B. Eicher. Oxford: Berg, 1998.

Clark, G. and L. Wagner. *Potters of Southern Africa*. Cape Town: Struik, 1974.

Clarke, Duncan. *Colors of Africa*. San Diego: Thunder Bay, 2000.

Colenso, John William. *Zulu-English Dictionary*. Farnborough: Gregg, 4th edition, 1967.

Conner, Michael W. and Diane Pelrine. *The Geometric Vision: Arts of the Zulu*. West Lafayette: Purdue University Galleries, 1983.

Conru, Kevin. *The Art of Southeast Africa*. Milan: 5 Continents Editions, 2002.

Contemporary African Music & Arts Archive, "Josephine Ghesa," University of Cape Town, http://www.cama.org.za/CAMA/countries/southafr/Makers/ghesa/HTML/

Costello, Dawn. *Not Only for Its Beauty: Beadwork and Its Cultural Significance Among the Xhosa-Speaking Peoples*. Unisa: Unisa Press, 1990.

Crabtree, Caroline and Pam Stallebrass. *Beadwork: A World Guide*. New York: Rizzoli, 2002.

Creative Proverbs from Around the World, "South African Proverbs," Franklin C. Baer, Baertracks, http://creativeproverbs.com/sf04.htm

Dagan, E.A. *Emotions in Motion: Theatrical Puppets and Masks from Black Africa*. Montreal: Galerie Amrad African Arts, 1990.

Davison, Patricia. "Some Nguni Crafts Part 2: The Uses of Horn, Bone and Ivory." In *Annals of the South African Museum*. Cape Town: Rustica Press, 1997.

Davison, Patricia, ed. "Ambiguity, Style and Meaning." In *Art and Ambiguity: Perspectives on the Brenthurst Collection of Southern African Art*, exh. cat. Johannesburg: Johannesburg Art Gallery, 1991.

Degli, Marine. "Zulu Sculpture." In *Sculptures: Africa Asia Oceania Americas*, edited by Jacques Kerchache, et al. Paris: Reunion des Musees Nationaux, 2000, p 38.

De Grunne, Bernard. *Mains de Maîtres*. Brussels: Banque, 2001.

Dell, Elizabeth, ed. *Evocations of the Child: Fertility Figures of the Southern African Region*. Cape Town: Human & Rousseau, 1998.

Derwent, Sue. *Zulu*. London: Struik, 1998.

Dewey, William. *Sleeping Beauties: The Jerome L. Joss Collection of African Headrests at UCLA*. Los Angeles: Fowler Museum of Cultural History, 1993.

Drewal, Henry John and John Mason. *Beads, Body, and Soul: Art and Light in the Yorùbá Universe*. Los Angeles: UCLA Fowler Museum of Cultural History, 1998.

Ellenberger, V. "The First Horses to be Seen in Basutoland." *Basutoland Witness* 9, no. 1 (1955): 6–7.

Elliot, Aubrey. *Tribal Dress: Beadwork and other Decorative Arts*. Cape Town: Struik, 1986.

———. Zulu: *Heritage of a Nation*. Cape Town: Struik, 1991.

———. *The Zulu: Traditions and Culture*. Cape Town: Struik, 1995.

Falgayrettes, Christiane. *Support de Rêves*. Paris: Editions Dapper, 1989.

Friedman, Hazel. "Ntwane Gimwane: Ntwane Grass Figures." In *Evocations of the Child: Fertility Figures of the Southern African Region*. Cape Town: Human & Rousseau, 1998.

Giesen, Johanna A.M. *Lesotho, Kingdom in the Sky*. The Netherlands: Afrika Museum, Berg en Dal, 1993.

Gillow, John. *African Textiles*. San Francisco: Chronicle Books, 2003.

Grossert, John Watt. *Zulu Crafts*. Pietermaritzburg: Shuter & Shooter, 1978.

Gwintsa, Veliswa. "Double Talk." In *Evocations of the Child: Fertility Figures of the Southern African Region*. Cape Town: Human & Rousseau, 1998.

Hammond, Tim, facsimile to the author by Mary Axworthy, 25 July 2004.

Hammond-Tooke, David. *The Roots of Black South Africa*. Parklands: Jonathan Ball Publishers, 1993.

Hammond-Tooke, David and Anitra Nettleton, eds. *Catalogue: Ten Years of Collecting (1979–1989)*. Johannesburg: Johannesburg Art Galleries, 1989.

Hammond-Tooke, W.D. *The Bantu Speaking Peoples of Southern Africa*. London: Routledge & Kegan Paul, 1937.

Havran, Agnes. "Catalogue list." In *Art and Ambiguity: Perspectives on the Brenthurst Collection of Southern African Art*, exh. cat. Johannesburg: Johannesburg Art Gallery, 1991.

Hoffman, A.C. and E. Bernard. *Bushman Engravings on Walking Sticks, Magic Sticks, a Calabash, and Ostrich Egg Shells*. Bloemfontein: Researches of the Nasionale Museum, 1969.

Hooper, Lindsay. "Some Nguni Crafts: Part 3, Wood-carving." *Annals of the South African Museum 70*, part 3 (May, 1981): 213–214, 230–235.

Hooper, Lindsay. "Domestic Arts: Carved Wooden Objects in the Home." In *Zulu Treasures: of Kings and Commoners*, exh. cat. Kwazulu: Kwazulu Cultural Museum and the Local History Museums, 1996.

Jolles, Frank. "Contemporary Zulu Dolls from Kwalatha." *African Arts* 27.2 (April 1994): 54–70.

———. "Zulu Earplugs." In *Zulu Treasures: of Kings and Commoners*, exh. cat. Kwazulu: Kwazulu Cultural Museum and Local History Museums: 1996.

———. "Zulu Earplugs: A Study in Transformation." *African Arts* 30.2 (Spring 1997): 46–60.

———. "Zulu Beer Vessels." In *Tracing the Rainbow: Art and Life in Southern Africa*, edited by Stefan Eisenhofer. Stutgart: Arnoldsche, 2001.

Kennedy, Carolee. *The Art and Material Culture of the Zulu-Speaking Peoples.* Los Angeles: UCLA Museum of Cultural History, 1978.

Klopper, Sandra. "Zulu Art." In *Catalogue: The Standard Bank Foundation Collection of African Art (1979–1986).* Johannesburg: University of the Witwatersrand Art Galleries, 1986.

———. "'Zulu' Headrests and Figurative Carvings: the Brenthurst Collection and the Art of South-east Africa." In *Art and Ambiguity: Perspectives on the Brenthurst Collection of Southern African Art,* exh. cat. Johannesburg: Johannesburg Art Gallery, 1991.

———. "The Art of Zulu-Speakers in Northern Natal-Zululand. An Investigation of the History of Beadwork, Carving and Dress from Shaka to Inkatha." Ph.D. diss., University of the Witwatersrand, Johannesburg, 1992.

———. "From Adornment to Artifact to Art: Historical Perspectives on Southeast African Beadwork." In *South East African Beadwork: 1850–1910. From Adornment to Artifact to Art,* edited by Michael Stevenson and Michael Graham-Stewart. Vlaeberg: Fernwood Press, 2000.

———. "Kings, Commoners and Foreigners: artistic production and the consumption of art in the Southeastern African region." In *The Art of Southeast Africa from the Conru Collection,* edited by Annie Pérez. Milan: 5 Continents Editions, 2002.

Klopper, Sandra and Karel Nel. *The Art of Southeast Africa.* Milan: 5 Continents Editions, 2002.

Krige, Eileen Jensen, and J.D. Krige. *The Realm of a Rain Queen.* London: Oxford UP, 1943.

———. *The Social System of the Zulus.* Pietermaritzburg: Shuter & Shooter, 1950.

Laband, John. "The Land of Zulu Kings." In *Zulu Treasures: of Kings and Commoners,* exh. cat. Kwazulu: Kwazulu Museum and the Local History Museums: 1996.

Levinsohn, Rhoda. *Basketry: A Renaissance in Southern Africa.* Cleveland Heights, Ohio: Protea Press, 1979.

———. *Art and Craft of Southern Africa: Treasures in Transition.* Craighall: Delta Books, 1984.

Levy, Diane. "Ndebele Beadwork." In *Catalogue: Ten Years of Collecting (1979–1989),* edited by David Hammond-Tooke and Anitra Nettleton. Johannesburg: University of the Witwatersrand, 1989.

Mack, John. *Africa: Arts and Culture.* New York: Oxford UP, 2000.

Magubane, Peter. *Vanishing Cultures of South Africa.* New York: Rizzoli, 1998.

Mangon, Marion, ed. *Ubuntu: Arts et cultures d'Afrique du Sud.* Paris: la Réunion des Musées Nationaux, 2002.

Mayr, Franz. "Language of Colours amongst the Zulu expressed by their Beadwork Ornaments; and some General Notes on their Personal Adornments and Clothing." In *Natal Government Museum, Annals,* 1 (1906–1908): 159–165.

———. "The Zulu Kafirs of Natal." *Anthropos* 2 (1907): 633–45.

Metropolitan Museum of Art. *African Beads.* New York: The Metropolitan Museum of Art and Simon & Schuster, 1999.

Miller, Penny. *Myths and Legends of Southern Africa.* Cape Town: TV Bulpin, 1979.

Morris, Jean and Eleanor Preston-Whyte. *Speaking with Beads: Zulu Arts from Southern Africa.* New York: Thames and Hudson, 1994.

Mphahlele, Es'kia. "Introduction." In *Art and Ambiguity: Perspectives on the Brenthurst Collection of Southern African Art,* exh. cat. Johannesburg: Johannesburg Art Gallery, 1991.

Mukondeni Fine Arts Gallery, "Owen Ndou," Mukondeni Fine Arts Gallery, http://www.mukondeni.com/html/Owen%20Ndou.htm

Murray, Colin. *Black Mountain: Land, Class and Power in the Eastern Orange Free State, 1880s to 1980s.* Washington, DC: Smithsonian Institution, 1992.

Nel, Karel. "Consonant with the Cattle-Culture: the Art of the Portable." In *The Art of Southeast Africa from the Conru Collection,* edited by Annie Pérez. Milan: 5 Continents Editions, 2002.

Nel, Karel and Nessa Leibhammer. "Evocations of the Child." In *Evocations of the Child: Fertility Figures of the Southern African Region.* Cape Town: Human & Rousseau, 1998.

Nettleton, Anitra. *The Traditional Figurative Woodcarving of the Shona and Venda.* Ph.D. diss., Johannesburg: University of the Witwatersrand, 1984.

———. "The Venda Model Hut." *African Arts* 18.3 (May 1985).

———. "History and the Myth of Zulu Sculpture." *African Arts* 21.3 (May 1988).

———. "Venda Art." In *Catalogue: Ten Years of Collection (1979–1989),* edited by David Hammond-Tooke and Anitra Nettleton. Johannesburg: University of the Witwatersrand, 1989.

———. "Dream Machines: Southern African Headrests." *South African Journal of Art and Architectural History* 1.4 (1990): 147–54.

———. "RE: Venda (?) Lady & Tsonga (?) Puppets." Personal email to Mary Axworthy, 15 July 2004.

———. "RE: Venda Objects." Personal email to Mary Axworthy, 15 July 2004.

Nettleton, Anitra and David Hammond-Tooke. "Art of the Pedi and Ntwane." In *Catalogue: Ten Years of Collecting (1979–1989),* edited by David Hammond-Tooke and Anitra Nettleton. Johannesburg: University of the Witwatersrand, 1989.

Nettleton, Anitra, Sipho Ndabambi and David Hammond-Tooke. "The Beadwork of the Cape Nguni." In *Catalogue: Ten Years of Collecting (1979–1989),* edited by David Hammond-Tooke and Anitra Nettleton. Johannesburg: University of the Witwatersrand, 1989.

Neufeldt, Victoria, ed. *Webster's New World Dictionary.* New York: Prentice, 1988.

Newberry, Charles. *Autobiography.* Unpublished, January 1912.

Newberry, Paul. "Newberry questions." Personal email to Mary Axworthy, 24 July 2004.

Newman, Diana L. *Catalogue.* Johannesburg: University of the Witwatersrand/Johannesburg Art Galleries, 1986.

Ngubane, Harriet. *Body and Mind in Zulu Medicine.* London: Academic Press, 1977.

Olupona, Jacob W. *African Spirituality.* New York: Crossroad Publishing, 2000.

Palgrave, K.C. *Trees of Southern Africa.* Cape Town: Struik, 1977.

Perani, Judith and Fred T. Smith. *The Visual Arts of Africa: Gender, Power, and Life Cycle Rituals.* New Jersey: Prentice Hall, 1998.

Pérez, Annie. *The Art of Southeast Africa: from the Conru Collection.* Milan: 5 Continents Editions, 2002.

Phillips, Tom, ed. *Africa: The Art of a Continent: 100 Works of Power and Beauty.* New York: Guggenheim Museum Library, 1997.

Powell, Ivor. *Ndebele: A People and Their Art.* Cape Town: Struik, 1995.

Preston-Whyte, Eleanor and Jo Thorpe. "Ways of Seeing, Ways of Buying; Images of Tourist Art and Culture Expression in Contemporary Beadwork." In *African Art in Southern Africa: From Tradition to Township,* edited by Anitra Nettleton and David Hammond-Tooke. Johannesburg: AD Donker, 1989.

Roberts, Margaret. *Indigenous Healing Plants.* Cape Town: Struik, 1990.

Robertson, Robert. *Zulu Izaga.* Christison Rare Books. http://www.antiquarian.co.za/Zulu%20Proverbs.htm.

Schoeman, H.S. "Re: Zulu Leather and Beaded Skirt." Personal email to Mary Axworthy, 11 March 2004.

Scott, Gillian. *Ardmore: An African Discovery.* Cape Town: Fernwood, 1998.

Sellschop, Susan, Wendy Goldblatt, and Doreen Hemp. *Craft South Africa: Traditional, Transitional, Contemporary.* Hyde Park, South Africa: Pan Macmillan, 2002.

Shaw, E.M. "The Basketwork of Southern Africa Part 1: Technology." In *Annals of the South African Museum.* Cape Town: The Rustica Press, 1992.

Sieber, Roy and Frank Herreman. *Hair in African Art and Culture.* New York: The Museum for African Art, 2000.

Sipusiso, C.L. *Zulu Proverbs.* Johannesburg: Witwatersrand UP, 1954.

Stevenson, Michael and Michael Graham-Stewart, eds. *South East African Beadwork 1850–1910, from Adornment to Artifact to Art.* London: Farmwood Press, 2000.

Taylor, Graham. "Basotho Pottery." *Sethala Magazine* 2. (10 May 1988) http://www.lesoff.co.za/artline/Traditional/BasothoPottery.htm

Thompson, Leonardo. *African Societies in Southern Africa.* New York: Praegar Publishers, 1969.

Toffoli, Hilary Prendini. "The Curse of Clocolan." *Style* (October 1995): 87–93.

Tubingen, Ernst Wasmuth Verlag. *AmaNdebele: Signals of Color from South Africa.* Berlin: Haus der Kulturen der Welt, 1991.

Twala, R.G. "Beads as Regulating the Social Life of the Zulu and Swazi." *African Studies* 10.3 (1951): 113-123.

Tyler, Rev. Josiah. *Forty Years Among the Zulus.* Boston: Congregational Sunday School and Publishing Society, 1891.

Tyrrell, Barbara. *Tribal People of Southern Africa.* Cape Town: Books of Africa, 1968.

Tyrrell, Barbara and Peter Jurgens. *African Heritage.* Johannesburg: Macmillan South Africa, 1983.

Valentin, Manuel. "Zulu Sculpture." In *Sculptures: Africa Asia Oceania Americas,* edited by Jacques Kerchache. Paris: Reunion des Musees Nationaux, 2001.

Van Heerden, Jannie. "Zulu Grassweaving." In *Zulu Treasures: of Kings and Commoners,* exh. cat. Kwazulu: Kwazulu Cultural Museum and Local History Museums, 1996.

Van Wyk, Gary. "Illuminated Signs: Style and Meaning in the Beadwork of the Xhosa- and Zulu-speaking Peoples." *African Arts* 36.4 (Autumn 2003): 12–33, 93–94.

Visona, Monica Blackmun, Robin Poynor, Herbert M. Cole and Michael D. Harris. *A History of Art in Africa.* New York: Harry N. Abrams, 2001.

Wanless, Ann. "Public Pleasures: Smoking and Snuff-taking in Southern Africa." In *Art and Ambiguity: Perspectives on the Brenthurst Collection of Southern African Art,* exh. cat. Johannesburg: Johannesburg Art Gallery, 1991.

Webb, C.de B. and J. Wright, eds. *The James Stuart Archive I.* Pietermaritzburg: University of Natal Press, 1976.

Webb, Virginia-Lee. "Fact and Fiction: Nineteenth-Century Photographs of the Zulu." *African Arts* 25.1 (1992): 50–59, 98–99.

West, Martin and Jean Morris. *Abantu: An Introduction to the Black People of South Africa.* Cape Town: Struik, 1976.

West, Martin and Michael G. Whisson. *Religion and Social Change in Southern Africa/Anthropological Essays.* Cape Town: David Philip, 1975.

Wood, Marilee. "The Girl Who Ran Away." In *Evocations of the Child: Fertility Figures of the Southern African Region.* Cape Town: Human & Rousseau, 1998.

———. "The Sorghum Child: Nguana Modula: South Sotho Child Figures." In *Evocations of the Child: Fertility Figures of the Southern African Region.* Cape Town: Human & Rousseau, 1998.

Wood, Marilee, ed. *Zulu Treasures: of Kings and Commoners.* Kwazulu: Kwazulu Cultural Museum and Local History Museums, 1996.

Woodhouse, H.C. *The Bushman Art of Southern Africa.* Cape Town: Purnell & Sons, 1979.

Zaloumis, Alex and Ian Difford. *Zulu Tribal Art.* Cape Town: Amazulu Publishers, 2000.

We'd love to make your life easier

4395 El Cajon Blvd.
San Diego, CA 92105

Phone: 619-518-9412